THE **QUINTESSENTIAL UNDERDOG** MOVIE...

BREAKING AWAY

Book Design & Production:
Columbus Publishing Lab
www.ColumbusPublishingLab.com

Copyright © 2024 by
Steve Basford

All rights reserved.
This book, or parts thereof, may not be
reproduced in any form without permission.

On the cover, Dennis Christopher as Dave Stohler crosses the finish line in a rehearsal for the movie, "Breaking Away". Courtesy: Indiana University Archives.

The artwork on the back cover is by Sirena Pearl. Her website is sirenapearl.com.

Paperback ISBN: 978-1-63337-864-3
E-Book ISBN: 978-1-63337-865-0

Printed in the United States of America
1 3 5 7 9 10 8 6 4 2

THE **QUINTESSENTIAL UNDERDOG** MOVIE...

BREAKING AWAY

A RETROSPECTIVE BY Steve Basford

TABLE OF CONTENTS

INTRODUCTION I
CHAPTER 1: The Cast 1
CHAPTER 2: The Brains Behind the Movie 9
CHAPTER 3: The Story 17
CHAPTER 4: It's About 53
CHAPTER 5: The TV Series 73
CHAPTER 6: Amy Wright, the Angelic Nancy 97
CHAPTER 7: Eddy Van Guyse, the Italian Villain 103
CHAPTER 8: In Their Words 121
CHAPTER 9: Post Script 169
PHOTOS 225
ACKNOWLEDGMENTS 233
BIBLIOGRAPHY 235
APPENDIX 237
ABOUT THE AUTHOR 239

WHY IS BREAKING AWAY STILL POPULAR TO THIS DAY?

BREAKING AWAY, released in 1979, is the quintessential underdog movie, earning numerous award nominations and ranking in multiple Top Ten lists. Why is it so popular, to this day?

IT HAS VERY GOOD performances, and it's about that age group. Barbara Barrie, Paul Dooley, they're just so great. They just really walked that fine line, especially Paul, of being extremely funny, but still real.

Amy Wright, the actress who portrayed Nancy

IT'S SO REAL, everybody loves the underdog winning ... "Hoosiers", "Rudy", and "Rocky", I love them ... and the humanity.

Eddy Van Guyse, Little 500 competitor and the Italian villain

I THINK IT'S THAT a lot of people can relate to the exhilaration and also the hard side of sports, and it also really is a movie that isn't so much about bike racing as it is about the relationships of these high school kids, and there are funny, funny points and poignant points, and there's a little bit of something for everyone. It's corny, but it's corny in a way that everyone can embrace.

Bill Brissman, multiple Little 500 champion and stunt double for Hart Bochner

I THINK IT definitely is the story of the underdogs being triumphant. It was heartwarming. And Dave's family, it's just typical Midwest values.

Debbie Broeking, Mini 500 competitor and extra in the movie

I THINK THAT THE nostalgia of the film helped the sleepy town that we were, but I also think it hits every sensibility that you've got; there's a little bit of a love story, but it's not too overblown; there's action, there's the kind of the villains in a way, which are the fraternity guys.

Doug Bruce, extra in the student union, Little 500, and the Cinzano 100 race scenes

IT GOES BACK to a coming of age, and everyone has to go through that. And they found a great way to make it funny to tie into a unique sporting event. And there's a victory at the end, which we all don't get in life.

Jim Kirkham, coach of the real-life Cutters team

IT'S GREAT ACTORS, like Dennis Quaid, and that was his first hit. And it just resonated with people, and it's funny, and it was a great script. An underdog movie, like my father told it, a sleeper.

Dan Levinson, son of associate producer Art Levinson

EVERYONE LOVES a good underdog story, whether it's a sports story or just a coming of age story. And this movie has both.

Dr. Ben Pearl, Little 500 competitor

IT'S JUST, I GUESS, a love story, maybe, and exciting, you want to know if the local kid is going to win? Just the whole idea that the local cutter kids could do that.

Dr. James Pivarnik, Little 500 competitor and racer in the movie

THE THEME IS TIMELESS, the growing up theme, moving on with life, that type of theme. It's just a good movie. There's no violence, other than Dennis Christopher getting knocked off of his bike. It's just a good family movie that has a great ending. And it just leaves you feeling good.

Carlos Sintes, one of the Italian racers in the Cinzano 100 race

I THINK IT'S THE identification of coming of age, that awkward stage between high school, college, what are you going to do with your life? Small town versus college, kind of the antagonist of the fraternity against a kid who's just trying to make it in his own town, and he's being bullied in his own town by these college kids.

Randy Strong, Little 500 Cutters team champion and extra in the Cinzano 100 race

Torin Kay-Mawhorr crosses the finish line to win the 2023 Little 500 race for the Cutters team, which was inspired by *"Breaking Away"*. *Photo Courtesy: Dr. Ben Pearl (1987 Little 500 rider)*

INTRODUCTION

I MUST BE IN the top 1% of movie goers. I will see movies of almost every genre other than horror or sci-fi, because I am fascinated by real people and real situations. There are plenty of exceptions to my rule; for example, I am the biggest fan of "Raiders of the Lost Ark" (which is very realistic except for Indiana Jones's high threshold of pain and a few minutes of special effects at the end), "Terminator", and the brilliant "Ex Machina" (who is to say that its plot won't happen some day?) While I see almost every blockbuster, I much prefer low-budget movies. For every "Mission Impossible", James Bond, and Marvel movie, give me movies such as "The Way", "A Walk in the Woods", and "Quiz Show" instead.

In August of 1979, I hit the jackpot when I saw "Breaking Away". It was shown on only two screens out of the 71 listed in my hometown newspaper in Columbus, Ohio, the *Columbus Dispatch*, and I saw it at the Raintree Cinemas, which, like many landmarks in the movie, has gone by the wayside. With summer the season for blockbuster movies—its competition included "Moonraker", "Alien", "The Amityville Horror", "Escape from Alcatraz", and "The Concorde-Airport 79"—it has been labeled a summer sleeper. In January of 1980, it was still showing at the second run theater at the shopping center across the street from my apartment, charging $1.00. The ad in the *Dispatch* had "HELD OVER!"

It is the story of Dave Stohler and his three friends, one year out of high school with no direction for their future, except that Dave is an elite bike racer obsessed with the Italian racers and Italian culture, much to the chagrin of his father, Ray, played by Paul Dooley. They are known as the Cutters, as their fathers cut the limestone for the Indiana University buildings. The movie checks all the boxes for me—real people, real dialogue, real situations, real locations with vivid scenery, and humor. We feel like we are part of the cast, as if the story is happening around us and we could join in the conversation any time. It is a movie that people of all ages can see; it annoys me when people say that they have seen an exceptional movie, only to tell their kids, "But, you can't see it!"

I feel that I have a somewhat cosmic connection to the movie. In November of 1978, I had traveled from my home in Columbus, Ohio, to Bloomington, Indiana—the site of the movie—to work the stats for Warner QUBE's cable broadcast of the Ohio State vs. Indiana football game. It was my first such Ohio State football gig for Warner, and it would be coach Woody Hayes's last win in his 28-year Ohio State career. Little did I know at the time that, three months earlier, my favorite movie was being filmed on the Indiana campus, including at the football stadium. Dave Stohler was the treasurer of the Latin Club in high school; I was the vice president of the Latin Club in high school.

Also, coincidentally, Paul Dooley was in Columbus on August 21, 1979, and gave an interview to the *Dispatch* entertainment columnist (note the appropriate first name) Dennis Fiely, with the headline " 'Little Film' Gets Lots Of Fame". Prophetically, Dooley was quoted in the story with, "I'm sure they're gonna want me to play this father in my next four or five pictures."; he would portray the dad in "Sixteen Candles", another movie where he has a heart-to-heart talk with his child, five years later. Interestingly, the ads in the *Dispatch* in the first few weeks have Rex Reed's quote of "One of the most funny, totally unique film experiences of this or any other year. You'd be dead wrong to miss it.", but the poster photo is the one on the Internet Movie Database (IMDb) page that shows the boys sitting on a hill, with a somber look on their faces.[1] It shows Mike

---

[1] https://www.imdb.com/title/tt078902/

INTRODUCTION

smoking; in the movie, he has a cigarette or a pack in several scenes, but he is never shown smoking. That poster, which is a common one identifying the movie and also hangs in the Indiana Memorial Union today, has a clever lettering:

BREAK
ING
AWAY

That lettering also appears in the trailer (which has the *M' appari tutt' amor* music that Dave will embrace). The narrative for the trailer exaggerates a bit: "Enrico Gimondi spends eight hours a day training to be the finest racer in all of Italy." The narrative concludes with "Somewhere between growing up and settling down. It happens to all of us."

The ad in the August 31 *Dispatch* edition had a different poster with a spoiler in it; it shows Dave winning Indiana University's Little 500 race, although it shows him with his arms in the air, holding the trophy in his right hand as he crosses the finish line.

On the 33to1.com website, Jeff LaFave, a 2013 graduate of Indiana University, wrote about its inception; filming would start shortly thereafter[2]:

> Citizens of Bloomington would only find about the film project on August 7, 1978 ... as Bloomington Mayor Frank McCloskey (a three-time congressman and initiator of the "Bloomington Transit" bus system) held a press conference in the City Council chambers with IU Foundation President Bill Armstrong (for whom the current Little 500 racing venue and IU soccer stadium is named), the British director [Peter] Yates, and members

---
[2] https://33to1.com/2014/04/17/column-35-years-later-can-breaking-away-still-compete/

of Twentieth-Century Fox [now 20th Century Studios], to make an announcement: a film called "Bambino," loosely based on the town's famous bicycle race.

Peter Yates was also the producer; the screenwriter was Steve Tesich, and the inspiration for the movie and the climactic bike race is David K. Blase, competing for the Phi Kappa Psi fraternity at Indiana University in 1962.

Note: many sources have the family name spelled as "Stoller"; the IMDb listing for the movie has "Stohler", and the listing for the TV series has "Stoller". The proof for the movie is the fact that the sign for the car lot that Ray owns has "Raymond Stohler, PROP.". The credits at the end do not show the last name of the three family members. The *Bloomington Herald-Times* has: "When Tesich went to pen the Academy Award-winning screenplay for Breaking Away, he called Blase and said he wanted to use his name in the film. The idea was shot down by the legal department at 20th Century Fox for liability purposes, so Tesich combined Blase's first name with Phi Psi team manager Bob Stohler."[3] The point was that it would have to be a biography in order to use "Dave Blase". An Indiana University website has "As an undergraduate, Bob was a four-year manager of the Men's Basketball Team under coach Branch McCracken. He participated as both a manager and rider in the Little 500 bicycle classic. In fact, he was the manager of the winning team in 1962 that was later depicted in the film, Breaking Away."[4]

I liked the movie so much that I raved about it to a coworker who was an avid bicyclist. He and I had seen the harrowing "Apocalypse Now", and he was quite shaken up when it was over. "Breaking Away" would be a calming experience for him. It is one of only two movies that I have

---

[3] https://www.heraldtimesonline.com/story/news/local/2014/04/22/35-years-later-the-man-who-inspired-breaking-away-is-still-biking/47726981/
[4] https://honorsandawards.iu.edu/awards/honoree/5694.html

INTRODUCTION

screened for a lady friend; she was an avid bike rider and triathlete, and I showed my VHS tape of it to her in my apartment. I asked her if the scene of Dave achieving a speed of 60 miles per hour on the highway was realistic, and she doubted that it was likely to ride that fast.

On a Mother's Day, appropriately, and I think that it was in 2021, I was in a bookstore in Dayton, Ohio, and found the DVD of "Breaking Away"; it is the best $6.00 that I have ever spent. Just as I had stumbled onto the movie in 1979, I found the DVD by chance; if I had really been focused on buying it, I could have searched on Amazon. The DVD case has "FAMILY FEATURE" on the top.

The movie culminates in Indiana University's Little 500 bike race, a 200 lap, 50-mile relay race as part of the "World's Greatest College Weekend". Sorry about the spoiler alert, but when Dave crossed the finish line to win the race, I got choked up when I saw it in the theater. Actually, I still do every time that I watch it. When I watch the scene where Mike bumps his head on a rock while swimming, I brace myself every time and still cringe.

I never missed the Siskel and Ebert movie review show. When they reviewed "Breaking Away", Roger Ebert said it was about real people—he and I are on the same wavelength!—and that he could relate to the local kids in a college town ("townies") from his youth in Urbana, Illinois, where his father was an electrician who helped build the University of Illinois campus. Gene Siskel pointed out that it had no big name stars and offered to send anyone who did not like it a REFUND! When they picked their best movies of 1979, Ebert picked it as his second best, and Siskel had it at number four, "the sunniest film of the year, a sweet slice of middle America." They both included it in their Best of the 1970s list, with Siskel calling it the most likable movie of the decade. Their original review show from 1979, their Best of 1979 show, and their Best of the 1970s show are available through web searches.

In Nell Minnow's interview on RogerEbert.com with Paul Dooley, she quotes him[5]:

> I did a tour when "Breaking Away" was about to come out. I went to all the major cities and Daniel Stern was with me and some of the other actors at different times. And I was interviewed by Roger Ebert and also by Gene Siskel, differently, separately. And they both had raved about the movie and then they met with me. The best quotes I ever got in my life are from Roger Ebert and Gene Siskel. Roger Ebert said, "to watch Paul Dooley in this part is to know he will win an Oscar." I'll always love the names Siskel and Ebert.

According to the IMDb, its budget was $2.3 million, and its gross was $16.4 million. By comparison, for "Apocalypse Now", the figures are $31.5 million and $96 million. It was nominated for the Oscar award for Best Picture. The other nominee about an underdog, "Norma Rae", had the second-lowest figures, $4.5 million and $22 million. "Apocalypse Now" had Marlon Brando, Martin Sheen, Robert Duvall, Frederic Forrest, Laurence Fishburne, Harrison Ford, Dennis Hopper, G.D. Spradlin, and Scott Glenn in its cast; the biggest name at the time in "Breaking Away" was Paul Dooley, though Jackie Earle Haley had made a smashing debut in "Bad News Bears" and its sequels. "Apocalypse Now" was filmed in the Philippines and is a story about war; "Breaking Away" was filmed in middle America and is a story whose conflict is between hometown boys and college students. Marlon Brando alone made over $3 million for "Apocalypse Now". Peter Yates's previous film, "The Deep", had an estimated budget of $9 million, and his following film, "Eyewitness", had a budget of $8.5 million.

---

[5] https://www.rogerebert.com/interviews/something-comes-out-of-me-that-has-a-fatherly-quality-paul-dooley-on-his-new-book-movie-dad

INTRODUCTION

How highly regarded was the movie? Its competition for the Oscar for Best Picture was "Kramer vs. Kramer" (the winner), "All That Jazz", "Norma Rae", and "Apocalypse Now"—yes, going head-to-head with Francis Ford Coppola. Steve Tesich did win the Oscar for Best Original Screenplay. Barbara Barrie (Best Actress in a Supporting Role), Peter Yates (Best Director), and Patrick Williams (Best Music, Original Song Score and Its Adaptation or Best Adaptation Score) also received nominations. Interestingly, Peter Yates had directed Dustin Hoffman, who won the Actor in a Leading Role award for "Kramer vs. Kramer", in "John and Mary", and had directed Robert Duvall, who was nominated for the Actor in a Supporting Role award for "Apocalypse Now", in "Bullitt".

Note: the year 1979 was very successful for the 20 Century-Fox studio; it also produced "All That Jazz", "Norma Rae", "Alien", "The Rose", and "A Perfect Couple" (starring Paul Dooley).

In the six years of 1978 through 1983, the only artists who were twice nominated for the Oscar for the Best Director are Peter Yates and Steven Spielberg.

Paul Dooley was named the Best Supporting Actor by the National Board of Review, which also named "Breaking Away" among its Top Ten Films of 1979. Dennis Christopher was one of 12 actors who were chosen by author John Willis among Screen World's Promising Actors of 1979, along with Bo Derek, Amy Irving, and Bette Midler, among others.

Seventeen sports-themed movies have been nominated for the Oscar for the Best Picture, and Dennis Christopher is the only actor to appear in two of them; the other was "Chariots of Fire", and both were from the 20th Century Fox studio. Five of the 17 were in a six-year span; "Rocky" was released in 1976, "Heaven Can Wait" in 1978, "Breaking Away" in 1979, "Raging Bull" in 1980, and "Chariots of Fire" in 1981.

It won the Golden Globe award for Best Motion Picture - Comedy or Musical. Dennis Christopher won the Most Promising Newcomer To Leading Film Roles award from the British Academy of Film and

Television Arts and received a Golden Globe nomination as New Star of the Year. Yates and Tesich also received Golden Globe nominations. The National Society of Film Critics said it was the Best Picture and honored Steve Tesich with the Best Screenplay award. Tesich won the Best Original Comedy award given by the Writers Guild of America. He won the Screenwriter of the Year, ALFS Award from the London Critics Circle Film Awards. The New York Film Critics Circle awarded it as the Best Screenplay.

The *New York Times* placed the film on its Best 1000 Movies Ever list. The American Film Institute placed "Breaking Away" eighth on the list of America's 100 Most Inspiring Movies, ahead of "Hoosiers" at 13th and "Rudy" at 54th, and eighth in the Sports movies category. Time magazine includes it among its All-TIME 25 Best Sports Movies, and the Associated Press ranked in a tie for 21st place in its Top 25 Sports Movies. In Esquire magazine, Kareem Abdul-Jabbar ranked it as the fifth-best sports movie. In 2020, Entertainment Weekly magazine picked it as the one film that best captures the spirit and story of the state of Indiana.

In 2020, the Hollywood Reporter's Chief Film Critic David Rooney included it in his "10 Under-the-Radar Summer Favorites", saying, "... it's also the sports movie for people who don't care about sports movies ...".[6] The "New York Times Essential Library Children's Movies" book by Peter Nichols in 2003 includes it in its top 100.

Columnist Jeff LaFave wrote:[7]

> Vogue magazine's staff review called it "one of the most totally unique film experiences of this or any other year." National critic Judith Crist called it "the feel-terrific movie of the year."

---

[6] https://www.hollywoodreporter.com/lists/thr-chief-film-critic-picks-10-under-radar-summer-favorite-movies-1304897/

[7] https://33to1.com/2014/04/17/column-35-years-later-can-breaking-away-still-compete/

INTRODUCTION

On ESPN's Top 20 Sports Movies of All-Time, it was ranked #14, with "Bad News Bears" (with Jackie Earle Haley) at 16th, and "Chariots of Fire" (with Dennis Christopher) at 17th. The story for its top 20 has "The scene where Dave (Dennis Christopher) rides to keep up with the truck is, along with Rocky's run through the streets of Phily, one of the two most inspiring training scenes in movie history."[8] It was in the midst of a run of highly acclaimed sports-themed movies; thirteen of the top 20 were released between 1976 and 1989.

The book, "1001 Movies You Must See Before You Die", lists only one movie directed by Peter Yates, and it is not "Bullitt"; it is "Breaking Away". The Sports Illustrated for Kids magazine in September of 2005 included it in The 20 Best Sports Movies For Kids. The Turner Classic Movies network considered it a classic, giving it its TCM premiere in February of 2016, following the airing of "Chariots of Fire", and showing it again on Veterans Day in 2018.

In his book, "Movie Dad: Finding Myself and My Family, On Screen and Off", Paul Dooley writes that when he attended the premiere in New York City, the audience gave it a standing ovation.

It was a ground-breaking movie about teenagers; John Hughes's first directing effort came five years later with "Sixteen Candles", which also had Paul Dooley as the dad. IMDb ranks "Breaking Away" as #4 in Best Cycling Movies; it was the third one chronologically, following the Italian movie "Bicycle Thieves" (1948) and a short movie "Vive le tour" (1962). Four of its other best movies were released in the 1980s: "BMX Bandits" (which had Nicole Kidman), "American Flyers" (written by Steve Tesich), "Quicksilver", and "Rad".

It was included in two documentaries by filmmaker Chuck Workman. One was his eight-minute, Academy Award-winning short, "Precious Images", which showed scenes from approximately 470 movies; the scene showing the four boys sunbathing at the quarry, their favorite hangout,

---

[8] https://www.espn.com/page2/movies/s/top20/no14.html

was featured. The other was "Words", which salutes Steven Tesich's writing by including the scene where Dave comes home early in the movie and greets Ray with "buon giorno, Papa". The Movie Database website describes "Words" with "This short film, released by the Writers Guild Foundation in 1987, honors the craft of screenwriting and the writers behind our favorite lines and cinematic moments. Written and directed by Academy Award winning filmmaker Chuck Workman, it was screened at film festivals and college campuses around the country to inspire writers and celebrate the importance of the written word in entertainment."[9]

Key participants describe it in superlatives. In multiple interviews, Paul Dooley said that it was the best movie that he ever made. The *San Luis Obispo Tribune* wrote:[10]

> During his long career, Dooley said "Breaking Away" is one of four or five films that really stands out. "It's the only great one I ever made," he said.

In a presentation in 2019, he added that it was the best script that he had ever read, with perfect casting, and Daniel Stern said that it was the most magical thing that ever happened to him. In the NPR interview "Bullseye" with Jesse Thorn in January of 2024, Dooley said that his role was his first big part.[11] On the AV Club website, he said that "… it's been my calling card ever since."[12] In his "Movie Dad" book, he writes that Ray was the best part that he ever had.

Appearing on the Great Day TV show on WISH-TV Channel 8 Indianapolis in 2019, Dennis Christopher said that it was the hardest

---

[9] https://www.themoviedb.org/movie/575030-words
[10] https://www.sanluisobispo.com/entertainment/tv-movies/article39500820.html
[11] https://www.npr.org/2024/01/09/1197956375/paul-dooley
[12] https://www.avclub.com/iconic-movie-dad-paul-dooley-talks-about-breaking-away-1845803434

INTRODUCTION

thing he has ever done, with the training and the opera singing.[13] In The Hollywood Reporter in 2015, he said, "I've never been involved in another project that has brought so much good will into my life. People are not over *Breaking Away*; they're passing it from generation to generation."[14]

At the world premiere at Indiana University 1979, Peter Yates told a reporter from WRTV-TV in Indianapolis that the movie was the best that he had ever done to that point—impressive, given that he had directed "Bullitt", "The Friends of Eddie Coyle", and "The Deep".

In his book, "Home and Alone", Daniel Stern wrote that "Peter Yates had just changed my life forever." Without "Breaking Away", would we ever know of Daniel Stern, who was broke at the time of casting?

The sneak previews were rousing successes. In John Schwarb's book, "The Little 500: The Story of the World's Greatest College Weekend", he writes, "Twentieth Century Fox's people also discovered they had something special, as the responses from Denver and two more sneak previews in New Orleans and Phoenix gave *Breaking Away* the highest test ratings in the studio's history."

A *Sarasota Herald-Tribune* article quoted cyclist Greg LeMond from Outside magazine. He picked it as his all-time favorite[15]:

> "The only true cycling classic. I used to race with a friend who could have been the inspiration for the film. He dressed and acted as though he were Italian. He even changed his name from Tony Comfort to Antonio Conforte."

---

[13] https://www.youtube.com/watch?v=U0BFpfNb7Xw
[14] https://www.hollywoodreporter.com/movies/movie-news/breaking-away-cast-reuniting-las-823728/
[15] https://www.heraldtribune.com/story/news/2008/06/05/classic-breaking-away/28641028007/

Speaking of underdogs, "Rocky" (also rated PG and with Sylvester Stallone's nickname as "The Italian Stallion") had set the stage three years earlier, winning the Oscar for Best Picture with an estimated budget of $960,000 and going up against heavyweight directors Alan J. Pakula, Hal Ashby, Sidney Lumet, and Martin Scorsese. When "Breaking Away" came out, "Rocky II" came out in the same year.

How many movies can you name for which the stars made appearances at reunions, presentations, and screenings multiple times, throughout the country, even 45 years after the release?

How many movies can you name that are based on a college event?

How many movies can you name that prompted the media to come to its venue as a result? The year after its release, the *New York Times*, *Washington Post*, and other newspapers came to cover the Little 500 race, along with camera crews from as far away as Mobile, Alabama.

How many low-budget movies can you name that were shown in a South American country, 31 years after its release?

The August 1979 edition of *Bicycling* magazine had Dennis Christopher on the cover as Dave on his bike with the caption "New Bike Racing Movie", and had an extensive review by Susan Weaver.

The 1981 race in the new Bill Armstrong Stadium received front page coverage by the *New York Times*, with a story and a photo. It reported that the university's news bureau issued 140 press credentials to 50 organizations. It cited Bill Brissman of Delta Chi, "… the rider who lost at the end of the race in the movie crossed the finish line with both arms in the air for his team's third consecutive victory."[16]

In 1982, the CBS network carried the race on a national broadcast, with Ken Squier calling the race and David Blase providing the color commentary. In the telecast, Squier referred to the movie several times,

---

[16] https://www.nytimes.com/1981/04/26/sports/indiana-s-little-500-speeds-into-the-big-time.html

INTRODUCTION

and the production showed scenes from the movie and included a taped interview between Squier and Blase at the quarry.

The state of Indiana sets the standard for underdog sports movies based on a true story. "Hoosiers"—about a small-town high school basketball team that won the state championship, inspired in part by the feat of the Milan High School team in 1954—followed seven years later, and "Rudy"—the story of Daniel "Rudy" Ruettiger, a walk-on football player at Notre Dame who had 27 seconds of playing time, recording one statistic—followed seven years after "Hoosiers". Both of those movies were directed by David Anspaugh and rated PG. Angelo Pizzo, who grew up in Bloomington, wrote and produced both movies. I also get choked up every time I watch "Rudy", when our hero gets his quarterback sack in a 27-second career, and when Jimmy Chitwood hits the state championship-winning basket in "Hoosiers".

What is "Breaking Away" about, a bike race? The race is the climactic ending of the movie, but a small portion. It's a story about class differences, honesty, pride, family, relationships, romance, and changing attitudes.

In other words, it's about life.

CHAPTER 1
THE CAST

DENNIS CHRISTOPHER is Dave Stohler, the most ambitious and confident of the four boys. Dave is obsessed with riding his bike, Italian culture, and the Italian racers, speaking and singing in Italian when he can. The role was perfect for him, as he had ambled through Europe before taking a huge risk to meet Federico Fellini, earning a role in "Fellini's Roma". Before "Breaking Away", he appeared in two movies directed by Robert Altman—"A Wedding", as Paul Dooley's son, and the compelling "3 Women". He was busy after "Breaking Away", though not in many high-profile theatrical movies. Exceptions were "Chariots of Fire", which won the Oscar for Best Picture, and Quentin Tarantino's "Django Unchained", which was nominated for Best Picture in 2013. He had the magic touch; all three films—"Breaking Away", "Chariots of Fire", and "Django Unchained"—won the Oscar for Best Original Screenplay. The year after the release of "Breaking Away", he starred in "Fade to Black" as another obsessed character, this time with an obsession for movies. Appropriately, he is half-Italian. IMDb shows his birth name as Dennis Joseph Carrelli and that he graduated from Monsignor Bonner High School, Drexel Hill, Pennsylvania. His older brother was the late actor/producer Vince Cannon; in the movie "Youngblood" (not the Rob Lowe movie), Vince's character is "Corelli".

DENNIS QUAID is Mike, the one with the biggest reputation. As the former quarterback on his high school football team, he calls the signals;

he is the leader of the pack, the enforcer when the boys get threatened by the students. He decides when it's time to fight. His stone-faced demeanor matches the limestone of the quarry; he is the most bitter of the four when it comes to leaving his school days. He is the only one who has a car, for the four boys to ride around in, although his brother is the actual owner. By far, of all the actors in the movie, Dennis became the biggest star afterwards. Previously, he had appeared in "September 30, 1955" with Dennis Christopher. He would reunite with Peter Yates in "Suspect". He appeared in a number of movies as real-life people, foremost in "Reagan" as Ronald Reagan, but also "The Right Stuff" as astronaut Gordon Cooper, "Wyatt Earp" as Doc Holliday, "Great Balls of Fire!" as Jerry Lee Lewis, "The Rookie" as pitcher Jim Morris, "American Underdog" as football coach Dick Vermeil, "The Express" as football coach Ben Schwartzwalder, "The Alamo" as Sam Houston, "Midway" as Vice Admiral William "Bull" Halsey, and as President Bill Clinton in the HBO film "The Special Relationship", for which he earned nominations for a Primetime Emmy Award, Golden Globe Award, and Screen Actors Guild Award. Other sports-related movies were "Everybody's All-American", "Any Given Sunday", "Soul Surfer", "Born a Champion", "The Hill", "The Long Game", "Our Winning Season", and "Tough Enough". Other noteworthy movies were "The Big Easy", "The Parent Trap", "The Day After Tomorrow", "In Good Company", "Flight of the Phoenix", "Yours, Mine & Ours", "Postcards From the Edge", "Jaws 3-D", "Traffic", and the "Footloose" remake. He received a Golden Globe Award nomination for his role in "Far from Heaven".

DANIEL STERN is Cyril, a tall, gawky kid and the most laid-back, a pacifist, quick with a wisecrack, constantly picked on by Mike. Ray makes an oblique remark that Cyril is the apple that doesn't fall far from the tree when he implies that Cyril's dad wasn't the greatest of stonecutters (and Dave smirks at the comment). But, you don't want to mess with Cyril when he gets a bowling ball stuck on his fingers. "Breaking Away" was his first movie, and he has been busy since. He had similar characters as the dumber and sillier of the Wet Bandits opposite Joe Pesci in two "Home Alone" movies and as the least-secure of the three buddies in the two "City Slickers" movies. He was the narrator in the TV comedy series "The Wonder Years". He was reunited with Dennis Quaid in "D.O.A." In his book, "Home and Alone", he writes, after reading the "Breaking Away" script: "... the story felt like me and my friends at the end of high school just a few years back, all of us having to break away from each other and our families to start our own lives.", and "The part of Cyril had some fantastic jokes, and I got lots of laughs, and I nailed the emotional scenes as well …." Upon landing the role, he had his first-ever airplane ride, to Los Angeles. In a Facebook posting in 2016, he wrote that, "Breaking Away changed my life forever. First movie I was ever in, made more money than I ever dreamed of (about $8,000) and made these incredible friends for life. Go Cutters!"

JACKIE EARLE HALEY is Moocher, the undersized, long-haired kid. He has a chip on his shoulder; make sure not to call him "Shorty", or you will see his mean streak. It helps that he likes to lift weights. He is small enough to climb out of the window in the back seat of Mike's car without opening the door. Moocher is mature; he lives in his home alone (Daniel Stern, take note). He is charged with selling the family house as his dad looks for work in Chicago, he does try to get a job, and he is about to get married. A story in *Entertainment Weekly* magazine states that Jackie initially went in to read for the lead role of Dave, but director Peter Yates decided to cast him as Moocher.[1] Jackie was the most nearly-mature of the kids in "The Bad News Bears", driving a motorcycle. His acting career made a big comeback when he appeared in "Little Children" in 2006, ending a 13-year gap in his movie appearances and earning an

---
[1] https://ew.com/article/2012/10/05/breaking-away-1979/

Oscar nomination for Actor in a Supporting Role. He worked for Martin Scorsese in "Shutter Island" and for Steven Spielberg in "Lincoln". He directed "Criminal Activities", in which he had a role, along with John Travolta.

PAUL DOOLEY is Ray Stohler, Dave's pot-bellied father. In his "Movie Dad" book, he writes that the character was so much like his dad that he could do the part in his sleep, and that he based it on his dad. He also writes that he has played at least 25 dads, sometimes grumpy, sometimes understanding, and once in a while, both. He has had a rich resume since "Breaking Away", most notably as Molly Ringwald's dad in "Sixteen Candles", which substantiates his "Movie Dad" autobiography. In addition to a wealth of TV credits, his movie credits include "Popeye", "Hairspray", and "Runaway Bride". He and Dennis Christopher played father and son in Robert Altman's "A Wedding" before "Breaking Away" and in the "Cherry Red" episode of TV's "Law & Order: Criminal Intent" in 2001.

BARBARA BARRIE is Evelyn Stohler, Dave's mother. She has a heart of gold, while Ray's heart is at risk for his diet that includes French Fries. She supports Dave in whatever he does, pointing out to Ray that he used to be sickly until he took up bike riding. We can assume that she was always a stay-at-home mom; she does the housework and yardwork, and there is no mention of her having a job. She played Goldie Hawn's mother in "Private Benjamin". Since "Private Benjamin" was made into a TV series, as was "Breaking Away", she has the distinction of appearing in two such movies. Interestingly, she appears in the opening and closing credits before Paul Dooley does. In addition to her Oscar nomination for the Best Actress in a Supporting Role, she was nominated for an Emmy Award for the Outstanding Supporting Actress in a Drama Series in 1981, for the "Breaking Away" TV series, thereby receiving both an Oscar and Emmy nomination for playing the same character.

THE CAST

ROBYN DOUGLASS is Katherine Bennett, the college student who is the object of Dave's desire as he pretends to be an Italian exchange student. The closing credits show "Introducing Robyn Douglass", as this was her first theatrical movie, following appearances in two TV movies within a year prior to "Breaking Away". She appeared in three theatrical movies—opposite the likes of Dudley Moore, Ryan O'Neal, and Steve Martin—and several TV movies after "Breaking Away". In a role-reversal twist, in 1984, she starred in the TV movie, "Her Life as a Man", with the plot as described on IMDb as "To land a sportswriting job on a national magazine run by a chauvinistic editor, an aspiring female reporter convincingly disguises herself as a man to get the inside story."[2] She grew up in San Francisco, a cosmic connection to Peter Yates's "Bullitt".

HART BOCHNER is Rod, the evil leader of the college kids who are always harassing the Cutters. Rod has no redeeming qualities, inciting violence against and insulting our heroes, and disrespecting coeds. "Breaking Away" was his second movie, following "Islands in the Stream" two years previously, and he went on to an extensive career, most notably in "Die Hard". He reunited with Paul Dooley in "For Your Consideration". His father was the actor Lloyd Bochner, whose career spanned 58 years. Interestingly, Lloyd appeared in one episode of the TV series "Hart to Hart" in 1980.

AMY WRIGHT is Nancy, Moocher's love interest and soon-to-be bride. "Breaking Away" was her fourth movie, and she appeared in eight movies that were released between 1978 and 1980. Her credits include "The Deer Hunter", "The Amityville Horror", "Stardust Memories" (with Daniel Stern), "Inside Moves", "Crossing Delancey", and "The Accidental Tourist". She has worked for the noted directors Woody Allen, Robert DeNiro, Richard Donner, John Houston, Lawrence Kasdan, and Joan

---

[2] https://www.imdb.com/title/tt0087403/

Micklin Silver. She was married to the late Rip Torn, one of my favorite character actors for roles such as Scully in "Summer Rental" and Patches O'Houlihan in "Dodgeball: A True Underdog Story".

JOHN ASHTON is Mike's unnamed brother, a policeman and the polar opposite of Mike. He continued his law enforcement roles as John Taggart in "Beverly Hills Cop", "Beverly Hills Cop II", and "Beverly Hills Cop: Axel F" alongside Eddie Murphy and Judge Reinhold. Like Paul Dooley, he appeared in John Hughes movies, in "Some Kind of Wonderful" as Eric Stoltz's character's father and in "She's Having a Baby". Other major roles were in "Midnight Run", "Little Big League", and "Gone Baby Gone". He appeared in "Honky Tonk Freeway" with Daniel Stern.

P.J. SOLES is Suzy, one of Katherine's sorority sisters. The closing credits list her as "Pamela Jayne Soles". She has a number of high-profile movie credits, such as Brian DePalma's "Carrie", "Halloween", "Stripes", "Private Benjamin" (with Barbara Barrie), and as the star in "Rock 'n' Roll High School". She had auditioned for the role of Princess Leia in Star Wars, but the part went to Carrie Fisher. She had met Dennis Quaid when they appeared in "Our Winning Season", and they were married in 1978 for five years, which includes the release of "Breaking Away". She appears significantly in only one scene, with minimal dialogue, but the scene has a major bearing on the story.

PETER MALONEY portrayed the doctor who attended to Ray after his meltdown. He has an extensive resume in TV, theater, and film, including appearing in "The Amityville Horror" with Amy Wright.

DR. JOHN RYAN was the real-life president of Indiana University at the time, and appears in one scene as himself. In 1978, Dr. Ryan allowed the filming of the movie to take place on campus. His other distinction

THE CAST

is that he hired the legendary men's basketball coach Bob Knight—who led the team to three national championships—shortly after he arrived in 1971. Oddly, both Dr. Ryan and director Peter Yates were born in 1929 and died in 2011. In an interview for WRTV in Indianapolis at the time of the filming, he said, "I think it's probably good for everybody to have a standby profession just in case you get fired from the one that you're in. Movie stardom isn't what I planned, but if it turns out that way, that's all right."

The movie had a cast of thousands, literally when including the locals who occupied the stadium for the finale. In fact, that turnout was below expectations, forcing Peter Yates to move the crowd around the stadium for the various scenes. Several other non-professional actors were instrumental in the movie. **EDDY VAN GUYSE** portrayed the Italian villain in the Cinzano 100 race; he still has the blue Colnago bicycle that he rode in it. **GARY RYBAR** was Dennis Christopher's stunt double and is a member of the Little 500 Hall of Fame. He was on the Delta Chi team that won the Little 500 race in 1974, 1976, and 1977, and placed second in 1975. One feature of his resemblance to Dennis Chrisopher was his nose. **TOM SCHWOEGLER**, a fraternity coach in real life, is in the credits as the Bicycle Coach and Mechanic. His Acacia team would win the Little 500 race in 1983 for the first time since 1961. **WILLIAM S. ARMSTRONG** and **HOWARD S. WILCOX** portrayed the two Little 500 Race Officials. Mr. Armstrong served as the Executive Director and president of the IU Foundation, and the current home of the Little 500—and of the men's and women's soccer teams—is named for him, the Bill Armstrong Stadium. Mr. Wilcox, while the director of the IU Student Foundation in 1950, was inspired to create the Little 500 race, which began In 1951. **BOB WOOLERY** is the retired president of the former Woolery Stone Co., and the grandson of its founder, Henry Woolery. The limestone mill is where Ray goes to visit his former coworkers, and Bob Woolery portrays the employee who greets him and jokes about making him an apprentice. Note: *The Bloomington Herald-Times* quoted him as saying that he "can never recall hearing the term 'cutter' before 20th Century Fox invaded Bloomington in the late 1970s to make Breaking Away."[3]

---

[3] https://www.heraldtimesonline.com/story/news/2003/12/29/old-cutter-woolery-still-loves-limestone/118288912/

CHAPTER 2

THE BRAINS BEHIND THE MOVIE

PETER YATES, the director, was born in 1929, in Aldershot, Hampshire, England. He started in theater, and, prophetically, his bio on IMDb has "In the early 1950's, he worked as a dubbing assistant, cutter …"[1] A theater cutter is an employee who works with the Costume Designer.

Interestingly, "Breaking Away" marked the halfway point of his theatrical movie career; it was his twelfth, with eleven before and eleven to follow. Before "Breaking Away", his most famous movie was "Bullitt", but "The Friends of Eddie Coyle", "The Deep", "Mother, Jugs & Speed", "For Pete's Sake", "The Hot Rock", "Murphy's War", and "John and Mary" before "Breaking Away" are also noteworthy.

After "Breaking Away", he produced and directed his second movie within four years that was nominated for the Oscar for the Best Picture in 1983, "The Dresser". He was also nominated for the Directing Oscar for "The Dresser". He was reunited with Dennis Quaid for "Suspect", which also had Cher, Liam Neeson, John Mahoney, and Joe Mantegna. He also directed "Roommates", "Year of the Comet", "An Innocent Man", "The House on Carroll Street", and "Eyewitness". When the *Washington Post* reported his death, it identified him as the director of the polar opposites "Bullitt" and "Breaking Away". What those two movies have in common is the fact that he liked to film his movies on location.

In addition to those actors already mentioned, the list of those who appeared in his movies reads like a Who's Who: F. Murray Abraham,

---

[1] https://www.imdb.com/name/nm0946811/

Jacqueline Bisset, Peter Boyle, Ellen Burstyn, Georg Stanford Brown, Michael Caine, Bill Cosby, Tom Courtenay, Tim Daly, Jeff Daniels, Robert Duvall, Peter Falk, Mia Farrow, Norman Fell, Albert Finney, Allen Garfield, Louis Gossett Jr., Moses Gunn, Larry Hagman, Marcia Gay Harden, Glenne Headly, Buck Henry, Dustin Hoffman, Linda Hunt, William Hurt, Louis Jourdan, Harvey Keitel, Ron Leibman, John Malkovich, Kelly McGillis, Steve McQueen, Penelope Ann Miller, Robert Mitchum, Ron Moody, Julianne Moore, Kate Nelligan, Nick Nolte, Peter O'Toole, Simon Oakland, Estelle Parsons, Mandy Patinkin, Robert Redford, Alex Rocco, Jan Rubes, George Segal, Tom Selleck, Robert Shaw, Sam Shepard, Maggie Smith, James Spader, Frances Sternhagen, Barbra Streisand, D.B. Sweeney, Jessica Tandy, Robert Vaughn, Eli Wallach, Sigourney Weaver, Raquel Welch, and Frank Whaley.

His last movie was a TV movie, "A Separate Peace" in 2004, and he passed away in 2011 at the age of 81. Of his 23 theatrical movies, 13 were rated PG (including one in 1963 indicated as "Approved"), six were rated R, three were rated PG-13, and one from 1967 had no rating. Even the ultra-tense "Bullitt" had a PG rating.

Time magazine reported that the Paramount studio made Yates an offer that he apparently could refuse, to direct "The Godfather":[2]

> The melodrama was right in keeping with the kind of picture Paramount had in mind. The company wanted a quickie exploiting the book's success, shot in modern dress in St. Louis on a relatively low budget of $2.5 million. To direct it, Paramount Production Chief Robert Evans approached Peter Yates, who had established his thriller credentials with Bullitt; Richard Brooks, who shot In Cold Blood; and even Greek Director Costa Gavras, the man who made Z. When, for

---

[2] https://content.time.com/time/subscriber/article/0,33009,903363,00.html

various reasons, none of these choices worked out, Evans went for a dark horse: Francis Ford Coppola, who was only 31.

STEVE TESICH was the Oscar-winning screenwriter. He was an alternate on the Phi Kappa Psi team that won the Little 500 race in 1962 with David Blase, and he competed on the teams that finished ninth in 1963, 11th in 1964, and fourth in 1965.

The *New York Times* has:[3]

> He was born Stoyan Tesich in Titovo Uzice, Yugoslavia on Sept. 29, 1942. His father, a professional soldier who opposed the ascendant Communist regime of Marshall Tito, fled the country after World War II, leaving Mr. Tesich and his older sister to be raised by their mother until the family could be reunited — which it was, in East Chicago, Ind., in 1957, where his father worked as a machinist until he died five years later.
>
> When he arrived in this country at 14, Mr. Tesich spoke no English …
>
> He attended Indiana University on a wrestling scholarship, though once there, his athletic interest turned to bicycling; like Dave, the hero of "Breaking Away," he was a racer. He majored in Russian literature, graduating in 1965, and moved on to pursue a Ph.D. at Columbia University.

At the Oscars ceremony, when Neil Simon as the presenter read the list of nominees for the Best Original Screenplay, Tesich received the loudest applause from the audience. As he came to the podium,

---

[3] https://www.nytimes.com/1996/07/02/arts/steve-tesich-53-whose-plays-plumbed-the-nation-s-identity.html

the orchestra played Felix Mendelssohn's "Symphony No. 4 in A major (Italian Symphony), Op. 90", which was prominent in the movie. Like Dave Stohler, he won a trophy. In his speech accepting the Oscar, he said:

> The last thing I want to say is that long before I actually saw America, my first glimpses of it were in a movie house in Yugoslavia. It was a western, "Stagecoach," and it seemed like a wonderful, endless frontier of a country where these good and evil characters fought it out for the soul of America. And after all these years of being here I am just so grateful to be given an opportunity to send back a film and to tell 'em that I find it very much like the place I had seen originally: The good and the bad still fight it out; the good still tend to win in the end.

He wrote the screenplay for "Four Friends" in 1981; the IMDb listing has a familiar ring to it:[4]

> A group of four friends form strong bonds while in high school in the early 1960s, then desperately cling to that love during the turbulent counterculture movement and social upheavals that marked the end of the decade. This story of four working-class kids in a small industrial town—who go their separate ways after high school in the innocence of 1961 and come together again at the end of the turbulent Sixties—is as much about the coming of age of America as it is about the changes the characters go through. The four friends of the title are thoughtful Danilo, a Yugoslavian immigrant with dreams of being a writer and a scholar; Tom, good-looking and athletic, who is bound for the army; cautious David who has mixed feelings about staying in town and joining the family mortuary business; and lovely,

---

[4] https://www.imdb.com/title/tt0082404/

ditzy, exasperating Georgia, who tries to inspire all of them with her longings for a life of Bohemian adventure. It is told through the eyes of Danilo, whose story is loosely based on the writer Tesich's own life growing up in Bloomington, Indiana.

Tesich and Yates worked together again on "Eyewitness" in 1981 and on "Eleni" in 1985. "Eyewitness" also had a familiar ring to it, with a humble janitor dishonestly claiming that he had seen a murder, in order to cozy up with an attractive TV reporter, played by Sigourney Weaver. Like "Breaking Away", it had different working titles, "The Janitor" and "The Janitor Doesn't Dance", before the change to "Eyewitness". In 1977, Yates had directed Tesich's play "Passing Game", about a basketball star, at the American Place Theatre. Tesich later wrote the cycling-themed film "American Flyers" in 1985, starring Kevin Costner. "American Flyers" has a character named David and the tagline, "They're four one-of-a-kind people taking a chance…and going after a dream that will change their lives forever." It takes place in Colorado; an early screening of "Breaking Away" had been wildly received in Denver.

He passed away in 1996 while on vacation in Nova Scotia. Whereas Ray Stohler was a candidate for a heart attack, that was the cause of Tesich's death.

CYNTHIA SCHEIDER was the editor, also the editor of the "Breaking Away" TV series and of "Eyewitness". She was the assistant editor of "Sorcerer", my favorite under-the-radar movie of 1977, and was married to Roy Scheider, the star of "Sorcerer" and many other notable movies. Interestingly, Roy was nominated for the Actor in a Leading Role Oscar for "All That Jazz" in 1980, the same year that "Breaking Away" had multiple nominations. Her only acting credit is in "Last Embrace", an Alfred Hitchcock-like story that starred Roy Scheider.

PATRICK WILLIAMS adapted the music. He has hundreds of credits on his resume. Interestingly, he was the composer of "Cutters", a TV series in 1993, which IMDb describes as "A sitcom about Harry Polachek's struggles to keep his Buffalo, New York barbershop open."

DAVID K. BLASE is in the credits as the "500 Race Announcer", but that understates his importance. Referring to the 1962 race that the Phi Kappa Psi fraternity won with a meet record, at the time, of 2:17:26, the *Bloomington Herald-Times* has:[5]

> While he was a student, Blase would walk down 3rd street singing Neapolitan songs and Italian arias. His dress aimed to mimic Italian style, building himself into a different character — someone far removed from the scrawny, self-proclaimed shrimp that Blase saw in the mirror.
>
> By the time he returned to Bloomington for his senior year in 1962, the IUSF [Indiana University Student Foundation] erased the rule for outside races and Blase was eligible again. He rejoined the team at Phi Kappa Psi, where he met a young Yugoslavian kid from the east Chicago area named Steve Tesich. The two bonded and trained together for the '62 race, which the Phi Psi team won handily. Blase rode a record 139 of the event's 200 laps, which were the most ever at the time.
>
> Blase served as a technical adviser during the film's production in the summer of 1978 and made a couple cameos, too. He was a rider in the Cinzano bicycle race late in the movie and served

---

[5] https://www.heraldtimesonline.com/story/news/local/2014/04/22/35-years-later-the-man-who-inspired-breaking-away-is-still-biking/47726981/

as the track announcer during the movie's big race scene filmed at the 10th street stadium.

On the Screenwriting From Iowa website, Tesich describes how meeting David Blase gave him inspiration:[6]

> I ran into a guy [in Bloomington] who was doing his Italian fantasy. I was riding a bike—I hear an Italian opera being sung behind me and I turn around and there's this guy climbing a hill singing. He starts talking Italian to me, and being Yugoslavian and knowing how tough it is on foreigners I really have pity on the guy. For a week I try to tell him what America is like, what it's like to be in Indiana and all this and I find out he's from Indianapolis [Indiana]. He grew up there and this whole fantasy was just kind of a daydream.

In an interview with Dr. Ben Pearl on the "Fit Foot" U podcast, David says that he had left Indiana University for a year to take a job in Indianapolis working with Italian doctors, and that he always liked opera. Steve Tesich's play about David, "The Eagle of Naptown" (Naptown is the nickname of Indianapolis) perhaps provides a clue for why Dave Stohler, coming home at the beginning of the movie, says to his parents in his Italian accent:

> Oh, the victory …she was easy. But the promoter…'fondatore' …He tells me that the Italians will be here maybe soon…and I will race with the best of them, Italianos. Like the nightingales they sing, like the eagles, they fly.

---

[6] https://screenwritingfromiowa.wordpress.com/2014/12/05/the-top-hoosierslavian-screenwriter/

The Art Direction was by **PATRIZIA VON BRANDENSTEIN**, whose credits include "Amadeus" (winning the Oscar for Art Direction), "The Untouchables" (Oscar nominee for Art Direction), "Ragtime" (Oscar nominee for Art Direction), "Postcards From The Edge", "Working Girl", "A Chorus Line", "Silkwood", and "The Candidate". In 2016, she received the Art Directors Guild's Lifetime Achievement Award at the 20th Annual Excellence in Production Design Awards. In addition to being in charge of cleaning up the quarry, she has a brief scene as the woman shaking a rug outside as Dave rides home in the beginning.

The camera operator, who masterminded the closeup shots in the Little 500 race among others, was **JAMES GLENNON**. His extensive list of credits includes "Star Wars: Episode VI - Return of the Jedi", "The Godfather Part II", "Ordinary People", and "The Conversation".

So, how did a director from England who had made the movie "Bullitt"—which had a famous, extended car chase through San Francisco (Yates's entry on IMDb states that he started out as a professional racing car driver); starred Steve McQueen, Robert Duvall, Jacqueline Bisset, and Robert Vaughn; and had explosions—make a movie that takes place in Bloomington, Indiana; whose chases are bike races; whose cast was largely unknown; and whose biggest explosion is a blown tire? It was an act of pure genius.

CHAPTER 3
THE STORY

IN HIS POEM "Locksly Hall", Alfred Lord Tennyson wrote, "In the spring a young man's fancy lightly turns to thoughts of love." In Bloomington, Indiana, the home of Indiana University, a young man's thoughts may also turn to classes, his future, and the Little 500 bicycle race.

That is, unless the young men are Dave, Mike, Moocher, and Cyril, four local boys. We will see that love is not a stranger to Dave and Moocher. They are in their last year as teenagers. They had jobs at the A&P grocery store, but Mike was fired and the other three quit out of solidarity. They are Bloomington's version of the Four Musketeers—"All for one, and one for all", as Mike says—most of the time. No classes for them, they are a year out of high school. They are taking a gap year, although there is no reason to think that the gap will last only a year. They have no idea what they want to do, except that they definitely don't want to go to college, instead hanging out at the quarry, where they can swim all day. When they sunbathe on Slant Rock at the quarry, they are positioned in order from left to right by their height—Moocher, Dave, Mike, Cyril (Daniel Stern is six-foot-four)—as if they are organized, which they are not. They are the tail end of the Baby Boomer Generation, but they don't fit the model. The Johns Hopkins University website has:[1]

> Being raised in a society with limited resources, limited jobs, and limited schooling inspired a generation of competitors:

---

[1] https://imagine.jhu.edu/blog/2022/11/17/the-changing-generational-values/

individuals who operated with a "work as hard as you can, then work even harder the next time" mindset.

According to liveaboutdotcom, some common workplace and worker values/mindsets associated with the Boomer generation are work-centric and workaholic, independent and self-assertive, goal-oriented and career-focused, competitive, and self-actualized. Together, these values and mindsets suggest a generation that prioritizes efficiency and efficacy in the workplace but has little regard for a work-life balance, with work tending to be the center of their lives.

The quarry is where their fathers, the real cutters, cut the limestone that was used for the university buildings that the rich kids occupy. The problem is that they can't escape the specter of college, as Indiana University is in their backyard. Everywhere that they look, they see "campus"; the realtor for Moocher's house is Campus Realty, Moocher gets a job, briefly, at the Campus Street Car Wash, even Dave's dad has sold out by calling his car lot Campus Cars. With the university ever-present, they are in constant conflict with the wealthy college kids, with each group having its turf.

They will not go to the Little 500 race, not even as spectators, since that would mean consorting with those students, who look down their noses at the poorer local kids. When the students call the local kids "cutters", it is an insult.

"Mike" and "bike" rhyme, but Mike and Dave are polar opposites. Mike was the high school quarterback, tall and athletic. When they occupy Slant Rock, Mike is the King of the Hill. Dave is short and slight, and has overcome a period of being sickly to be an elite bike racer. Mike talks a good game, but Dave has self-confidence, enough to pursue an attractive coed, who should be out of his league.

THE STORY

Dave eventually gets a job cleaning the cars on Ray's car lot, but, as an expert at repairing bikes, that would have been ideal for him; as the saying goes, "Choose a job you love, and you will never have to work a day in your life." Moocher will land a job at the car wash, but lose it in a matter of seconds. Mike and Cyril are appalled when Moocher is starting that job:

Dave: *Guess what? The Italians are coming.*
Mike*: Guess what? Moocher's going?*
Cyril: *Dave, you've got to talk to him.*
Dave: *Where are you going, Mooch?*
Cyril: *He's getting a job!*
Dave: *So?*
Cyril: *So? HE'S GETTING A JOB.*
Mike: *Campus Street Car Wash. Going to wait on college boys. Don't forget to smile, to get a tip. Look, I thought we were going to stick together.*
Moocher: *I need a job, Mike.*
Cyril: *Don't go, Mooch! They only let you out on weekends and national holidays!*
Mike: *Hey, don't forget to write!*

The four boys actually have little in common, other than being slackers, but they have displayed some athleticism; they like to swim, and their dives into the swimming hole at the quarry are actually impressive. Dave is obsessed with the Italian bike team, riding a Masi bicycle and wearing a yellow Campagnolo cap. While Mike is the former quarterback, Cyril played basketball in high school and thought that he might get a scholarship offer; Moocher lifts weights. Cyril is actually taller than Mike; if his posture were better—he is often slumped—he might exhibit more confidence.

It would make sense that the nickname "Cutters" carried over from real-life Indiana. However, IMDb has:[2]

> The production team decided to call the Bloomington townies "cutters" because they felt the actual local nickname ("stoners" or "stonies") would draw a parallel to drug references for viewers who were not raised in the area.

The Cutters' turf is the quarry, where they retreat in the opening scene to enjoy a swim, with Mike singing a song about working at the A&P. Dave has a huge trophy, after another bike race victory. The quarry is their place to escape from the college culture, swim and sunbathe in a simple setting, while honoring their fathers' work at the same time. Instead of retreating to a watering hole to celebrate, they go to the Long Hole, in the quarry known as Sanders or Rooftop Quarry, off East Empire Mill Road. In the opening scene, Dave passes on joining his friends for a swim. In the Pressbook for the movie, Dennis Christopher said that he had never learned how to swim. Later on in the movie, Dave will have to aid in rescuing Mike in the water after a mishap.

We learn that Moocher's parents are in Chicago, as his father is looking for a job. We learn that Cyril is the good-natured goofball of the four. We learn later that he took the college entrance exam with Dave.

They ponder their future:

Cyril: *When you're sixteen, they call it sweet sixteen. And when you're eighteen, you get to drink and vote and see dirty movies. What the hell do you do when you're nineteen?*
Mike: *You leave home.*
Cyril: *My dad says Jesus never went further than fifty miles from his home.*
Mike: *And look what happened to him.*

---

[2] https://www.imdb.com/title/tt0078902/

THE STORY

You leave home? That may not be foremost in the boys' head, although Mike may be yearning to leave for Wyoming.

Dave rides home on his Masi bike that he had won in a race, carrying his trophy and singing "Libiamo ne'lieti calici" from the opera "La Traviata" by Giuseppe Verdi, in Italian. His singing is a little off-key, but his voice will improve the next time that he sings. The fact he had been the treasurer of the Latin Club may have kick-started his love of Italian culture. He calls out to the *bambini* (children) who are playing on the sidewalk. Nancy calls out to him to ask if Moocher is home, but Dave is lost in thought. There is a small girl playing on Nancy's doorstep, but we will not learn who she is. Dave's Italian persona has riled at least one neighbor. As he passes by, a woman sitting on her front porch says to her husband: "He was as normal as pumpkin pie. And now look at him. His poor parents."

The scene cuts to his poor parents in their house on South Lincoln Street; actually his father, Ray, is the only one who is miserable over Dave's actions. He always looks as if he has swallowed a teaspoon of vinegar. He is swatting flies, whose presence he attributes to Dave's cologne, which is Neapolitan Sunset, Evelyn tells him. Evelyn is managing Ray's diet by giving him grapefruit, a salad, and see-through coffee, because the doctor says that he has a bad heart. Ray, the used car salesman, has his pocket protector, which contains a "Campus Cars" business card.

Evelyn is the open-minded one of the two parents; there may be a genetic connection between her and Dave in their light-colored hair. When Evelyn and Ray talk about Dave, we get the obligatory "When I was his age ..." speech.

> Evelyn: *He was very sickly until he started riding around on that bike.*
> Ray: *Yeah, now his body's fine but his mind is gone. He used to be a smart kid. I thought he was going to go to college.*

Evelyn: *I thought you didn't want him to go to college.*
Ray: *Why should he go to college? I didn't go to college. When I was nineteen I was working in the quarries ten hours a day.*
Evelyn: *Most of the quarries have closed.*
Ray: *Yeah, well, let him find another job.*
Evelyn: *Jobs are not that easy to find.*

Even worse for Ray, Dave acts like an Italian.

Ray: *But, Evelyn. Look what's happened to him. He's turned into an I-tie; Ciao, Papa. Ciao, Mama. A-ree-da-ver-chee. That's Ity talk. I used to think it was funny at first, not funny anymore.*

On cue, Dave arrives with his huge trophy from the race that he has just won. He is in his Italian-accent mode.

Dave: *Buon giorno, Papa.*
Ray: *I'm not Papa, I'm your Goddamn father.*
Dave: *Buon giorno, Mama.*
Ray: *And she's your Goddamn mother.*

Evelyn admires the trophy:

Evelyn: *Isn't this a lovely trophy, dear?*
Ray: *Oh, yeah, so what? I've lived fifty years, and I never got a trophy.*
Dave: *You never got a trophy, Papa?*
Ray: *Nope, I never got one.*
Dave: *I give you this one. You are Numero Uno, King Papa.* [gives him a kiss on the cheek.]
Ray: *Don't do that.*

THE STORY

Note: appropriately, Paul Dooley was in fact age 50 at the time of the filming. Ray never won a trophy, but Paul Dooley won the 1979 National Board of Review Award as the Best Supporting Actor for "Breaking Away". Ray does not exhibit positive parenting; he should be supporting his son's success instead of acting with sarcasm. To say that he is uncomfortable with Dave's kiss on the cheek is putting it mildly.

Dave goes to the bathroom to shave his legs. He puts his album, OPERATIC ARIAS BY ENRICO GIMONDI—the cover has a photo of Enrico Gimondi, the fictitious opera singer, and whose name is inspired by the Italian cycling legend Felice Gimondi—on his record player and plays Figaro's "Largo al factotum" from "The Barber of Seville".

His room is a shrine to Italian culture. On his door, he has a poster of the Roman Colosseum, with "Italia" at the top. In his room, he has a map of Italy and a green-white-and-red Italy flag on his window. He has posters of Italian racers, including one above his bed's headboard of the Cinzano Racing Team, his heroes. Ironically, the Cinzano colors of red, white, and blue replicate America's. He has a Cinzano decal on the headboard, an empty Cinzano bottle, and a Cinzano ashtray for the cat's food. Rocky Balboa had his pet turtles, Cuff and Link; Dave has named the cat Fellini, replacing the name of Jake that Ray had given it.

The inspiration for Dave renaming the feline to Fellini was described in the Pop Entertainment website. Dennis Christopher was traveling through Europe on a one-way ticket with no plans and about $79 in his pocket when he stumbled into a Federico Fellini set in Rome. He engaged with Fellini, a risky venture, and ended up with a role as The Hippie (Uncredited) in "Fellini's Roma", which came out in 1972.[3]

In an interview with the Huffington Post, Christopher said that Fellini "… used to call me 'Bambino,' which is funny, because that was

---

[3] https://www.popentertainmentarchives.com/post/dennis-christopher-an-actor-s-life-from-fellini-to-breaking-away-to-django-unchained

the original title of *Breaking Away*. He took a great fondness to me."[4]

Dave has several trophies from races that he has won, and he keeps his bike suspended from the ceiling, but, true to his hometown, he has a "BHS South Panthers" decal on his window, denoting his Bloomington high school.

When Nancy comes to Moocher's house, which has peeling paint and sparse furniture, on her way to work (yes, *she* has a job), he starts to lift weights, barely listening to her.

> Nancy: *You know what?*
> Moocher: *No, what?*
> Nancy: *I'm leaving home, that's what.*
> Moocher: *What? Where are you going?*
> Nancy: *About 5 blocks south.*
> Moocher: *Oh.*
> Nancy: *I found this nice little place to rent, it's so cute, I could scream. My folks said I could have some of their furniture from the basement.*
> Moocher: *All right.*
> Nancy: *I thought maybe you could give me a hand, moving.*
> Moocher: *Oh sure, if I'm not too busy. You know. How's the job?*
> Nancy: *You know what. Frank said if I keep up the good work, it will just be a matter of time before I become head cashier.*

Moocher, busy doing what? To Nancy, leaving home is moving a few blocks south. Moocher says that he will walk her to her job, apparently not worried that they will be seen together. At the quarry, he had denied to Mike that he was still dating Nancy.

The next scene has Ray trying to sell a college kid what he calls the best car on his lot. The car lot is called "Campus Cars"; his sign has "Cars With a College Education". His clientele is the rich college kids. He

---

[4] https://www.huffpost.com/entry/dennis-christopher-a-life_b_3698096

does have a Volkswagen Beetle on the lot, a foreign car! He has written sales-pitch slogans such as "HOMECOMING QUEEN", "ENGLISH MAJOR", "GRAD SCHOOL SPECIAL", "MAGNA CUM LAUDE", "FRESHMAN RUSH", and "VARSITY SQUAD" on the windshields, a nod to his potential customers.

The students' turf is the campus. Both groups cross into the other's turf occasionally, igniting a conflict when they do. Early in the movie, Mike has pulled a prank by pretending to be trapped in a refrigerator in the quarry. Peter Yates had extended underwater scenes in "The Deep", but this one lasts a few seconds. When the students arrive, Mike is stunned when one of them performs a masterful dive off of the 65-foot Rooftop ledge, and yells out to them. A student yells back, "Hey, Cutter", giving us the first mention of the term, but without context yet.

> Mike: *They've got indoor pools and outdoor pools on campus, and they got to come here … Come on, let's get out of here. If they're going to come here, then we're going to go on the campus.*

The students have dared to trespass on their turf. The Cutter boys drive toward the campus, Mike saluting the Marlboro billboard on the way. He has a pack of Marlboros on top of his dashboard. The contrast from quarry to campus is similar to Dorothy entering the Land of Oz. They pass the tennis courts on North Fee Lane, in sight of Assembly Hall, the arena that houses the men's basketball team that had won the national championship a few years earlier. Cyril is taken by the coeds; he shouts out, "Hi there, what's your major?" He wonders what it is like to kiss a co-ed; it is a foreshadow, as Dave will be able to tell him what it is like in a few days. They cruise near the auditorium on East 7th Street, where the premiere of the movie will take place. Near the Musical Arts Center on North Eagleson Avenue, they accidentally run over the frisbee that Rod, Katherine, and others are tossing, then Mike puts the car into reverse to run over it again when Rod insults him. The monetary damage is minimal, but for Rod, it is the principle: the Cutters–only Dave is wearing a shirt, a white tank top–in a beat-up car have dared to come onto his turf. As the boys drive away, Katherine's expression shows that she is miffed at their actions. Moocher had tried to warn Mike not to provoke the students, saying, "Hey, we're on their turf, Mike." This is conflict #1 between the Cutters and Rod's posse. Dave pokes his head out the car and is instantly smitten with the attractive Katherine.

In the next scene, as they watch football practice from a hill outside the stadium, Mike shares that when the students call them Cutters, it's a dirty word. Ironically, without the original cutters, the boys' fathers, the students would not have their majestic buildings.

Later, Dave is on campus, near the current location of the Sample Gates, relaxing beside his bike. Why is he on campus? Because he has conflicting thoughts about going to college? Luck smiles on him; he sees the same Katherine, who was tossing the frisbee, leave a class at Franklin Hall on Kirkwood Avenue. "Mamma mia", he says; no translation is necessary. Katherine is radiant, and so is the light behind Dave, perhaps from lighting of the production. When she takes off on her scooter, a notebook falls off of the back. Fittingly, her scooter is a Vespa, manufactured by Piaggio in Italy, and it has a USA decal on it. "Vespa" means "wasp" in Italian; it would have been bizarre if there were a scooter named "Mosca", a word that Dave knows well. Note: in a handwritten 1989 letter by Robyn Douglass, stored in the Indiana University Archives, she wrote that she still had the Vespa and that it had been ridden by Steve McQueen during his filming of "Bullitt". She also wrote that she still had her sorority shirt, and she suggested that Indiana University create a museum dedicated to the movie.

Dave hops on his Italian-made Masi bike, fetches the notebook, and takes off to chase her down, dodging traffic while going the wrong way on a one-way street, with Mendelssohn's *Italian Symphony No. 4 in A Major, Op. 90, "Italian": IV. Saltarello: Presto* accompanying him.

THE STORY

Note: in an interview with Bob Babbitt, on his babbittville.com website, Dennis Christopher said that Steve Tesich had said that it would be impossible for him to pick up the notebook while cycling.[5] Dennis proved him wrong.

Dave is on his two-wheel vehicle, and Katherine is on hers. He has her notebook in his mouth, but still calls out "Signorina" to her. Dave had been practicing from a book, "Italian Phrases", at the time; he can't let Katherine see it. He makes a right turn from South Hawthorne Drive onto East Third Street and passes the Biology Building greenhouse.

Note: in an example of Peter Yates's creative directing, Brad Cook of the Indiana University Archives said:[6]

> "... in that scene that I mentioned earlier where he notices the girl, drops a book and she goes off on a motor scooter and he gets on his bike grabs the book and goes after her, you'll notice that in one place, they're riding west to east on that road between the Union Building and Owen Hall, and in the very next scene, they're riding the other way."

Dave finally catches up to her when she arrives at her sorority house on East Third Street, the Chi Delta Delta. In real life, it was the Delta Delta Delta house, so the change in lettering on the building was minimal. In front of the sorority house is a rack filled with bicycles. Note: Google Maps shows that it's faster to travel the route by bicycle than by car, and even more so in 1978, since the route today does not cut through the campus. Even though Dave had poked his head out of the car at the frisbee incident, Katherine does not recognize him as one of the boys who made her angry. He is also *incognito*; wearing a racing

---

[5] https://babbittville.com/classics-dennis-christopher/
[6] https://indianapublicmedia.org/news/breaking-away-celebrates-40th-anniversary-of-premier.php

outfit, he does not project as a Cutter. Out of breath, he talks to her in an Italian accent, "Is yours, no?" She is amazed at the effort that he went through. She asks if he is an exchange student; he pauses, then decides that by saying yes, he can charm her. He introduces himself with the first name that pops into his head, Enrico Gimondi from the opera album. This may have inspired the basis for the movie "Mrs. Doubtfire", where Robin Williams, with his fake female British accent, concocted his name by seeing the newspaper headline, "Police Doubt Fire Was Accidental". Thus begins Dave's big lie. Luckily for him, she does not recognize the name of the opera singer. If Google had existed in 1979, she may have done a background check on the name. She introduces herself as Katherine Bennett and likes the sound of "Katherina", as Dave/Enrico repeats her name. As a Cutter, he knows that Katherine is out of his league, but as a student, she is not.

The music of *M'appari tutt'amor* begins. It translates to "She appeared to me, full of love" and is an aria from Friedrich von Flotow's romantic comic opera, "Martha". It carries over into the next scene, as Dave sees Katherine again by accident. He is riding his bike blissfully in the woods of Brown County State Park, east of Bloomington on State Road 46, without his hands on the handlebars, arms spread out as if he is conducting the orchestra. Then, a tire bursts, and as he is fixing it, Katherine drives by, in Rod's convertible, of course. She is leading a pack of students as they train on their bikes. She recognizes Dave and calls out to him, slowing down to the point that the students nearly run into the car.

When Dave gets home, he moans that he is in love, though apparently not giving the details to his parents. He now has everything that he could desire—freedom, no job, no schoolwork—and he has two love affairs, with Katherine and with his bicycle.

He is so smitten that he sends flowers to Katherine at her sorority house, where his chase with her notebook had ended. Rod and Katherine bicker in Rod's convertible.

THE STORY

Rod: *Suzy says this guy sent you flowers.*
Katherine: *So what? You never sent me flowers.*
Rod: *Who is he, Kath?*
Katherine: *Just some crazy guy I met. God, I don't know what's gotten into you.*

Note: this will not be the last time that Suzy creates friction in Dave's pursuit of Katherine. At this point, Dave is just a crazy guy to Katherine, although he charmed her when they first met. That will change. Dave and Rod never come face-to-face, and are never together until the final race, but Mike will spar with Rod a few times.

The tightness of the four boys is starting to show cracks. Dave and Moocher have love interests, which they don't share, initially. Cyril thinks about taking the college entrance exam with Dave.

Dave is on his doorstep working on his bike when the postal carrier drops off the mail. Evelyn is working in the garden; the flowers in the front of the house are red and white, which, along with the green grass, display the colors of Italy's flag. Dave opens his magazine and sees the news, "Team CINZANO to Race in Indianapolis" for a 100-mile race, which sets him into a state of ecstasy. The magazine includes a photo of the Cinzano Racing Team, his heroes. He yells to Evelyn that "The Italians are coming!" and jumps on his bike to catch up to the postal carrier to give him a kiss on the cheek.

Dave is so psyched that he knows that he has to challenge himself in order to compete in the race. He rides his Masi Gran Criterium through the Morgan-Monroe State Forest to a point 50 miles from Bloomington and races on the main highway, State Route 37. Actually, the "Bloomington 50" sign was made just for the movie. Prophetically, the Little 500 race is 50 miles in length. An 18-wheel semi-truck passes him on the highway; it has "CINZANO" on the back. Dave is able to use the draft of the truck to speed down the highway, and the truck driver helps him by signaling his speed with his fingers … first, four fingers for 40 miles per hour, then five fingers when Dave hits 50 miles per hour. He thinks that he has lost Dave when he can't see him in his rear-view mirror, only to see Dave appear moments later. There is a terrific long camera shot from hundreds of feet away showing Dave pacing the truck; it symbolizes a Dave-and-Goliath competition. Just when the driver sticks out five fingers plus another to indicate that they have hit 60, a highway patrol officer pulls him over for exceeding the 55 miles per hour speed limit. The truck driver waves at Dave as he is pulled over; for Dave, a male adult has shown him some respect. Luckily for Dave, there is no law for riding a bike at 60 miles per hour. The music from "Symphony No. 4 in A major (Italian Symphony), Op. 90" by German composer Felix Mendelssohn accompanies him on his chase.

Dave passes a sign that has "WELCOME TO BLOOMINGTON: HOME OF INDIANA UNIVERSITY". On one hand, he is home. On the other hand, it is a reminder that his home is the site of a college career. Looking at his watch, he is thrilled with his time. He takes his water bottle and sprays his head in celebration.

After a shower at home, Dave listens to a recording of Italian phrases and their translations, "It's hot today, isn't it?" and "Do you think it will rain?" These will come in handy later. He greets Fellini, the family cat, who is on his bed. He dumps some food into an ashtray with "CINZANO" written on the sides. Apparently, Fellini understands the Italian language; Dave says, "*Mangiare*" (eat).

The boys take Moocher to his first day at the car wash on South Walnut Street; Mike and Cyril give him a hard time about it, and Moocher says that he needs a job. Why? Because he has plans to get married? Dave doesn't rag on Moocher; they exchange a happy signal that shows that they are on the same wavelength. It was Moocher who had said early in the movie, "You know there ain't many places that will hire all four of us." The owner tells Moocher that he's late, and he apologizes. The owner tells

THE STORY

Moocher, "Don't forget to punch the clock, Shorty", upon which Moocher does just that, wrapping a towel around his hand and smashing the clock face to pieces. Moocher's job lasts about ten seconds, and he jumps back into the car with his friends, who give him three cheers as he tosses the towel in the air and welcome him back to the club of unemployment.

Note: on IMDb, Daniel Stern was quoted with:[7]

> "I knew I wanted to act when I was around 14. The only other thing I can really remember wanting to do besides acting was a gas station attendant. At the time that seemed like a great job—wash the windows, pump the gas …"

If he had gotten the job, would he have punched the clock?

The boys are enjoying a pizza on the sidewalk downtown on North Walnut Street—the Tovey's shoe store is prominent in the background—and Mike's brother, the campus policeman, double-parks his car and tells Mike to stop hot-rodding on campus, or else he will take the car back. That would be a big deal, and not just to Mike; the car is their means of going to the quarry, and it has the rack on the top that is used to take Dave to his races. Mike begrudgingly says "alright … alright … alright", preceding Matthew McConaughey's signature tag line by several years. It must be a Texas thing.

After his brother leaves, Mike says to the guys that they should let off some steam by taking a trip to Terre Haute tomorrow. Actually, Terre Haute is the home of another college, Indiana State University. If they had made the trip, they may have run into Larry Bird, who was winding up his stay there.

Dave has told Cyril about Katherine. Cyril joins Dave in his room to strum on his guitar, which his father was sure that he wouldn't master, to prepare for Dave's serenade of Katherine.

---

[7] https://www.imdb.com/name/nm0827663/bio/

Dave rides his bike, carrying Cyril with him, to Katherine's sorority house at night to serenade her as she looks out from an upper floor window (Romeo and Juliet, from different backgrounds?). With Cyril accompanying, Dave sings *"M' appari tutt' amor"*. He even goes to one knee, as if proposing. Cyril shows that he has a good set of pipes as he joins Dave to sing "Martha, Martha" (the opera is "Martha"). Katherine does not recognize Cyril from the frisbee incident. Katherine is charmed and comes outside as her sorority sisters applaud, joining Dave on a ride on his bike. Her sorority is Chi Delta Delta, but she is wearing a Sigma Tau Omega shirt from Rod's fraternity; its light blue color matches Rod's Mercedes. Returning to the sorority house, Katherine thanks him and gives him a kiss, on his lips! Contrary to the adage that it is better to give than receive, Dave is more thrilled with receiving a kiss than by giving one, which he did on the cheek of his Goddamn father and the postal carrier. Note: this scene took two days to film; Peter Yates calmed Dennis Christopher down by giving him some alcoholic drinks. Apparently, Dave was safe enough to drink-and-ride. While Dave was the recipient of a kiss, how did the night turn out for Ray and Evelyn? Stay tuned.

Meanwhile, Suzy, who is wearing an appropriate pink Chi Delta Delta shirt, has called Rod: "Oh, hi Rod. I was just wondering if you knew that there was a guy here with a guitar serenading Kath." Rod and company speed over—in his Mercedes convertible, of course—to rough up the intruder, but when they arrive, only Cyril is there. Suzy had said that it was a guy with a guitar instead of two guys, so Cyril is the obvious suspect; he tries to outrun the fraternity guys, but he is outnumbered five-to-one.

P.J. Soles, who played Suzy, explained this part in the book "Dennis Quaid" by Gail Birnbaum:

> That part came about quite by accident, according to P.J.: "I went away on location with Dennis and they had one entire scene with locals in Bloomington, Indiana, and they cast

hundreds of people and they couldn't find anyone to read three lines!" she explained. "Peter Yates asked if I'd do that small part, so I said sure."

While Dave is serenading Katherine, Evelyn is seducing Ray at dinner, with six candles—"Sixteen Candles" would come a few years later for Paul Dooley—on the table. She goes to Dave's room and puts his Enrico Gimondi opera album on the record player, playing the same song that Dave is singing to Katherine, "*M' apparì tutt' amor*". In an earlier scene, she had been listening to it and swooning while waxing the floor. As she extinguishes the candle flames with a snuffer, Ray helps in his debonair style, by licking his fingers. In their bedroom, Evelyn continues the romantic evening; she takes the flowers out of her hair. Ray is smitten, and, in his debonair style, he removes his pocket protector. We can only guess what happens next; she has been reading the scandalous "Valley of the Dolls" book. Note: Paul Dooley's previous film was "A Perfect Couple", directed by Robert Altman, in which he plays a middle-aged, divorced, well-dressed, mustachioed man who is courting a young singer whom he met through a dating service; he was quite romantic, not cartoonish at all.

The next day, Mike is angry at the look of Cyril's bruised face. Cyril tries to downplay the trouble to protect Dave, but Mike won't have it.

Mike: *What kind of car did they drive?*
Cyril: *It was a Mercedes convertible.*
Mike: *Was it blue?*
Cyril: *Yes.*
Mike: *I've seen that car. All right. They want a fight, we're going to give them a fight.*

Dave says that he can't join in the hunt for the fraternity guys, hiding the fact that he has a date with Katherine.

Mike, Moocher, and Cyril reach campus at night, and Mike sees Rod in his convertible with his new girlfriend. Mike even drives in reverse so that he can give Cyril a good look and ask him if Rod is the one who beat him up.

Girl: *Who are they?*
Rod: *A bunch of Cutters.*
Girl: *What are Cutters?*
Rod: *Townies.*

Rod says only that Cutters are townies, but he doesn't show his true colors by saying that it is a derogatory term.

Mike sees Rod's parked car at the student union and parks his car, blocking Rod's car. It must run in the family; Mike's brother had double-parked his car in his first scene at the courthouse square. Mike leads the boys into the student union—despite Cyril saying, "I don't think we can go in there"—where Rod and his girlfriend have already reached the dining hall. The boys enter in their shabby clothes, drawing stares, disapproving looks, and "a bunch of cutter kids" whispers from the students. One of the students is wearing a black hoodie with "Little 500 Indiana" and two checkered flags on the back. Is that a foreshadow, the first mention of the storied event?

Dave and Katherine are on a dinner date in another part of the building. Mike thinks that he sees Rod in the bowling alley. In typical Mike fashion, he barges in instead of opening the door for people leaving, but it isn't Rod. Cyril somehow manages to get a bowling ball stuck on his fingers; he tries to hide it under his shirt. They go back into the dining area, where Cyril comes face-to-face with Rod's new girlfriend.

Cyril: *What's your major?*
Girl: *Soc* [Sociology]
Cyril: *Uh, Soc. That's a nice major, Soc.*

THE STORY

Rod appears with a tray of food and drinks. It is the second time that the Cutter boys have dared to trespass on his turf. It is the third time that Cyril hedges on the truth with Mike, not identifying Rod, after making a positive ID of Rod when they passed him in their cars.

Rod: *What are you cutters doing here? Did you get lost?*
Mike: *No.*
Rod: *Then why don't you get lost now?*
Mike (to Cyril): *Is that him?*
Cyril: *No, no, I don't think it is. No.*
Moocher: *Let's get out of here.*
Rod: *Smart move, Shorty.*

The camera cuts to Mike for a second; he looks at Moocher to see his reaction. We know what's coming next. Moocher grabs a towel from a passing student, wraps it around his fist as he had done when he punched the clock at the car wash, and punches Rod while dumping Rod's tray of food on him. Note: Jackie Earle Haley had some real-life experience. In the Pressbook for the movie, he said, "It's not easy being an actor before you're even in your teens. I had problems with school. The other kids were jealous of me and somebody was always trying to beat me up."

An all-out fight breaks out, with the Cutter kids outnumbered, as always, ten-to-one. The fact that the three of them—actually two of them, since Cyril is a pacifist—would be greatly outnumbered had been no concern to Mike. Cyril defends himself by swinging the bowling ball that is still stuck in his fingers. Dave and Katherine had been nearby on a date; Katherine is nearly in an Italian mode, wearing a white dress and a red ribbon in her hair. They come to the fight, but Dave knows that they have to scram to avoid being seen by his buddies. Windows and dishes are broken, and the fight ends only when Mike's brother and other police show up. It's a Cutter vs. a fraternity guy as Mike's brother restrains Rod. Rod says that the Cutters started it. Mike's brother gives Mike an angry look.

Who really started it? Mike had initiated the first conflict by insisting that the boys go on campus, although there is no indication that they were going to do any harm, after the students dared to come to his quarry. The Cutter boys would not have come looking for Rod if Rod had not engineered the first altercation by attacking Cyril.

In the next scene, university President Ryan has called a meeting with a group of students in his office, expressing his displeasure at the incident, which he says is not an isolated one. [Note: In an interview with WTIU television during the filming, we learn that it was actually the office of the Chancellor, Herman Wells, since it was a bigger office and Dr. Wells was out of town.] He says that if they want to tangle with the locals, it will be in the Little 500 race, allowing a local team to compete for the first time. Rod is crushed by the decision. The original plan was to use Dr. Ryan's voice in the scene, but a faulty audio take resulted in his voice being dubbed over. The Indiana University Archives has a document of a telephone conversation where Peter Yates described the dubbing: "My reason for changing the voice is merely to add extra dialogue. It would not have been possible to get him to go to L.A."

Appropriately, that chapter is the twelfth of the 23 chapters on the DVD, a turning point with 11 scenes before and 11 scenes after.

A battle starts in the very next scene. The boys go to the quarry, where they quarrel about the race and about their potential splintering apart as friends. Dave says that he doesn't want to be seen with the college students, and that he plans on getting a job, because he needs the money. Why does he need the money? To pay for a college education? Rod, Katherine, and other students show up. It is curious that Katherine is with Rod, given her spat with him and the fact that she has a new, charming boyfriend. Dave sees Katherine and ducks out of sight. Mike and Rod lock eyes, and Mike points to the water to challenge Rod to a race, one length across and one back. Mike is in his cut-offs, and Rod is in his swimsuit. Mike takes the cigarette out of his mouth, and they dive in. It is no contest; Rod is on the swimming team, while Mike is a football player more than a year removed from the gridiron. Rod wins easily, even taunting Mike by swimming backstroke on the return lap. Katherine is angered by the scene and leaves. Mike is committed to finishing anyway, and he recklessly bumps his head into a rock. Even though he is bleeding, he turns to keep swimming, before finally floundering. The irony is that the quarry and its rocks, the Cutters' domain, have inflicted injury and embarrassment on Mike. The boys dive in to save Mike; with Katherine having left, Dave doesn't have to worry about being discovered. The three scenes at the quarry have evolved from one of relaxation and celebration to one of provocation to one of conflict and pain.

Mike is on a losing streak; he has been busted by his brother, he has argued with Moocher, who challenged his authority, he has been told by Dave to cut it out, and he has lost a swimming competition to a hated fraternity guy. He can't understand why Moocher and Dave would want to get jobs alone, why Cyril would be walking near the sorority houses by himself, why none of the others would join him on a trip to Terre Haute, and why Dave doesn't want to compete in the Little 500 race.

At some point, Dave has told Moocher about his sham job with Katherine. As they walk past the Indiana Theater on East Kirkwood Avenue—the theater now known as the Buskirk-Chumley Theater, which has shown the movie in multiple years, including on the Little 500 weekend in 2024, 45 years later after the movie's release—Dave tells Moocher that he has to come clean with Katherine, upon which the soon-to-be married Moocher gives him advice on relationships. Dave is so absorbed in his dilemma with Katherine that he doesn't hear Moocher say that he is getting married. By chatting with Moocher as they walk in downtown, Dave is actually taking a chance that Katherine does not come by. Moocher had been seen with a necklace with a cross on it a few times earlier. Fittingly, as Dave and Moocher talk, we can see a church reflected in a store window.

> Dave: *I tried calling her to tell her, but I just couldn't.*
> Moocher: *She's going to see you in the 500, you know. You know, if she really likes you, she just won't care.*
> Dave: *What a mess. Moocher, you're a Catholic, aren't you?*
> Moocher: *Yeah.*
> Dave: *You ever go to confession?*
> Moocher: *Twice.*
> Dave: *Did it make you feel better?*
> Moocher: *Once.*

Certainly, Dave must realize that he can't continue the ruse forever. At some point, Katherine would ask: Where do you live? What classes do you take? Who is your friend with the guitar?

One day, Dave happens to be riding in town when he sees Moocher and Nancy going into the courthouse; he smiles at the thought that they are there to get a marriage license. Nancy realizes that she is a dollar short on the $5 fee, but the resourceful Moocher comes to the rescue. She has a job, he does not.

> Moocher: *What do you think they are going to ask us?*
> Nancy: *Nothing we can't answer, I suppose.*
> Moocher: *I wonder if I have to have a job to qualify.*
> Nancy: *I don't think so. I think it's mostly blood and relatives that they're interested in.*
> Moocher: *Blood and relatives ... well, that's great. I got both of them.*
> Nancy: *Oh, Fudge. You know what?*
> Moocher: *No, what?*

THE STORY

> Nancy: *I only brought four dollars.*
> Moocher: *Well, it's only five. I'll tell you what, we'll go Dutch.*
> Nancy: *On a marriage license?*
> Moocher: *Sure, why not.*

Dave waves to Ray, who is test-driving a Ford Pinto with a family on board, and Ray ignores him again. Dave speeds up to dodge a bus and get through a traffic light that has turned red, and Ray hits the brakes, causing the car to stall. Ray can't get it to start, and he glares at Dave. He is slumped on the steering wheel and moaning as the Pinto is towed, with the customer's family along for the ride. Coincidentally, the Pinto's last year of existence was a year after the movie was released.

At home, Ray vents to Evelyn in their bedroom. Dave, in his bed, hears Ray and suffers.

> Ray: *He couldn't find a job to save his life. He's worthless, Evelyn. I tell you, I die of shame every time I see him, goddamn lazy freeloader.*

Ray visits his former coworkers at the limestone mill, and they let him do some of the cutting work that he used to do. He is in his element now. He says, "I'm only here for a visit, but if I wanted to start over again, I could pick up right where I left off." Is he considering returning to the job that was laborious but fulfilling, or just appreciating the good old days? In the job that he loved, where he would use his hands, he had a steady check, but now he has a business that has peaks and valleys and no guarantees. While he labors to re-experience that job, he is still wearing his short-sleeve shirt and tie. The men exchange small talk about their sons, and Ray says that his son is "fine" (!).

Ray and Evelyn stroll downtown, passing by Nick's English Hut and the Baskin-Robbins ice cream shop on East Kirkwood Avenue. Ray has a huge stain on his tie; according to the original script, it came from eating forbidden food at a restaurant. Evelyn suggests that Ray give Dave a job at the car lot. Ray isn't so sure, but the next scene shows Dave at work on the lot, cleaning the cars. After a long first day, he is tired but not miserable; he goes out to train instead of heading home. On another day, he sees his jobless friends drive by, free as birds, and he sees Rod and his fraternity buddies out on a bike ride. The Mendelssohn music adds to his dismay.

The day of the Cinzano 100 race is approaching. At the car lot, Dave asks Ray for the day off, but Ray refuses. Dave is crushed. A student shows up with three buddies, pushing the red convertible that Ray had sold him, saying that Ray gave his word on a 90-day guarantee. Dave jumps in, saying that if Ray gave his word, he has to honor it, because they are poor but honest. As the students push, Ray pushes back. Like the Cutter boys, he is outnumbered by college students. The student says, "All I want is a refund." Ray spews "Refund!" five times, then the scene shifts to him in bed, where he is about to get an injection from his doctor; he says "refund" meekly four more times. This should rank up there with Robert DeNiro's "You talking to me?" in "Taxi Driver" (only four times) as the most famous repeated line in movie history.

Dave feels responsible for Ray's ailments and says that he will skip the race against the Italians, but Evelyn won't have it. She shows Dave her passport, which she has never used but keeps in case she has to prove her identity. It is an allegory from the perfect mother about not missing opportunities.

The race starts near the Fireside Inn, the hotel that the filming crew used. Racing against the Italians, Dave is gambling that he won't be discovered by Katherine. If he had won, any publicity could have ended his ruse. The four Cinzano team racers arrive to applause from everyone, including Dave; they wear black outfits with a little white trim, while Dave's outfit has red and green with white trim, the colors of Italy.

THE STORY

Cleverly, as the racers take off, they pass a sign that has "DO NOT PASS". Did Dave construe that as a sign to not pass a college entrance exam? One of the funniest scenes in the movie comes as a pack of racers approaches a railroad track, and a dog is on the other side. The dog is able to scurry across the road in the nick of time. Note: this scene reminded me of the one in the movie "Funny Farm", when Chevy Chase is trying to sell his house, and the prospective buyers pull up. Already loving the idyllic setting in the snow, they are sold when a deer prances by; inside the house, Chevy Chase had seen the couple outside and radioed a friend to "cue the deer", letting the deer out of its cage. Did Peter Yates stage a similar trick with the dog? Amusingly, no, it was just a coincidence. The dog should have gotten in the credits, but did not, nor did Fellini/Jake. Dr. Nicole Kraft, a professor of journalism at The Ohio State University, wrote a book called "Always Get the Name of the Dog: A Guide to Media Interviewing", referring to the directive that, if you are a reporter and report on a story that involves a dog, no detail is too small; always get the name of the dog.

The music, Gioachino Rossini's The Barber of Seville, accommodates the action; it is invigorating when the racers burst out at the start and mellow in the long shots where the racers appear to be gliding.

Keeping pace with Dave in one sequence is the real-life David Blase. Several Delta Chi fraternity racers and Troy Stetina (who went on to become a noted guitarist) are in the pack. Shortly, the pack is Dave and the Italians, with Dave rankling them by chatting in Italian with the phrases that he had learned, "It's hot today, isn't it?" and "Do you think it will rain?" Eddy Van Guyse's villain character leans over and flips his gear shift, slowing Dave to a crawl. The villain later gives Dave an insulting gesture. Dave is able to recover and catch up again, but, just when the music reaches its most joyous moment, the villain pulls another dirty trick; he sticks his pump into Dave's front wheel, causing Dave to tumble into the ditch, bloodying his nose, injuring his legs, and knocking him out of the race. It could have been worse; if Dave had been on the outside, he would have fallen onto the pavement. The route had been lined with cheering fans, but the Italian picked a spot that had no witnesses. Dave looks at the pack leaving him and is distraught, betrayed by his heroes, who taunt him with "Bravo, bravo" as they ride away. The race sequence, which lasts five minutes, took seven days to film.

Eddy Van Guyse said that the pump-sabotage scene took only two takes. He was actually born in Belgium and had to lose 20 pounds and gain a tan to look Italian. He told Peter Yates that the bikes that were delivered for the Cinzano 100 race were all wrong—such as having big tires, straight bars, and reflectors—upon which Yates made him the technical advisor for the movie and had him recruit racers to play the other three members of the Cinzano team. Eddy recruited three friends from Chicago, the bespectacled triathlete Carlos Sintes, John Vande Velde (a two-time Olympian), and Pete Lazzara (the only real Italian of the four) to fill the roles. Eddy's Delta Chi team had finished tenth, second, fifth, and second in his four years of 1969 through 1972 competing in the Little 500 race. He is also in the Little 500 Hall of Fame. In the "Fit Foot U" podcast with Dr. Ben Pearl, Bill Brissman, the stunt double for Hart Bochner in the Little 500 race, said that he was in the mass of riders at the start, and that he had to make sure that he was not detected, to avoid any confusion.

Dave's friends had come to the race to cheer him on, so they have mended their differences after the argument at the quarry. They give Dave a ride home; Mike delivers a reality check:

Mike: *Well, I guess you're a Cutter again, huh? Just like the rest of us?*
Dave: *I guess so.*

Moocher tries to cheer Dave up by telling him, "You've still got the 500", subtly not saying, "We've still got the 500".

THE STORY

Dave comes into the house hobbling, alarming Evelyn and confounding Ray by calling him Dad instead of Papa. Dave had brought his bike into the house through a side door in the beginning of the movie after a victory, but, symbolically, comes through the front door without his bike after this loss. There are red and white flowers on the coffee table, but no sign of green; the Italian influence has faded. Dave comes to tears and hugs Ray after telling him that he didn't win a trophy because everybody cheats, he just didn't know. Prophetically, Lance Armstrong's confession will come decades later. In his "Movie Dad" book, Paul Dooley wrote that hugging Dave was the hardest scene that he had ever played and the most emotional one that he had ever done, based on the relationship with his own father.

Dave realizes that if his heroes can't be genuine, then he should. He had talked to Moocher about confession, so he arranges a meeting with Katherine and confesses his true identity. She slaps him out of anger.

Dave has gone through a rollercoaster of emotions. He has had a rift with Mike; while at his job at Ray's car lot, he sees his three friends drive by, still free to cruise around; he has had an emotional breakup with Katherine; his heroes, the Italian racers, have turned out to be cheaters; and his dad is recovering from his meltdown. Ray comes to his rescue.

They walk through the campus, where Dave says that he won't go to college and that he is proud to be a Cutter. Ray says, "You're not a Cutter. I'm a Cutter". They head back home, newly reconciled as father and son. Dave is not a Cutter, he's not Italian, and he's not a college student, so what is he?

He's still an avid bike rider. For the Little 500, the boys are given a run-down, single-speed AMF Roadmaster set up for track racing. They gather on Dave's porch; as they talk, appropriately, someone rides by on a bicycle for a few seconds, actually riding the wrong way on the one-way South Lincoln Street. Mike had said that Dave would ride the entire race; the fact that he has a pack of cigarettes in his T-shirt pocket does not speak well for his conditioning. Dave is discouraged at the condition of the bike, and more so overall is Mike, who sounds like Rocky Balboa when he said to Adrian, "I can't do it … I can't beat him … I mean, who am I kidding, I ain't even in the guy's league."

> Mike: *The hell with it. Get off, Cyril. At least we got invited. I'll just take it back.*
> Dave: *You seem relieved, Mike. What's the matter, don't you think we can win any more? Why not?*
> Mike: *Well, maybe those guys are better than us.*
> Dave: *Well, maybe they are, but that's the first time I heard you say anything like that.*
> Mike: *That's the first time I ever felt that.*

Why is Mike discouraged? Because he lost a swimming competition? Dave's choice of words, "don't you think we can win", is interesting.

After overhauling the bike, Dave cruises out of the garage and into the light to take it on a test-drive on the Little 500 track at Tenth Street Stadium, alone on the track except for one other rider. The stadium was Indiana University's first Memorial Stadium for football through 1959, dedicated in 1925 but demolished in 1981 and redeveloped into an arboretum. Patrick Williams's inspiring music accommodates him.

Dave is happy again. As he relaxes on a sidewalk on the courthouse square, enjoying a snack, the shadow of Katherine gives him a jolt. She is also happy; she tells him that she is leaving for a job in Chicago and has reconciled with her parents, to the point that they will travel to Italy. She wishes him well. She has gone through some of the stages of grief: denial, anger, and acceptance.

On the day before the Little 500 race, Moocher is at dinner with the Stohlers. Ray gives the shocking news that he is going to be a father again, Evelyn is going to be a mother again, etc. We should have guessed this from the fact that Evelyn has a flower in her hair again. They present Dave and Moocher with T-shirts that have "CUTTERS" on the front. Ray has continued his transformation; he is wearing a striped shirt with a striped tie for the first time.

Now Dave is on a winning streak; he has reconciled with Katherine, he and his dad have a true understanding of each other, and he has a sibling on the way. Ray is healthy enough to return to work and happy for one of the few times in the movie, the first being when he conned a college student on a sale and the second when he labored at the mill for old time's sake. He is apparently happy with becoming a father again; does he have any choice? Evelyn is happy with growing her family. The Cutter boys are reunified. Katherine is happy. Rod's team is confident.

It's the day of the Little 500 race. Tenth Street Stadium is filled with fans, although at least one of them has brought in contraband, a cooler in violation of the rules. Dave couldn't beat the Italians, but now he takes on the Greek system. Will he ride all 200 laps, the entire 50 miles? Will Jackie Earle Haley fall "short" of victory, as he had in "The Bad News Bears"?

Before the start, everyone sings The Star Spangled Banner, followed by "Indiana, Our Indiana", Indiana University's official fight song and a reminder that the race is still in the college's domain. During The Star Spangled Banner, we see eleven rows with three bicycles in each row on the track and one bicycle by itself in the back, the Cutters' bicycle. Thirty-three teams are selected in qualifications trials to compete in the race, so the #34 on the Cutters' helmets, the bike, and the back of their T-shirts is appropriate. It is also appropriate in that 3 of the 4 boys plan on sitting out the race.

Rod is the leader of the Sigma Tau Omega team and has the pole position. His team heads to its pit with their arms around each other's shoulders, marching as a team. At least our heroes resemble a team, with their matching CUTTERS T-shirts. There is no indication that Rod knew that Dave was the one who stole Katherine from him or that Dave had the alter ego. Instead of competing for the same girl, they are competing for an athletic prize and respect. It is the only time that they come face-to-face, or, more appropriately, side-to-side. Rod had messed with Cyril after the serenade and fought with Mike and Moocher in the student union melee. Now, he is matched up with Dave in a nonviolent scenario.

For the first time, the Cutters are on campus without any harassment, even with their T-shirts identifying them. They and the fraternity guys are equals now in one respect; every team must use an AMF Roadmaster bicycle. There is still a hint of Italy–a green bicycle, white T-shirts, and a red helmet. Just as Dave had to give up his Italian persona, so too does he have to forgo his Italian Masi bicycle for an American-made one. Rod is accustomed foreign vehicles, too, driving a Mercedes. Although, the fraternity guys have the advantages of a stationary bike to help them keep limber and a coach to give them advice, but the Cutters have no such perks, not that they would use them. Who has more money, the better car, the better education is irrelevant; the question is who is tougher. The odds are now 33-to-1 against the Cutters, or more accurately, 132-to-1 if Dave goes solo. In the men's NCAA basketball tournament, a #16 seed team has upset a #1 seed twice; could a #34 seed upset the #1 seed in this race? Even though Dave had shown that he can keep pace with the world-class Italians, it would be unrealistic to expect him to run the race alone.

Dave's right knee is wrapped, a carry-over from the Cinzano 100 race injury. The ceremonial pace car to escort the competitors around the track is another light blue convertible, but an American-made car. Dave starts in last place, but quickly breaks away to a three-quarter lap lead, as Rod tells his teammates in the pit, "He won't last." The radio broadcast adds authenticity, with the broadcaster identifying the Delta Chi, Acacia, and Phi Psi teams among the leaders.

A potential tragedy strikes when an accidental collision knocks Dave to the track. He gets back on the bike, but is in agony. Clearly, the boys had no Plan B; the others didn't train for the grueling race and probably hadn't ridden a bike in years. Dave comes to the pit, but, to the exasperation of the public address announcer, David Blase, none of his teammates take over for him. Mike is still in his funk; Cyril hands a helmet to him, who hands it right back. Cyril helps Dave off the bike, and Dave pushes Mike away in anger. Dave yells at Mike, "Get out there, Mike! Get on the bike!", another rift at the most crucial time. Mike, the only famous athlete of the four as a high school quarterback, won't contribute to the team. Moocher jumps on the bike for some exhausting, but vital laps, pumping his short legs on the unaltered bicycle. Rod is on the sidelines when Moocher passes by and breaks into laughter—"The little guy is on the bike!" Yes, Rod, the same little guy who punched you in the student union. Cyril takes over for Moocher. At least Cyril was prepared; he is the only other one wearing gloves. With Dave out, Rod tells his teammates, "It's our race."

Mike mutters, "It's all over". Nancy is there for moral and wellness support; she gives a cup of water to Cyril after his set. It is the first time that she has interacted with the other boys; in the beginning of the movie, Moocher had told Mike that he wasn't seeing Nancy any more.

Rod rides by Mike—still disengaged, sitting on the sideline—and says "Nice try, kid". Rod's final insult to Mike backfires, just as what happens whenever Moocher is called "Shorty". Mike, who had no intention of taking a turn on the bike, is angered by the slight and jumps on the bike to take over for Cyril, who tumbles to the ground in exhaustion. Mike still has it, his athletic ability, and he makes up significant ground. His brother shouts to him, "Go, you Cutter, go!"

Dave is getting his ankle wrapped and his right knee re-wrapped by a nurse. He has blood on his lower left leg and a bloody left ankle. Boston Red Sox fans may relate it to the bloody right ankle of Curt Schilling, who pitched a win for the underdog team that rallied from a three-games-to-none deficit 25 years later against the Yankees and went on to win their first World Series in 86 years.

Evelyn is at the race from the start, and Ray shows up later. Dave sees Evelyn and Ray, who gives a salute. Angry that Cyril says "At least we showed them", he says, "Showed them what?" and demands that Mike come in so that he can get back in the race. It's the only time that Dave has been angry at Cyril, or had a reason to be. He has his friends tape his feet to the pedals, which commits him to finishing the last 15 laps by himself. Evelyn yells, "Go, son, go damn you!", then covers her mouth in embarrassment. Rod is in his team's pit and yells to his teammate on the bike, "Pick it up, he's back in the race!" He's worried now, so he demands the bike for the last shift. As Dave makes up ground, Rod is really worried; he looks at him over his left shoulder, realizing that he may be in trouble. As Satchel Paige said, "Don't look back. Something might be gaining on you."

In the scene where a coach—played by Tom Schwoegler, who coached the Acacia team in real life—gives advice to a rider in the pit, the extra on the stationary bike wearing a MERCHANTS NATIONAL BANK jersey is James Pivarnik, whose interview appears in this book.

As the white flag is waved at the final-lap mark, Rod has a one-length lead and keeps it at the third turn. Coming off the last turn, it's fraternity brother vs fraternity brother in reality; Gary Rybar (Dave's stunt double) and Bill Brissman (Hart Bochner's stunt double) combined for five first place finishes for Delta Chi between 1976 through 1981. Rybar had suggested to Peter Yates that Brissman would be perfect as the stunt double. Rod veers a tad too much to the outside, and Dave sneaks on the inside, sprinting to the finish line to win by a nose—or more aptly, by about half a wheel—raising his arms just before he crosses, with Patrick Williams's triumphant music accommodating him. This is the point where I get choked up every time that I watch it. It is the second time that Dave has pedaled without his hands on the handlebars, the first being his blissful ride through the woods after connecting with Katherine. Just like the end of his race against the Italians, being on the inside worked out

THE STORY

better for Dave. In the "Fit Foot U" podcast interview by Dr. Ben Pearl, Bill Bissman said that he told Gary Rybar, "I will let you come under me", leading to the perfect execution of the wide angle.

The sequence of the final two laps was successfully filmed in the first take, and it had no cuts, no zooms into the faces of the two riders. Peter Yates had made a comment to Eddy Van Guyse, who played the Italian racer who knocked Dave out of the Cinzano 100 race, that even if a take is a "keeper", he likes to have multiple takes in order to make choices. This one was a real keeper. In a "Fit Foot U" podcast interview by Dr. Pearl, Eddy tells the story that Peter Yates's instruction to Bill Brissman was "Don't win! You can't win, you understand?".

The sprint evokes memories of Dave Wottle's kick finish down the backstretch in the Munich Olympics, six years previous to this filming. The Britannica website has that Wottle:[8]

> ... was far back in the field for most of the 800-metre race. Yevgeny Arzhanov, a Soviet runner who had not lost an 800-metre race in four years, was leading down the stretch. Less than 20 metres from the finish, Wottle made his final move and caught up to Arzhanov. As the two athletes neared the finish line, Arzhanov stumbled and fell, allowing Wottle to win the gold medal.

Mike, Cyril, and Moocher do a celebratory dance, and Mike jumps into Cyril for a bear hug, probably the only time that they connect without Mike giving Cyril a put-down. It is the only time in the movie that Mike is happy, and he makes up for it big time. It was his first win in a competition since being the quarterback about a year and a half before this moment. Ray and Evelyn come to celebrate with Dave, Nancy comes to hug Moocher, and even Mike's brother comes to reconcile with Mike

---

[8] https://www.britannica.com/biography/Dave-Wottle

with a hug. Mike had lamented that a cutter was something that he never got a chance to be, but today, he wears his CUTTERS shirt proudly. Cyril has his first moment of athletic glory since his basketball days; he had lost out on a scholarship, but he is a winner today. He is clapping and gets pats on the back, but he looks like a subdued pre-1983 North Carolina State basketball coach Jim Valvano, who was looking for someone to hug after winning the national championship in a huge, last-second upset. When Cyril gets home, he may say, "Hey, Dad, I didn't fail!" Rocky Balboa had his Adrian, the boys have their version of celebrants.

Dave had overcome his sickliness, Moocher didn't let his lack of size hold him back, Cyril found something to succeed in, and Mike reclaimed his athletic ability. They didn't need to find their brain, but they found their heart and courage.

All that is left is the award ceremony, with Dave lifting the huge trophy over his head. Note: billionaire Mark Cuban, a student at Indiana University at the time, says that he was in the crowd of celebrators at the trophy presentation, but the camera zoomed into his roommate and captured only the side of his head.

The boys had demonstrated that they were in fact a team, out of necessity when Dave was injured. In a team construct, the members don't have the same skill set, they just need to contribute to the best of their abilities.

What if Dave and the Cutters had lost the race? I think that in-house audiences would have started a riot.

In a feel-good movie, the good guy gets the girl in the end, but Dave doesn't, as Katherine is leaving Indiana University. But wait!

At the end, several months have passed since the Little 500 race in April. A new academic year has begun, and Dave has in fact enrolled at Indiana University, off to his new adventure. He beat 'em AND he joined 'em. We see that Evelyn is very pregnant. In his final sequence, Dave is on campus and meets a French coed, who asks him for directions to the bursar's office. The scene is outside the Indiana Memorial Union, where Dave was on a date with Katherine before the fight started. The roles are reversed; she is the foreign student, but a real one. They share a connection; she has a bike, too, not a scooter. Dave continues to be on a roll. He is smitten, and they ride their bikes through the campus. Dave has made a clean break from the Italians; he is now all-in on French culture. He has crossed the border from Italy to France, and he has crossed the border into the college campus.

> Dave: *I was thinking of taking French, but it's my first year. Have you ever seen Le Tour de France?*
> Girl: *No.*
> Dave: *No! Mon Dieu. The French riders ... they are the best! Poulidor, Anquetil ...*

The camera cuts to Ray, who has mounted a bike and ridden to the campus; now, he is comfortable being among the limestone buildings. Ironically, Ray had never gone to college, and we expect Dave to do well at Indiana University; in real life, Paul Dooley graduated from West Virginia University, while Dennis Christopher briefly attended Temple University.

Ray sees Dave and the coed on their bikes riding in the opposite direction. Ray, who had called Dave a weirdo, a bum, stupid, worthless, and a lazy freeloader, now calls out to him with, "Hi ya, big shot!" The next-to-last shot is a freeze-frame of Ray, flummoxed that Dave has now turned French by calling out to him, "Bon jour, papa!".

What would have been fitting is, on the screen ... *FIN*.

CHAPTER 4
IT'S ABOUT...

WHAT IS "BREAKING AWAY" about? It is a story about class differences, honesty, pride, family, relationships, romance, and changing attitudes.

IT'S ABOUT CLASS DIFFERENCES
The Cutter kids worked at the A&P, and their fathers are blue-collar workers, which seems to be the destiny for the kids, too; the students will go on to be white-collar workers.

Rod drives an immaculate, German-based Mercedes convertible. Mike has a classic, two-door, American-made Buick Skylark. It is two-toned, but not by design; it is gold-colored with a red door, an obvious Frankenstein-patch job from a junkyard, has dents in the front hood and both fenders, and the body has splotches of missing paint. It spews exhaust when speeding away, and it has only one headlight that is working. It probably did not come from Ray's car lot, since it runs so well otherwise. The car has a bike rack on the roof, a symbol of his friendship with Dave, the only bike rider of the four. The car isn't even his, as his policeman brother threatens to take it away if Mike keeps hot-rodding on campus.

The students come to the university from anywhere. Rod's Mercedes convertible has a Texas license plate, and his new girlfriend is from elsewhere, as Rod has to explain to her what a Cutter is. The students wear Izod shirts in everyday life, and suits when they are called on the carpet by President Ryan; the Cutters wear comfortable teenage-type attire. Mike has the 1950s Marlon Brando look, with a pack of cigarettes rolled up in a sleeve of his T-shirt, which has a ripped pocket. In the book "Dennis Quaid" by Gail Birnbaum, Dennis said that Marlon Brando was his idol for a while; he had hung out with Brando when his brother, Randy, was acting in "The Missouri Breaks" and had coached Brando on the mandolin.

When the Cutter boys come to campus in Mike's beat-up car, the contrast leaves them in envy:

Moocher: *They sure look like they've got it made.*
Mike: *That's because they're rich.*

The evil Rod thinks that he can play the field. Even though Suzy had phoned him to tell him that someone is serenading Katherine, he has already found a new girlfriend. In this scene, in his convertible, of course:

Rod: *You haven't pledged any sorority yet?*
Girl: *No.*
Rod: *You should. Most frat guys won't go out with dormies. I'm the exception.*

There is even a small business versus corporate element; when Dave rides downtown, he passes a Ford dealership while Ray is test driving a modest used car with a customer.

In the Little 500 race, the students have colorful T-shirts with sponsor ads—such as "MERCHANTS NATIONAL BANK", "ARBYS", "1st NATIONAL BLOOMINGTON", "ROGER'S BLDG SUPPLY", "FAIRMONT FOODS", "KITTLES", and the mega-companies of "MARATHON OIL", "CUMMINS" and "Coca Cola"—on the front, and their number and lettering on the back. Another sponsor is "WHITESIDES", the store that appears in the background near the courthouse in a few scenes. The Cutters have white T-shirts with homemade

IT'S ABOUT...

"CUTTERS" lettering on the front and their number 34 on the back. Apollo Creed had his red, white, and blue trunks with white stars; Rocky Balboa had plain white trunks with red trim. At least, Rocky had a sponsor; "SHAMROCK MEATS INC" is on his robe.

IT'S ABOUT HONESTY

Except for Mike and Evelyn, the main local characters have some extent of dishonesty. Ironically, there is no display of dishonesty by the students, Rod and Katherine, though Suzy is devious.

In the opening sequence, Mike says that his brother had seen Moocher with Nancy, and Moocher emphatically denies it—"It wasn't me, I'm not seeing her anymore"—and throughout the movie doesn't share with his friends that he could be marrying her. But, when Nancy comes to Moocher's house, which is for sale, he is delighted to see her. He checks the street to make sure that nobody saw her. Moocher keeps his love affair with Nancy a secret, only discovered when Dave happens to see them enter the courthouse.

Dave pretends that he is a foreign student in order to court Katherine. He moaned to his parents that he was in love, but there is no indication that he gave them the details. If he had, Ray may take a different view of him.

After being warned by his brother to stop hot-rodding on campus, Mike says to the guys that they should let off some steam by taking a trip to Terre Haute tomorrow. Dave is able to hide his fling with Katherine from Mike, but he has confided in Cyril; he needs Cyril to accompany him and play the guitar on his serenade of Katherine. Cyril says that it's a good idea, but Dave shoots him a look. Moocher says that he is busy; does he also know about Dave and Katherine? The Monroe County Courthouse, where Moocher will eventually make an important trip, is across the street. Cyril says that he is busy after all. Mike says that he may go by himself.

After Cyril gets beat up by the frat guys following the serenade, the boys are together the next day.

Mike: *He won't tell me who did it.*
Cyril: *It was dark. All I can tell you for sure is that they all wore Brut aftershave and reeked of Lavoris.*
Mike: *Well, what were you doing there by yourself?*
Cyril: *I was just walking.*

It is the second time that Cyril has covered up for Dave, keeping a secret from Mike. Mike wants revenge, so he says that they will look for Rod and fight. Again, Dave makes an excuse for not joining, "I have to be somewhere." He and Cyril exchange a look again; Cyril knows that Dave can't risk interacting with the students on campus.

One day at the quarry, the college kids show up. Dave has to hide out of view so that Katherine can't see him. When he tells Ray that he learned that everybody cheats, well, Dave, you were dishonest with Katherine.

Ray is the prototypical unscrupulous used car salesman: "You know, those college boys ain't so smart. I sold one of my worst cars to one of them today," he tells Evelyn. Even his tie isn't legit; he wears a clip-on. When he is test-driving a car with a customer and hits the brakes in an intersection to avoid crashing into Dave, the car stalls and won't start again, needing a tow. Ray shifts into damage-control mode:

Ray: *Oh, damn. You know what I did? I think I put premium gas in this baby by mistake. It hates expensive gas.*

When he's on the car lot with a student customer, and Dave calls to him in Italian, he pretends not to know him and asks the student if that kid on the bike is a friend of his; he can't jeopardize a sale! He has his sales pitch down pat:

IT'S ABOUT...

Ray: *It gets thirty miles to the gallon. Of course, the mileage you get may vary. It's a beaut, right? Right. Boy, you sure know how to pick 'em. Frankly, this is the best car on the lot. Quality product.*

Naturally, the car is a convertible. When the student tries to return the car, needing help from buddies to push it into the lot, Ray again pretends not to know Dave, who has intervened and says, "We're poor, but we're honest." Actually, Dave has been dishonest in portraying himself as an Italian student to Katherine.

Mike is the only one of the four boys who doesn't hide anything. He kas no filter on his feelings. His monologue about the college football player he will never be is as honest as they come.

IT'S ABOUT PRIDE

Pride takes several forms in the movie.

When Dave takes the job cleaning the cars on Ray's lot, he is clearly proud of his work, as he looks over the cars at the end of the day. He uses the word "proud" when he tells Ray, "Hell, I don't want to go to college, Dad. To hell with them. I'm proud of being a Cutter."

Dave is proud of his race victory trophy, and so is Evelyn; not so for Ray, until he gets jolted into reality late in the movie. Ray takes pride in that he sold the worst car on the lot, but it's a false pride. At the end, he proudly changes the name of his car lot from "Campus Cars" to "Cutter Cars".

More pertinently, the Cutter fathers had every right to be proud of their work. The state stone of Indiana is, of course, limestone. As described on the Smithsonian Magazine website:[1]

> The Hoosier State's first commercial limestone quarry was established in 1827. Demand for limestone skyrocketed in the

---

[1] https://www.smithsonianmag.com/science-nature/indiana-limestone-americas-most-prized-building-materials-180982119/

1890s, after massive urban fires razed buildings across Chicago and Boston. Indiana limestone was the ideal rebuilding solution, flame-resistant and up to the country's first building codes, says Todd Schnatzmeyer, executive director of the Indiana Limestone Institute of America. Architects and sculptors quickly came to love the stone—dubbed "the Nation's Building Stone"—for several reasons. It's chemically pure and consistent, at over 97 percent calcium carbonate, which makes it highly uniform; it's a freestone—you can cut, carve or mill it in any direction; and it stands the test of time, because its uniformity gives it the same strength in all directions. What's more, compared with other high-quality deposits, such as those in Alabama, Indiana limestone is both accessible and vast. "Indiana limestone has gone into literally tens of thousands of building projects across North America and the world," Schnatzmeyer says.

In Bloom magazine, Scott Russell Sanders, a distinguished professor emeritus of English at Indiana University writes:[2]

"I was bemused by the fact that Cutters were treated in the film as a derogatory term for townies when, in fact, in the stone industry the cutters were the next to the top of the hierarchy," says Sanders. "The highest are the carvers, and right below them are the cutters. These were the foremen who knew the stone so well they knew what to cut and where to cut. It actually was an honorific to be a cutter."

The Cutter boys are poor, but they have their pride. They wear their Cutter T-shirts proudly for the Little 500 race. As they watch the Indiana

---

[2] https://www.magbloom.com/2018/03/blooms-greatest-hits-how-true-was-breaking-away/

IT'S ABOUT...

Hoosiers football team practice in Memorial Stadium, Mike is depressed by the sight of athletes who are about the same age as he is.

> Mike: *You know, I used to think that I was a really great quarterback in high school. I still think so, too. I can't even bring myself to light a cigarette, 'cause I keep thinking I should stay in shape. And you know what really gets me, though? I mean, here I am, I gotta live in this stinkin' town, and I gotta read in the newspapers about some hotshot kid new star on the college team. Every year, it's going to be a new one, and every year, it's never going to be me. I'm just going to be Mike. Twenty-year-old Mike. Thirty-year-old Mike. Old mean old man Mike. But these college kids out here, they're never going to get old or out of shape…'cause new ones come every year. And they're going to keep calling us 'cutters.' To them it's just a dirty word, to me it's just something else I never got a chance to be.*

Mike is saying that he would be proud to be a stone cutter, like his father. When he is outclassed by Rod in a swimming race in the quarry, he won't give up, even though the contest is over; going all-out, he rams his head into a rock, producing blood, but he keeps swimming until his friends come to his rescue.

Moocher gets called "Shorty" twice, and reacts with anger each time. When he gets a job at a car wash, the manager calls him "Shorty" and tells him to punch the clock; he does just that. When the boys confront the students in the student union after Cyril gets beat up, Moocher says that they should leave, until Rod calls him "Shorty", igniting a fight. Dave and Katherine are eating at the same place when Mike, Moocher, and Cyril barge in; if Dave gets seen, his ruse is over.

The fight is a catalyst for the rest of the movie; it leads to a meeting between the students and Indiana University's President Ryan, in his office. The students are wearing their Sunday-best suits and ties; even a coed is there.

> President Ryan: *Most of you will only spend four years here. But to a lot of us, Bloomington is our home. And I don't like the way you boys have been behaving in my home. If you feel compelled to compete with the kids from the town, you'll do it in a different arena. We've decided to expand the field of this year's Little 500 bicycle race to include a team from the town.*
> Rod: *But, sir, they're not good enough.*

The camera cuts to Mike's brother, the campus policeman, who is clearly not pleased by the affront. Rod would have no way of knowing if the Cutters are good enough to compete in a bicycle race; he is saying that they are not good enough as human beings, which is worse.

IT'S ABOUT FAMILY

Interestingly, the Oscar winner for the Best Picture, "Kramer vs. Kramer", was also about family, with an only child and a rift between husband and wife.

Ray and Evelyn are the Archie and Edith Bunker of "Breaking Away", evoking the parents in the 1970s TV show "All in the Family" of the same decade, except that Evelyn is more subtle than Edith. In fact, one of the chapters on the movie DVD is titled "All in the Family". Note: Roger Ebert said that Ray was not that much like Archie Bunker. While Archie railed against multiple ethnic groups—which includes his Polish son-in-law, Mike—Ray is bedeviled by his son, who thinks he's Italian. The generation gap between Dave and Ray is massive—bicycle versus car, unemployed versus employed, physically fit versus cardiac candidate, slacker versus The Greatest Generation.

IT'S ABOUT...

Ray: *He wanted a year with those bums, so I gave him a year.*
Evelyn: *It hasn't been a year yet.*

Evelyn: *I'll talk to him, dear. I'll tell him he either has to get a job or go to college.*
Ray: *College! So he can thumb his diploma at me.*

Ray can't handle Dave's Italian persona; he is taken aback by Dave shaving his legs and squeamish when Dave kisses him on the cheek. In those days, it was not unusual for a father to refer to his son as a weirdo, a bum, stupid, worthless, or a lazy freeloader, as Ray does at various times. Dave has no chores around the house; he is free to ride his bike, swim, and hang out with his friends all day.

Evelyn is on Dave's side and keeps the peace between Dave and Ray. When Dave says that he should skip the race against the Italians, since Ray is recovering from a meltdown, Evelyn talks him out of it. She shows Dave her passport, which she never used except to be used as ID if needed. She never got to pursue her dream of seeing the world, but that doesn't mean that Dave shouldn't pursue his dream. Dennis Christopher shared that Barbara Barrie agreed to do the film only if she could create a scene that was meaningful to her; the passport scene is it. Evelyn has a romantic soul; she waxes the floor while *M' apparì tutt' amor* plays. Dave wishes that he had siblings, a thought that freaks out Ray—a second child 19 years after having Dave?

Evelyn: *He says Italian families stay together.*
Ray: *Evelyn, we are not Italian.*
Evelyn: *So, I know, I know. It's just that I come from a big family myself, and it really was kind of nice. He thinks we should have another child.*
Ray: *What?*

At the end of the movie, the Stohler family will be adding another metabolism. Dave loves his dad despite their differences. His only episode of frustration is severe when Ray tells him that he can't have the day off to race against the Italians. Mike's brother is a policeman and threatens to take away Mike's car if he doesn't stop hot-rodding on campus. At the quarry, we learn why Moocher was alone in the house when Nancy visited:

Dave: *You hear from your folks, Mooch?*
Moocher: *Yeah, my Dad called. He says there's a lot more jobs in Chicago. He hasn't got anything yet, though. Wanted to know if the house was sold. He could use the money, something fierce.*

Dave considers Moocher like family; he tells him, "You can come and live with me when it's sold." Cyril has a father who is supportive, in an interesting way:

Cyril: *I was sure I was going to get that scholarship. My dad, of course, was sure that I wouldn't. When I didn't, he was really understanding, you know. He loves to do that. He loves to be understanding when I fail. 'That's OK, Cyril, I understand.' He even bought me that guitar because he was sure I'd never learn to play it.*
Dave: *Well, I'm supposed to take this college entrance exam.*
Cyril: *Are you going to go to college?*
Dave: *Hell, no. I just want to see if I can pass.*
Cyril: *Maybe I'll take it too and flunk it. My dad's birthday is coming up.*

Note: Cyril's guitar does come in handy, as Daniel Stern was accomplished in playing it. In his book, he writes that he taught himself to play the guitar from Paul Simon's epic playbook. He later met Paul Simon when they appeared together in "One-Trick Pony", in which he had a bit part as a Hare Krishna character in an airport.

IT'S ABOUT...

Other than these, we don't know anything else about the families, whether Cyril's mother or Mike's parents are in their lives. We don't know if Moocher or Cyril is an only child, like Dave. Without a parent around, or in Cyril's case only a seemingly hands-off father around, nobody is pushing Mike, Cyril, or Moocher to get a job. In the celebration after the race, Mike and his brother embrace. Cyril is happy and claps his hands, but is by himself; his understanding father is not there. We know that Nancy lives with her parents, and if she does move to that apartment, it would be perfect for her and Moocher, once he sells the house. Dave is a member of the Baby Boom generation, but the Stohler household does not have two-and-fraction children (yet?).

On a date, Dave talks about his fake family in Italy, giving her a glance to see if she is buying the story. He asks Katherine about her family, which nearly brings her to tears:

> Dave: *My Papa, he tells me, figlio mio, we are fishermen in our family for as far back as I can see. You, you can do what you want, you go to America. Say hello to the new world for me. My Papa!*
> Katherine: *It's kind nice to hear of somebody who misses his parents.*
> Dave: *Certo, I miss. Just like you miss your Mama and Papa.*
> Katherine: *I ... I don't miss them. I went as far as I could to get away from them.*
> Dave: *But they miss you. Hey, at home they sit, and they look at your photo. And they say, ah, how we miss our Katherina, our bambina.*

IT'S ABOUT RELATIONSHIPS

The four boys have a strong friendship relationship, but, as is common in relationships, conflicts can happen. Symbolically, while the two previous scenes at the quarry had the four boys basically within arm's length from each other, in the third scene, they are spread apart. An argument boils over at the quarry after they learn that they will be in the Little 500 race. That should be a unifying moment for the boys, but Dave says that he doesn't want to be seen with the college kids; the real reason is that he would be discovered by Katherine. This provokes Mike's anger; for the first time, the others have challenged Mike as the leader of the pack.

> Moocher: *Doesn't it take four people to have a team anyways?*
> Mike: *Well, we got four. I mean, don't we? I mean, we all enter just to get in, and Dave rides the whole thing, and we win.*
> Dave: *Yeah, yeah, yeah, sure. Look, Mike, I'm going to be working that day, okay?*
> Mike: *Working.*
> Dave: *Yeah. I'm going to get a job.*
> Mike: *By yourself?*
> Dave: *Yeah, I need the money.*
> Mike: *Hey, hey, thanks a lot, Dave. That's really great. You're a real pal. You know that? I bet you won't be working on the day of the Italian race.*
> Moocher: *Mike, the time comes when we just all have to go our own ways, you know?*
> Mike: *Oh, you're a real adult, aren't you? B-town boy grows up.*
> Moocher: *It's going to happen sometime.*
> Mike: *Oh, yeah. Is that what Nancy said?*
> Moocher: *You can just leave her out of this.*
> Mike: *Just shut up, would you? I wasn't talking to you in the first place.*
> Moocher: *Hey, well, I don't give a goddamn. You're not the quarterback here, Mike.*
> Mike: *Well, at least I was once. Which is a hell of a lot better being a midget all my life.*

IT'S ABOUT...

> Dave: *Cut it out. Just cut it out.*
> Mike: *You know, I think you're just afraid of those college guys.*
> Moocher: *Oh, and you're not, right, Mike?*
> Mike: *The only thing I'm afraid of is wasting the rest of my life with you guys.*
> Cyril: *I thought that was the whole plan. That we were going to waste the rest of our lives together.*

Dave starts to talk to Cyril in Italian, but Mike cuts him off, telling him that he is sick of his Italian antics. When Mike says that Dave rides the whole thing and "we win", so much for teamwork! The fact that he has a cigarette in his hand is not encouraging. Mike sarcastically calls Dave a real pal for having the nerve to get a job or to get one by himself.

Dave also challenges Mike when the boys examine the bicycle that they are given for the Little 500 race, and yells at Mike when he gets injured in the race and Mike won't get on the bike. Cyril never challenges Mike, though he has subtle comebacks.

IT'S ABOUT ROMANCE

Appropriately for Dave, Merriam-Webster has this about the origin of "romance":[3]

> The story of the word romance begins as the fifth century is coming to a close, and the Roman Empire with it. The story's key players are the inhabitants of Gaul, a region comprising modern-day France and parts of Belgium, western Germany, and northern Italy—a region one British isle short of the western reaches of the Roman Empire. The Gauls speak a Latin-derived language that we now call Gallo-Romance, but that

---
[3] https://www.merriam-webster.com/wordplay/ah-romance-a-word-borne-to-english-on-the-breastplates-of-chivalry

the Gauls themselves refer to as Romanus, from the Latin word meaning "Rome" or "Roman."

In Old French, the Latin Romanice is adapted as romans or romanz. The new word is a noun, and it refers not only to Old French itself but also to works composed in it. It's the Middle Ages now, and the romans/romanz composed are often narratives written in verse and chronicling—what else?— the affections and adventures of gallant and honorable knights. Romans/romanz takes on a meaning referring specifically to metrical treatments of the love and times of the chivalrous, and the fate of the Modern English word romance is sealed: its close association with tales of love join it forever to love stories, both true and merely dreamt of.

Dave is hopelessly in love with Katherine, Moocher gets engaged to Nancy, and Evelyn has a romantic soul, inspired by Dave's romantic soul to the point that she seduces Ray. She has been reading the scandalous Valley of the Dolls book.

We know that Cyril had a thing for Dolores Reineke, but had "lost all interest in life" when he had seen her at the quarry with fat Marvin (interestingly, his character's name in the two "Home Alone" movies is Marv). He likes to flirt with the coeds; twice, he asks, "What's your major?"

IT'S ABOUT CHANGING ATTITUDES

Through a series of turning points, several characters gradually begin to change their way of thinking.

When Mike keeps swimming after bumping his head on a rock, drawing blood, instead of gloating, Rod has an expression of either concern or sympathy, or that he knows that Mike is genuinely tough. This Cutter may not be good enough, but he is tough enough. In the award

IT'S ABOUT…

ceremony after the Little 500 race, everyone is cheering, even Rod's teammates. Rod gets a contrite look on his face, then joins in the applause.

When the boys examine the bike on Dave's porch to compete in the Little 500, Mike is humbled; it comes after being busted by his brother at the dining hall fight and losing a swimming race. In the Pressbook for the movie, Dennis Quaid said, "When I first read the script, I hated Mike because of the jock part of his character. He could play a sport but was not much of a person in his relationship with others. But as I got into the role I saw how he changed. He became a more sensitive person. Throughout most of the film his problem is that he is unable to express his feelings to his friends. But at the end he's able to let go. His old jock values that used to work no longer do and he lets them go."

Dave realizes that the Italian racers aren't the subject of his idolization or role models when they foul him twice during the race, first messing with his gear shift and later knocking him off his bike into a ditch and out of the race, producing bumps and bruises. When Dave hobbles into the house, Ray knows that something is amiss, because Dave calls him Dad instead of Papa. When Dave says that "Everybody cheats. I just didn't know", Ray says, "Well, now you know", and his expression shows that, while it was not Dave's intention, cheating applies to him, too. When Ray asks him where the trophy is, Dave breaks down in tears and hugs Ray, calling him—not Papa, not Dad—but "Daddy". Ray is taken off-guard, first patting Dave on the back before giving a full embrace. Evelyn is moved to tears at the sight of the two bonding.

Dave realizes that he has to tell Katherine the truth, and he arranges to meet her on campus at the Rose Well House, another structure made of limestone, in the Old Crescent area. For Dave, the third time that he plans a meeting with Katherine will not be a charm. Perhaps Katherine was expecting a romantic moment. The Indiana Memorial Union website has:[4]

---

[4] https://imu.indiana.edu/event-planning/spaces/rose-well-house.html

... the Rose Well House came to be known as a place for romance. It was a popular spot for marriage proposals, and eventually it became a campus tradition for couples to kiss in the Rose Well House at the stroke of midnight. According to campus lore, a woman was not considered a true coed until she had undergone this rite of passage. Today the tradition of romance continues, but with a modern spin. Now it is said that if you kiss someone in the Rose Well House at the stroke of midnight, that person will be your romantic partner for life.

Why is Dave wearing an Indiana University sweatshirt? Is it a foreshadow? Katherine notices his preppy clothes and a different hairstyle and that he is not wearing his cornicello, but does not notice right away that Dave doesn't have an Italian accent. Dave confesses who he really is, that he went to Bloomington High, that he is a Cutter. He had been the treasurer of the Latin Club in high school, consistent with his love of Italian culture. The *M' apparì tutt' amor* music, which he sang in the serenade, plays slowly, as if sadly. At first, Katherine thinks that he is kidding. She starts to tear up and rail on him, but turns away, only to come back and give him a hard slap on the cheek. If the slap looks realistic, it is, and it took multiple takes. It would be interesting to see if the multiple takes exist in outtakes, to compare to the eight slaps that Andie MacDowell gives Bill Murray in "Groundhog Day". In the podcast, The Film Scene with Illeana Douglas on the Popcorn Talk Network, Dennis Christopher related that after each slap, they had to apply makeup to get the red out.[5]

After Dave is betrayed by the Italian racers, he takes down the posters in his bedroom, as Fellini stays faithfully Italian on his bed. Ray tells Dave to take a walk with him on the campus, where they have a heart-to-heart talk. Ray is still wearing his pocket protector. They stop outside

---

[5] https://www.youtube.com/watch?v=reTaBlSoIbo

IT'S ABOUT...

the Herman B Wells Library, with its double towers of Indiana limestone and located a stone's throw from the stadium where the Little 500 race will take place. We can see students hitting the books inside the library; symbolically, there is a limestone wall between those learning and those who didn't or won't go to college. Dave admits that he and Cyril took the entrance exam to apply for admission to Indiana University, and did all right, but emphatically does not want to go to college to mix with the rich kids. As they head home, Ray puts his arm on Dave's shoulder for only the second tender moment between the two.

Dave's change at the end of the movie is stark; he is a freshman student at Indiana University after emphatically saying that he doesn't want to go to college.

When Dave, though exhausted from work, says that he still needs to train on his bike instead of going home, Ray shows a look of respect.

Dave's come-to-the-truth realization from his race against the Italians is a turning point for Ray, too. He becomes all-in with the boys competing in the Little 500 race, and he arranges the "CUTTERS" T-shirts for the team, although Evelyn probably did all the work. During the race, he cheers on the boys while listening to the radio broadcast in a car on his lot, yelling "That's-a my boy!". He is even enjoying a pizza that appears to be a large, judging by its box, which would put a crimp in his healthy diet. It's a double about-face for him—Ity food and from the Noble Roman's pizzeria. He realizes that he should head to the race, and he joins Evelyn cheering on Dave, though his fist-pump is weak, having no practice.

When the boys had driven Dave home from the Cinzano 100 race, Cyril had said, "I feel like one of those dwarfs, you know, like when they think that Snow White's dead." For Ray, he has changed from Grumpy to Happy at the end. He has changed the name of the car lot from "Campus Cars" to "Cutter Cars", written on a sign against a background of an outline of the state of Indiana and with a star representing the city of Bloomington. That sign is modest, but his red "CUTTER CARS" sign with "Raymond Stohler, PROP." on the street is impressive. He is both minding his health and embracing his son's passion; he hops on a bicycle and heads to the campus, where he sees Dave riding with a coed and now speaking French, off to his next adventure, perhaps.

Ray had taken to heart what Dave had hoped for, that they expand their family. At the dinner table before the Little 500—Moocher is there, too—Ray explains that he is going back to work after his meltdown, but he won't come to the race:

> Ray: *If you eat so much, Moocher, how come you're so damn small?*
> Moocher: *It's my metabolism, Mr. Stohler. I eat three times a day, and my metabolism eats five times a day.*
> Ray: *Well, I go back to work tomorrow.*
> Dave: *You mean you're not going to come and see us race?*
> Evelyn: *He thought he might bring you bad luck if he comes.*
> Ray: *Well, I've just got work to do. That's all. Besides, there might be another metabolism to feed around here.*
> Dave: *You mean we might be a father?*
> Ray: *No, I might be a father, and your mom might be a mother, and you might be a brother. You see, that way I keep it all in the family.*
> Moocher: *Wow. Hey, I didn't think people your age…*
> Ray: *Uh, the next word might be your last, kid.*
> Moocher: *You must be very happy, Mr. Stohler.*
> Ray: *Of course, I must. Do I have any choice?*

As Ray mounts his bicycle for the ride into campus, Evelyn turns to the camera to show that she is very much pregnant. Ray has even trusted Evelyn to handle the business at the car lot, keeping it all in the family. In his new state of relaxation, he is not wearing a tie, nor had he when walking through campus with Dave.

IT'S ABOUT...

Even Katherine, the victim of Dave's sham, comes to terms with herself. Near the end of the movie, she surprises Dave, who is enjoying a snack on the sidewalk downtown. She says that she has gotten a job in Chicago; she is leaving college, while Dave is on the threshold of entering college. She has forgiven Dave, realizing that he had given her some inspiration:

Katherine: *And I'm going to Italy after all. With my parents.*
Dave: *That's great, Kath. I wish you a nice trip.*
Katherine: *You too.*
Dave: *I'm not going anywhere.*
Katherine: *I don't know about that.*

CHAPTER 5
THE TV SERIES

A TV SERIES by the same name was created for the 1980-1981 season, airing on Saturdays starting on November 29, seven months after the 1980 Oscars ceremony that honored Steve Tesich and had several other nominees for the movie. The delay to November was due to the 1980 Screen Actors Guild strike. Shaun Cassidy had the role of Dave, and it was shot in Athens, Georgia, instead of Bloomington because of the climate.

It was canceled after eight episodes and was rerun by the Arts & Entertainment cable channel a few years later. In a 2002 interview with the Indiana Daily Student, Barbara Barrie described why the TV series did not do as well as the film:[1]

> "It was politics. The big honchos at ABC all changed in the middle of the first season. It was the tradition for the new people, unless shows were out-and-out hits, to end everything and start over. We were doing quite well, and then suddenly, one day we were just shut down. That's what we figured, anyway."

According to my hometown newspaper, the *Columbus Dispatch*, the first episode was moved to Sunday, opposite an NFL game and a movie, due to the local affiliate carrying the Ohio State men's basketball game that

---

[1] https://www.idsnews.com/article/2002/04/breaking-away-mom-dishes-about-her-experiences-making-the-film-5b9c3213dcea0

Saturday. The following week, it was on Saturday, opposite the Barbara Mandrell Show on NBC, and opposite the "WKRP in Cincinnati" show and the Tim Conway Show on CBS. The Television Highlights section of that *Dispatch* had, "TV's Warmest New Show … BREAKING AWAY! … Shaun Cassidy Stars!"

Joseph Ruben, who directed Dennis Quaid in "Our Winning Season", directed one episode. He also directed the 1980 movie "Gorp", which starred Dennis Quaid and had a role for Lisa Shure, who played the French coed at the end of the "Breaking Away" movie. It was Lisa's only other theatrical movie. Stan Lathan directed two episodes; he had directed one episode of the TV show "Barney Miller", which had Barbara Barrie as Barney's wife. Jack Bender made his debut as a director by directing one episode, and his extensive credits include the TV series "Northern Exposure", "Beverly Hills, 90210", "The Sopranos", "Lost", "Game of Thrones", and "Ally McBeal", and, interestingly, the TV movie "The David Cassidy Story".

In the series, we learn Mike's last name—unlike the movie, he is identified as "Michael Carnahan"—and that Cyril has a sister named Laura, and that his mother is in fact very much in his life. We learn that Moocher's real name is George, the same as his father. That may be an oblique reference to Babe Ruth, whose nickname was "The Bambino" and whose real name was George Herman Ruth.

Barbara Barrie and Jackie Earle Haley carried over their roles as Evelyn and Moocher. For the TV series, Barbara was nominated for an Emmy award as the Outstanding Supporting Actress in a Drama Series; how interesting that the TV series was considered a drama! John Ashton returned as Mike's brother for two episodes, showing his name as "Roy".

Shaun Cassidy played Dave. He had several TV credits, most notably "The Hardy Boys/Nancy Drew Mysteries". His only theatrical movie was "Born of Water" in 1976. Shaun had a more athletic physique than the scrawny Dennis Christopher.

THE TV SERIES

The veteran actor Vincent Gardenia played Ray, who always seems to be wearing a tie and reading the newspaper whether at home or in the office. When venting to Evelyn, he calls Dave "your son". The role was perfect for him in that he often portrayed exasperated characters, though as Ray, he rails against the Italian-leaning Dave despite his own unique accent. He was born in Naples, Italy. He was twice nominated for an Academy Award for Best Supporting Actor, for the baseball manager in "Bang the Drum Slowly" and for Cher's father in "Moonstruck". By the way, which movie had the better slap—when Robyn Douglass slaps Dennis Christopher, or when Cher slaps Nicolas Cage in "Moonstruck"? Other notable movies were "The Front Page" and "Death Wish". How ironic is it that both Vincent Gardenia and Paul Dooley appeared in "Death Wish"? He reunited with Steve Tesich for the TV series; he had appeared in "The Carpenters"—about a dysfunctional family—both the play at the American Place Theater in New York City and a 1973 TV movie. In 1992, he suffered a fatal heart attack at the Benjamin Franklin Hotel in Philadelphia, Pennsylvania, which is Dennis Christopher's home town.

Tom Wiggin played Mike. He played Whitey Ford in the TV series, "The Bronx Is Burning", and his list of TV series includes "St. Elsewhere" and "All My Children".

Thom Bray, a Justin Long look-alike, played Cyril; he also appeared in the "Private Benjamin" TV series with Barbara Barrie, giving him another credit in a series based on a movie. He is not nearly as tall as Daniel Stern, and his character in the series is much more prominent, with his insecurities and his father's low expectations a recurring theme. He often wears a Chicago Cubs shirt, jacket, and cap, and does a great impression of Howard Cosell several times in the series.

Shelby Brammer, who played Nancy, had appeared in "Kramer vs. Kramer", which won the Best Picture Oscar award in the same year that "Breaking Away" was nominated.

The series had several prominent actors who appeared in a few episodes.

Jeff Daniels played a student who buys a car from Ray, who talks him out of a guarantee. That car stalls after a confrontation with the Cutter kids. His one episode was his third acting credit and came a few years before his breakout appearance in "Terms of Endearment".

Olympia Dukakis played a waitress in a diner in the pilot. She reunited with Steve Tesich; she had appeared in his play "Baba Goya" in 1973. She and Vincent Gardenia portrayed Cher's parents in "Moonstruck". She played Dustin Hoffman's mother in "John and Mary", directed by Peter Yates. She appeared in "Rich Kids" with Paul Dooley, and both she ("Cop at the Precinct") and Paul ("Cop at Hospital") had uncredited roles in "Death Wish". One of her major roles was in "Steel Magnolias".

Dominique Dunne played Paulina, Dave's potential love interest, in four episodes. Tragically, a few years later, she was murdered.

Interestingly, the title of several of the episodes mimics other artistic works.

THE PILOT

The series is set up as a "prequel" to the events of the movie. The pilot has the four boys on the verge of graduating from high school.

The episode begins at the quarry, where they used to watch their dads working. Dave has a paper route, earning some money while enjoying his bike rides. Ray rants that Dave was never on a team, but he smiles when he sees Dave reading a Playboy magazine on the porch. Dave points to the magazine and says to Evelyn, "Isn't she beautiful?", but, in fact, he is referring to the La Strada bicycle in the bicycling magazine that he has slipped inside the Playboy magazine. Evelyn says that they can't afford the $1,295 bicycle, but Dave says that he hopes to win one in his first race, in Kokomo.

The boys go to a diner, where they tussle with college kids who come in with their large radio blaring. One of the college kids calls Moocher

"Shorty", so we know what happens next. After getting some punches in, Moocher smashes the radio. Luckily for the college kids, Mike's brother shows up to break up the fight.

From contributor David Goren, a fellow author:

I was a student at Georgia, when they shot the TV show. The restaurant was The Grill, on College Avenue. On the corner, you can see it, was a vacant restaurant. That was the Varsity, a very famous hamburger place known more for its original location across the street from Georgia Tech, in downtown Atlanta. There is also another in Athens that still exists today. That building sat vacant for a year. The next year it was a video arcade back when they were a huge deal, and I spent a lot of time there. Bob Russo, whom I met and spoke with, owned The Grill and other Athens restaurants, including Russo's Gyro shop, where I sat next to Vincent Gardenia.

Dave goes on campus to buy a ticket for the Aida opera, but since he is a Cutter and not a student, he can't afford the ticket. Fortunately, a coed fights with her boyfriend, who throws his ticket on the ground, scooped up by Dave. He wears a cape to the opera, and the coed shows up. Dave is moved to tears by some of the story. Leaving the opera, the coed asks Dave if he is an exchange student. Similar to the movie, he borrows a familiar name and says, Yes, he is Enrico La Strada! Her name is Anna Carrelli, borrowing from Dennis Christopher's real name of Carrelli.

David Goren: *I would stop to watch a scene once in a while. One night, I was returning from the library and saw the filming of this scene at the Fine Arts Building.*

Ray doesn't go to the boys' high school graduation ceremony, sitting in his car outside the school instead. In the ceremony, Mike wins an athletic award. They converge on the postal carrier to see if they receive letters from Indiana University to show whether they are accepted. The letters are there; Mike, Moocher, and Cyril open theirs and are discouraged that they were denied. Dave smiles at his letter, then says that he was denied, too. Later, Cyril tells Dave that he noticed that Dave's envelope was the only fat one, was he actually accepted? Dave confesses that he was, but they will stick together as a team.

Dave lies to his parents that he did not get accepted to college. What will he do, they ask? He will make some money, but his goal is to be the best at something, just as his dad was the best stonecutter. Evelyn later tells Dave that she found the letter while cleaning his room; she gives him advice on making decisions.

At his physical, required by his insurance company, Ray fails miserably and is given a list of forbidden foods—pork chops, lamb chops, roast beef, cheese, etc.—by his doctor. Evelyn clears out the freezer and posts the list on the refrigerator. When Dave sees the nearly empty refrigerator and their meager dinners, he thinks that the family is down to its last dollar. When Dave offers his cheeseburger to Ray, Evelyn says that they can't afford it; what she means is that they can't afford the risk to Ray's health. A clever angle is that Evelyn said that she gave the food to the Reineke family; in the movie, Cyril had a thing for Dolores Reineke, but had "lost all interest in life" when he had seen her at the quarry with fat Marvin.

Dave wins the big race—Rossini's The Barber of Seville accompanies him—charging back after a tire blows up. Dave shows up at the Stohler house with the huge trophy and the bike that he has won. The other boys show up as the Three Wise Guys bearing gifts, bags of groceries. Dave says that he had some money saved from his paper route, so here is everything on the list of forbidden foods—salami, cheese, pancake mix, pork chops! He says that he can sell his bike and buy more food. Ray is in heaven, he hugs Dave, and says, "That's a my boy!" It's Evelyn's turn to be befuddled.

THE TV SERIES

THE "AMERICAN DREAM" EPISODE

This episode has the themes of honesty and relationships. The title may also be a nod to Peter Yates, who had directed the Edward Albee play by the same name at the Royal Court Theatre in London.

A group of fraternity students knows how good a quarterback Mike is, and they convince him to join their intramural football team, sneaking a Cutter onto the team. They arrange for a coed, Liza, to pretend to be friendly with him, and they go on dates.

Dave sees Mike practicing with the team, wearing an Omega Nu shirt. Dave is not happy with Mike's actions, which include going to the movie with Liza instead of his friends. Nancy learns that the students are just using Mike when she hears coeds talking about it at her job at the beauty parlor. She tells Moocher, who confronts Mike and the fraternity guys. Mike blows Moocher off, one of the students calls Moocher "Shorty", and we all know what happens next. Mike and Moocher have a falling-out.

At the big football game, Mike has led the team to a 21-7 lead at halftime when Nancy shows up and chews him out, confirming what she heard at the beauty parlor. Mike decides to get revenge on the students by deliberately fouling up. He convinces Cyril to be the center, knowing that he is a lousy snapper, and the team loses. Moocher shows up, and a long shot shows Mike apologizing, without dialogue, and all is well.

A concurrent subplot, in the Honesty spectrum, is the realtor covering up the flaws in Moocher's roof (it leaks, but she said that it was new), the boiler, and the floor when a prospective husband and wife come to see Moocher's house, to Moocher's disapproval. The couple returns later without the realtor, and Moocher tells them about the flaws. When the realtor finds out and visits Moocher, he fires her.

"American Dream" in this episode refers to the topic discussed by Professor Manchester, played by the distinguished actor Jeff Corey, in a class that Dave attends—without a pen or notepad—on the sly to see if he likes college. He says that he has free time—Mike is playing football with the fraternity guys, Moocher is selling his house, and Cyril is looking for jobs. Unaware that there is a Cutter in the class, Professor Manchester talks about the Cutters (drawing laughter from the class) being challenged to achieve the American Dream. Dave is obviously soured on college, but he returns on a day to find out that there is a midterm exam; he has to borrow a pencil from the professor! At a chance encounter at a diner, the professor tells him that his essay had great promise; that he has a nice, refreshing point of view, and that he liked what he wrote about the American Dream being attainable. He tells Dave that he is glad to help straighten out the glitch that caused Dave not to show up as registered in his class.

Dave goes to work cleaning the cars on Ray's lot, wanting a piece of the pie that Professor Manchester says is escaping the Cutter kids in the American Dream. When Ray is outside, Dave examines Ray's balance sheet and finds the missing $96.34 that neither Ray nor Evelyn could find. The kid has an aptitude, but Ray tells him to find something else, anything, to interest him.

One scene does not mesh with the movie. In the movie, the Stohler house had only one story, making it easy for Dave to move from the dining room to the bathroom–where he shaves his legs–to his room, from which his Italian opera music can fill the house. Evelyn was able to put the record on in the scene where she seduced Ray. However, in the series, it is a two-story house.

Another bonus for Dave is that he has met a coed in the class who could be a soul mate—Paulina Bornstein from New York; her dream is to be a stand-up comedian. She calls him "Paisan" and tells him that it is normal for kids not to know what they want.

THE "KNOWING HER" EPISODE
This episode is about honesty and relationships.

THE TV SERIES

Cyril laments to Dave that he has trouble getting dates. They go to an art museum, and Cyril is thunderstruck at the sight of an attractive young lady who smiles at him; he tells Dave that he is going to marry her. Dave pushes Cyril to talk to her, and Cyril does chat up Jeanne Lindsay. He makes her laugh.

Evelyn has read in the Indiana University course catalog about a real estate class, which can lead to her getting a license. Ray is not happy with the $300 fee, but after a tiff, Evelyn does become a coed.

Mike convinces Cyril to call Jeanne. At home, he goes into a closet and calls her for a date; she thinks that he is charming and agrees. Mike loans him his car, insisting that it comes back clean and with a full tank of gas. Cyril struggles to drive the car, making Mike nervous. When they meet, Jeanne asks him if he is a Cutter, and he says that he is the son of a Cutter. The date ends with them holding hands, and she lets him kiss her. They have more dates.

To Mike's disapproval, Moocher has taken a job as an usher at a movie theater; his job entails making sure there is no talking, no smoking, no customers putting their feet on the seats, calming crying babies—which should come in handy, as he is considering marriage—removing the gum, and cleaning the johns. His supervisor is a slimy, college-type guy who says that his job is to supervise and says, "You're a Cutter, aren't you?". Moocher tells his buddies that the job stinks, but he won't quit.

In a clever twist, when Moocher applies for the job, the marquee shows that "Wild Times" is the feature. "Wild Times" was a TV series that had only two episodes in January of 1980.

By accident later, Dave sees Jeanne kissing another guy. He tells Cyril about it, that he has learned from Paulina that Jeanne "likes a lot of guys". Cyril, who has bought a ring for her costing $3.50, gets mad at Dave.

At the theater, Moocher's job gets worse. He has to tell a group of college students to take their feet off the seats and stop throwing popcorn.

One of them calls him a midget usher. When the supervisor shows up, he high-fives his buddies, throwing Moocher under the bus. He spills a drink for Moocher to clean up and tells him to take a crack at cleaning it up, which is the same as calling him "Shorty", so we know what happens next. Moocher is back among the unemployed.

Cyril has confronted Jeanne, who makes excuses about needing to take a trip to see her aunt in Dearborn, and won't let Cyril drive her. He decides to wait outside her dormitory for hours until she shows up. When she shows up with a guy, Cyril is beginning to wonder if it's over between the two of them. He goes to Dave's house, Dave's not there, so Ray gives him advice on girls, sharing his experiences. Ray later tells Dave that he made the story up.

Evelyn has been raving to Ray about her teacher, Bob Doughtery, whose wife had passed away, and says that he needs someone to show him around town. Bob comes to the car lot in need of a car, and Ray does his usual underhanded sales job, while Dave looks on disapprovingly. After Bob flatters Ray by saying that he learned from Evelyn about how great their marriage is—that he bought an engagement ring after selling his first car, that he worked double shifts at the quarry to buy a house before Dave was born, and what a great dancer he is—Ray rips up the paperwork and sells him the car that he really wants. Dave is impressed with this side of Ray that he has never seen.

Cyril confronts Jeanne for the last time, saying that he knows that she went to Louisville with some guy. Jeanne says that she is sorry that she lied, that she likes a lot of guys, that she does what she wants, that she is a big girl, and that Cyril is a wonderful guy. Similar to the slap scene in the movie, Cyril calls her a little tramp, completely out of character for him. As she walks away, he says to himself that he didn't mean it.

At the game arcade, Dave cheers Cyril up, saying that there will be other girls. The episode ends when an attractive blonde smiles at Cyril, who gives her the OK sign.

THE TV SERIES

THE "KING OF THE QUARRY" EPISODE
This episode is about family.

Moocher says that his dad has a job at a toaster factory in Chicago, and that he might be joining his dad for a job there.

A college kid comes into Ray's car lot, Campus Clean Used Cars, and tells Ray that he would like him to be a guest speaker for his architecture class, talking about limestone cutting, a job that Ray had for 25 years and knew more than anybody. Ray says that it is unlikely. At home, Ray tells Evelyn that he won't do it. Evelyn and Dave think that it is a good idea.

At the quarry, the Omega Nu fraternity members are preparing for a regatta where the vessels are bathtubs. But, they are on the Cutters' turf, so the Cutters overturn their bathtub pontoon. Mike is attracted to one of the coeds, and they exchange smiles.

Moocher talks to his dad on the phone, and the plan is for Moocher to start on Sunday.

On a long bike ride, college students harass Dave, whom they recognize from the quarry. Dave gets revenge by loosening the pontoon on the students' roof, causing it to fall onto the road.

Ray and Dave go to the limestone factory, where Dave convinces Ray to do the guest speaker appearance. Evelyn and Dave will go with him. As he dresses up at home, Dave gives him a flower (a gardenia?) for his lapel. When Ray gives his speech, a student challenges him on the value of limestone, saying that it is boring and not cost-effective, while concrete is cheaper and faster to make. Ray says that the student sounds like a car salesman, and loses his temper. The local newspaper prints a story about Ray's blowup, which causes the Stohler home phone to ring all day and all night.

Moocher has a talk with Nancy about taking the job in Chicago; it pays $6.50 per hour, which is "a lot of money". Moocher really doesn't want to go, but can't bring himself to tell his dad. Nancy wants to spend an evening together with him. Moocher tells the guys that he doesn't want to take the job. They go to the roller rink, where Mike sees the coed from the quarry and skates with her, holding hands while the song "The Rose", from the movie of the same name that was released in 1979, plays. The boyfriend shows up, and they scuffle.

At the quarry, the students have come again. The Cutter boys decide that they will enter the bathtub regatta. Mike hesitates, but agrees when he sees the coed and the evil student kiss.

The boys go to Lowell's antique store and buy a bathtub for the regatta. Dave dickers the price down, just like his dad would do. Mike is wearing jersey #34, a foreshadow of the Little 500 race. They paint "SS CUTTER" on the bathtub.

The race is on Sunday, the day that Moocher is supposed to start his job in Chicago. Moocher and Nancy have a serious talk as he is packing. Moocher says that his dad has allowed him to delay starting the job until Monday.

At the quarry, Moocher coaches the guys on how to navigate the bathtub.

The boys help Moocher pack, but leave when Nancy shows up. They kiss, but Moocher can't say "I love you".

Dave comes home from a ride, then is crushed, because the bathtub is crushed; it accidentally gets hauled away in a garbage truck! Ray goes to the antique store and dickers with Lowell on the price on a replacement, getting a lower price because he is leasing it, and getting the delivery cost thrown in. He makes Lowell swear not to tell anyone, but Lowell does tell Evelyn.

Ray tricks Evelyn into taking a nice, leisurely drive, when in fact he is taking her to the regatta. The race is a relay, with Mike and Cyril in the first leg, and Dave and Moocher in the second. The boys are wearing T-shirts that have "CUTTERS" lettering, just like in the movie. The prize is the "King of the Quarry" trophy, a glorified toilet seat. The student organizer announces that Rule #1 is that there are no rules. Despite fraternity guys interfering with the Cutters by jumping in the water and rocking their ship, the Cutters win the race. The head fraternity guy shakes Dave's hand, and Dave is presented with the coveted "King of the Quarry" trophy, which he gives to the real King of the Quarry, Ray.

The episode finishes with another happy ending, as Moocher has called his dad to tell him that he is not going to join him in Chicago.

THE "HEART LIKE A WHEEL" EPISODE

This episode is about relationships and class differences. The title is the same as a song and album by Linda Ronstadt in 1974. Interestingly, three years later, a movie by the same name and with a familiar theme was released; IMDb has "Shirley Muldowney is determined to be a top-fuel drag racer, although no woman has ever raced them before. Despite the high risks of this kind of racing and the burden it places on her family life, she perseveres in her dream."

Similar to the Cinzano truck scene in the movie, Dave is racing all-out on the highway, with Rossini's The Barber of Seville in the background. This time, it's his friends who are timing him, as Cyril shouts 35, then 45, then five fingers for 50 miles per hour. Two fraternity guys drive up to harass the Cutters and challenge them to a race at a stop light. Mike lets them take off, tricking them into getting pulled over by a motorcycle cop. In an editing glitch, a road sign shows Route 29, which runs through Athens, Georgia; the University of Georgia was used for the series, which still was identified as Indiana University.

Moocher is shown at home, very despondent. He hopes that Nancy is there, but she isn't. They are getting more serious. She sneaks into his house to make meals for him.

At Cyril's house, the fraternity guys pull up to Mike's car to spar with him, then tell him that they have let the air out of his rear tires.

With his tires restored, Mike goes to campus looking for the fraternity guys. He tries to go into a building, but the security officer won't let him.

Dave is getting cozier with Paulina. He asks Evelyn if he can invite her—a college girl!—to dinner at his house.

Cyril talks about a guy named Bobby, "a jerk", who is getting married right out of high school. Moocher says that he is not going to get tied down! Mike razzes Dave for having Paulina come to his house for dinner.

Nancy comes to Moocher's house and is amazed that Moocher has cleaned the kitchen.

Ray brags to Dave that he sold a "catastrophe, a real stinkeroo" to a college kid, a car with a 440 engine that guzzles gas and will drive him to the poor house. When Paulina comes to dinner, Ray is not impressed with her; she is a non-stop talker, and Ray is not. She manages to charm him. After a bike ride back to campus, she surprises Dave with a kiss.

Mike and Cyril go looking for the fraternity guys and find them. They agree to a five mile race on Old Quarry Road. Dave tells Mike that the fraternity guys have an advantage with their new car with the 440 engine.

Moocher wants Nancy to move in with him. The guys show up, impressed by the clean house. Nancy wants to tell the other guys about moving in, but Moocher cuts her off, making her mad. Mike offers to give her a ride home; she thought that she already was home. Nancy is understandably angry, but says nothing.

Now Mike is discouraged about the race; he compares himself to his beat-up car and wants to call the race off. Dave says that he just needs a bigger engine, and he will get it.

At home, Dave is sluggish at the breakfast table. He tells his parents that he got in after 4:00 after his night with Paulina. Ray is happy that his son is becoming a man. Dave says that he wants a car, which Evelyn says is a wonderful idea. Dave later comes to Ray's lot and gets a car with a V8 engine, not the four cylinder car that Ray wants to give him.

Dave has been avoiding Paulina; when she comes to his house, he says that she is not his girlfriend, though he likes her a lot and thinks about her all the time, that she is just a friend. They hug as friends.

Moocher shows up at the beauty shop where Nancy works and tells her that he is sorry about his recent behavior. Paulina is able to get Moocher and Nancy back together.

Mysteriously, the race between Mike and the fraternity guys is back on. Dave, Paulina, Moocher, and Nancy go to the site of the end of the race, where college kids say, "Well, well, we've got some real live Cutters here!" Cyril gives Mike a pep talk, and Mike forces Cyril to ride with him in the race. Cyril is beyond nervous. He tells Mike that James Dean died in an automobile crash, an oblique reference to the movie "September 30, 1955", which was about James Dean's death and had Dennis Quaid and Dennis Christopher.

Meanwhile, Ray and Evelyn want to take a ride in Dave's new car, but it won't start. Ray looks under the hood, and freaks out when he sees that the engine, the V8 engine, is missing.

Mike wins the race easily, tricking the fraternity guys into thinking that he has taken a back road. Dave and Paulina hug, Moocher and Nancy make up, and Moocher tells the guys that they are thinking of getting engaged.

Later, back at the Stohler house, with the boys on the porch, Ray looks under the hood of the new car and sees that somehow, it has an engine again.

The episode ends with Moocher reaffirming to his friends that he is engaged! Since the TV series is a prequel to the movie, this doesn't jive with the movie, where Moocher emphatically denies to Mike in the opening scene that he is seeing Nancy.

THE "RAINY NIGHT IN GEORGIA" EPISODE

This episode is about relationships. The title is the same as the song popularized by Brook Benton in 1970. Interestingly, this episode does not feature Dave on his bike; he is seen riding into the car lot briefly.

Dave says that it will be hard to find a job that will hire all four of them. He quizzes Evelyn for her upcoming all-day real estate exam, and she leaves for it. When she comes home after the exam, she puts on a poker face, but ends the suspense by saying that she passed! On top of that, her teacher offered her a job, and she will soon be among the employed.

She tells Ray that they should take a vacation before her job starts, going to her brother's condominium in Florida on the beach, which is available. Ray wants to know who will run the car lot; has he ever had a day off? Not surprisingly, they have never been to Florida. The answer to who will run the car lot is Dave, not that Ray is comfortable with that, of course.

Dave gets some training from Ray. When Ray lists a car for $900, Dave says that is too much, since Ray had paid only $100 for it from an auction in Evansville. Clearly, Dave doesn't know the business. He will get a 10% commission from any car that he sells.

Dave brainstorms on running the business; he hires Mike as a mechanic, Moocher to do the cleaning, and Cyril to do the sales. They will split the profits four ways. Dave wears a pocket protector, jacket, shirt, and a tie—not a clip-on tie like Ray's—and turns into a true professional; he tells Mike that he wants a full report in writing after road-resting every car. Dave wants the others to wear a tie, which they don't even own. They are late for their first day of work. Mike is miffed by the change in character that Dave is showing; it is not the way that Ray operates.

Before leaving for their trip, Evelyn tells Dave, "I have absolute faith in you. So does your father.", four years before Tom Cruise's mother said something similar in "Risky Business": "Just use your best judgment. We trust you."

Ray has taken a top-of-the-line car that gets 30 MPG on the highway for the trip, not his own car. Driving through Georgia, they run into a huge rainstorm, and Evelyn notices that the windshield wipers on the top-of-the-line car are grossly sub-standard. Then, she asks, is that smoke coming out of the engine? This station wagon is in similar shape as the Griswolds' in "National Lampoon's Vacation". They make it to a repair shop, and the mechanic says that it will take two days for the parts to arrive from Atlanta, since they discontinued this model a few years ago. Evelyn whispers to the mechanic to make sure that he orders new wiper blades.

Ray and Evelyn have to stay at the ritzy Whitehall Inn while they wait out the delay. In the dining room, they chat with Mr. and Mrs. Puffer. Note: I recognized Muriel Moore, the actress who portrayed Mrs. Puffer; she was the juror in "My Cousin Vinny"—which was also filmed in Georgia—who said, "Fry them!" She was a magnet for Oscar awards, too; she appeared in two films that were nominated for the Best Picture: "The Big Chill" and "Driving Miss Daisy", which won the award.

Meanwhile, back in Bloomington, the used-car business is brisk. Dave chats up an attractive coed named Michelle Simmons and sells her the best car on the lot for $500, exactly what her father gave her. A male customer takes a test drive in a car and comes back saying that it has no pickup. Mike jumps in the car with him and proves him wrong by driving like a maniac. The frazzled customer agrees to buy the car for Mike's price of $700 despite it being the "biggest turkey on the lot", as Mike says. Cyril and Moocher congratulate Mike, but Dave is mad at Mike.

Back in Georgia, Ray is bed-ridden with a bad back after carrying the bags. His car now needs additional parts, which need to come from Savannah.

In Bloomington, Dave has become more demanding of his friends/employees. He wants them to show up at 7:30 to take inventory, wear a tie, and work at night. He says that Mike should have bagged his lunch instead of going out to lunch. The other boys ask Dave what happened to the money from the two cars that they sold, and Dave says that he used it to buy more cars. Michelle brings back her car that has conked out and wants her money back in 24 hours, not quite as emphatic as a REFUND! Dave finds out that Mike didn't test-drive the car as he was supposed to. When Dave tells Cyril to shut up, Cyril says, hey, Mike is the only one who can tell him to shut up. Mike angers Dave by saying that Ray only pawns off lemons to college kids who are too dumb to know that they are being ripped off.

Later, Moocher shows up at the car lot at night. Dave tells Moocher that all the cars really are clinkers. Dave says that he expects his employees to …, but Moocher cuts him off and says that they are not his employees, they are his friends.

Back in Georgia, Ray has suddenly become romantic. In their room, they dance, and he says that maybe they can come back next year if her boss will give her a couple of days off. Evelyn is struck by the beautiful moon. Note: coincidentally, or not, eight years later, Vincent Gardenia will play an Italian character named Cosmo in "Moonstruck", and a scene has a character named Raymond waking up by the brightness of a full moon and telling his wife, "Look … It's Cosmo's moon!"

Back in Bloomington, Michelle shows up again and surprises Dave with a kiss. Why? Because the great mechanic (Mike) had come in early and made a minor fix to her car. Dave apologizes to Mike, who says that the cars that Dave had bought at the auction were shabby, but the engines are good. All is well with the boys; Dave is no longer the tyrannical boss. He says that the ties that they were wearing can go, upon which Moocher removes the clip-on tie that he probably borrowed from Ray.

Ray and Evelyn are back on the road, but Evelyn is so happy with Ray's transformation that she says that they should turn around and go back to Bloomington, and so they do. When they pull into the car lot, Ray is confounded by the sight of the extra cars.

THE "LA STRADA" EPISODE

This episode is about honesty and relationships. The title (The Road, in English) is a nod to the movie of the same name, directed by Federico Fellini.

Moocher comes to Mike's house to show him that Nancy has found a job in the newspaper for the boys to investigate, painting a new restaurant.

Moocher stays for breakfast, and Roy observes Moocher's big appetite. Mike is wearing a #34 jersey. They go to fetch Cyril to join them for the interview. They go looking for Dave, who had already gotten up at 6:30.

Dave is out on a long ride on his La Strada bike that he won in his first race. He races another bicyclist, while the same Mendelssohn music from the movie's truck scene plays. Mike, Cyril, and Moocher spot Dave on the road and see the guy force Dave off the road and into a ditch. After a confrontation, the guy says that he is Jack Riley from the Indianapolis Road Club. He gives Dave a lecture on not letting someone pass on a curve. He has raced in Italy, and says that Dave is good, damn good, perhaps Dave can train with him in Indianapolis and race with him in Chicago, St. Louis, and Kenosha. Mike, Cyril, and Moocher are jealous that Dave has made a new friend. Note: Jack Riley was played by Mark Metcalf, who portrayed the evil Doug Neidermeyer in "National Lampoon's Animal House", another rare movie that was filmed on a college campus.

At home, Ray is peeved that Evelyn made him a poached egg, instead of his customary scrambled eggs that have milk and butter. Dave comes home and says that he is invited to join a race club and is looking into a job, to his parents' delight.

The boys talk about the painting job that starts tomorrow, but Dave says that he has to train for a race. They argue about Dave joining the race club. Mike says that he always drives Dave to races, and walks out in anger. Mike keeps talking about Dave and "that damn bike". It looks as if it will be the team of just Mike and Moocher doing the painting.

Without a car ride, Dave decides to go to the race in Indianapolis on a bus, and Cyril says that he will join him. Mike and Moocher see Dave and Cyril at the bus station, where Dave tells them that his $1,200 La Strada bike has been stolen. He asks Roy, the campus policeman who is Mike's brother, to help find the bike.

Note: this evokes similarities to two other movies. One is the Italian movie, "Bicycle Thieves", in which a poor man gets a job hanging posters—similar to the Cutters painting the restaurant—but has his bicycle, his only means of transportation, stolen. It is a father-and-son story, too, as his young son accompanies him on his hunt for the bicycle. In the Oscars awards, it earned the Special Foreign Language Film award and was nominated for the Writing (Screenplay) award. The other is "Pee-wee's Big Adventure", in which he dreams about winning the Tour de France and has his bicycle stolen by someone he knows.

The four boys are busy at work painting, with Dave upset that he should be looking for his bike. When the restaurant owner makes a remark that college kids could do the job better, Mike says that they will get the job done in the week as promised.

Evelyn convinces Ray to cheer up Dave. In Dave's bedroom, Ray tells Dave the story of when he was a young stone cutter and had his tools, given by his father, stolen. He thought about getting a new job, but bought a new set. They weren't as good as the old set, but everything turned out fine.

Moocher is at Mike's house for dinner when Roy tells Mike to come outside to the back yard. Roy has discovered that Mike stole the bike.

Cyril finds out later and tells Moocher that he is going to tell Dave. Mike shows up at the restaurant; he has found the bike! Mike says that he will drive Dave to Indianapolis, but first he confesses that he stole the bike, after pressure from Moocher and Cyril. Dave can't understand why Mike would do that, and, for probably the first time ever, slugs him. Dave rides off, and Mike chases him, finally getting Dave to let him drive to Indianapolis. Dave wants to know why Mike did it. We learn that Mike has been jealous of Dave for many years, that Dave would lie about getting low grades in high school to be one of the guys, that he knows that Dave was accepted to Indiana University. Why didn't Dave go to college? Dave says that he was scared.

At the start of the race, Mike wishes Dave good luck. Rossini's Barber of Seville music plays as the race takes off. Dave and Jack Riley bump each other multiple times, and when the music reaches the same point as in the dirty trick scene in the movie, Dave bumps Jack, and both land in a ditch and out of the race. Dave recites the same lecture about not letting someone pass on a curve. There are no hard feelings, they shake hands, and Jack says, "Welcome to the club." Dave thanks Mike for being there to see how well he did.

When they arrive home, Dave is asleep in the car. Mike tells Moocher and Cyril that Dave did great. Mike says that he did good, too. Dave wakes up and puts his arm around Mike. All is well.

Ray and Evelyn are in bed, and Evelyn says that she had gone to the bank and seen something curious in their savings account. Ray doesn't want to talk about it. She says that Ray withdrew $1,200 one day but replaced it the next day. Perhaps he wanted to buy something, like an Italian bicycle. He says that the bank must have made a mistake. Evelyn kisses Ray, who asks why, but asks her to do it again.

THE "GRAND ILLUSION" EPISODE

This was the eighth episode; it was not aired, but is available online.

The title is a reference to the celebrated French movie directed by Jean Renoir, who passed away in 1979, the year that "Breaking Away" was released. Like the ending of the movie, this final episode entails a relationship with a French woman.

Dave brings his bike downstairs from his bedroom, and goes on a ride while singing "Figaro". He sees an attractive woman riding on a bike coming the opposite way, and she says "bonjour", causing him to crash into a cluster of trash bags. He loses her, was she an illusion? He finds her and follows her to a hotel, where he sees a poster that she is Francoise Jobert, a Cycling Champion. Now, he is inspired to sing the French song, "Alouette".

At home, Evelyn is sharing how happy she is about her realtor job. Ray reads in the newspaper that the city is being invaded by French people to make a television commercial. Evelyn knows who Francoise Jobert is from commercials and says that Dave has pictures of Francoise in his room. Dave comes home and says he has seen a vision, a rhapsody. He is speaking French now.

Evelyn tells Ray that she knows of a parcel of land that they could buy, then sell to the university on a hunch. It would cost $5,000. Ray says that he wouldn't even consider looking at the land.

Cyril goes to his high school with books in his hands and eavesdrops on his former English teacher, Mr. Fields. [Note: I recognized the actor's voice, he was Lou Walker, who played the cook in one of my favorite movies, "My Cousin Vinny", where one of his lines was "You mean to tell me you never heard of grits?" He also played the security guard in the "Heart Like a Wheel" episode.] Cyril and Mr. Fields chat, and the teacher asks him why he is not in college.

He tells his friends that Mr. Fields thought that Cyril was a born writer, that writers didn't have to go to college. Cyril says that he used to write about a subject that inspired him, that subject being Mike, his fights, his touchdowns, his girlfriends. This may be a nod to Steve Tesich, whose "Eagle of Naptown" was about the athletic exploits of his friend, David Blase.

Dave tells his friends about meeting Francoise, which they doubt. Cyril has a list of things he'd like to do for inspiration—a two-fisted brawl, get drunk, and have a passionate adventure with a girl whom he will never see again.

Dave and Cyril go to the hotel to try to see Francoise. Dave sees her getting into a sports car with a guy after giving him a kiss. Dave gives a message and his address to the desk clerk, but she tosses it away after Dave leaves.

At the arcade, Cyril has decided that he wants to be a tough guy, so he asks Mike to coach him. Mike teaches him how to walk and how to look tough with his eyes. Mike tells him to start a brawl. Cyril challenges a guy to give up the pinball machine, and it works! He challenges another guy who calls Moocher "Shorty", but this time, the guy roughs up all three of them.

Ray agrees to check out the parcel of land that Evelyn talked about. Talking to the owner, Ray says that he is in the transportation business. The owner says that an alumnus has offered $23,000 for the land. Ray's cigar drops out of his mouth.

The boys go to Dave's house to pursue Cyril's goal of getting drunk on Ray's booze. Paulina is already there, as Dave had invited her, and Cyril cozies up to her. Dave lies to his friends, saying that he is going to have dinner with Francoise in her room at the hotel.

Evelyn tells Ray at the car lot that a bigwig in Chicago has bought the land. They come home to find Cyril drunk.

Paulina comes to Cyril's house. Cyril says that his parents went to the movies, which is the only reference that his mother is very much part of his life. Paulina has become Cyril's muse in encouraging him to write, so he takes off in his new endeavor. She makes up a story about a girl and a guy, and the girl thinks that he is a nice guy and kind of cute.

At the hotel, Dave sees Francoise in the lobby. She spills the contents of her purse, and he helps her. She gives him a kiss! Dave has a keepsake from the encounter, a bottle of her perfume. The desk clerk says that he can give it back to her next summer in Paris.

Paulina keeps hinting to Cyril that she likes him. He tells her that he likes her idea about a guy and a girl having a relationship, but a long term one.

Dave reads what Cyril has written and likes it. Cyril tells the guys that Paulina did the typing. Mike challenges Dave to prove that he had met up with Francoise. Dave shows them the bottle of perfume and says that it must have fallen out when they were "rolling around the floor kissing", a *double entendre* if there ever was one. He wraps up the episode by saying, "Would I lie to you?"

CHAPTER 6

AMY WRIGHT, THE ANGELIC NANCY

THANKS TO Dan Levinson, the son of Art Levinson, the associate producer, I was able to interview Amy Wright in July of 2024.

Where does "Breaking Away" rank among your favorite movies?
Amy: Oh, I think it's a great movie. I don't rank movies, I just like movies, or don't really remember them or how well they held up, or whatever. But for "Breaking Away", I'm very, very happy to have been part of it. I remember when we were making it, we were sitting around with the editor, Cynthia Scheider, and she said the line, "This is a really nice little movie, I have really no idea where this is going to fit in, or how well it is going to do, or what it is at the end of the day." A lot of times, when you are making films, I have heard several actors say that they don't know what this movie is going to turn you into. So, it was nice that it came out so well.

Why do you think the movie is so popular, to this day?
Amy: It has very good performances, and it's about that age group. Barbara Barrie, Paul Dooley, they're just so great. They just really walked that fine line, especially Paul, of being extremely funny, but still real. It was fun to experience all those fans in the crowd for the bike races.

How was the cast to work with?
Amy: Everybody was fun. A lot of them had the beginning of their careers … Dennis Quaid and Daniel Stern.

Specifically, how was Jackie Earle Haley?
Amy: Oh, well, he was lovely. He's a wonderful actor, and he was fun.

When the movie was over, as you've worked with the cast, did you get a sense that these actors were going to take off in their career?
Amy: I didn't really think that, because we were all young. It was one of the first films I was in, and the first films that they were in. So, you never know. I didn't say, "Yeah, I was in The Deer Hunter with Meryl Streep, and everybody said, oh, she's going to be a huge star, that was obvious." [Laughs]. I don't remember thinking about it that way. Everybody was just having a good time and excited, at the start of their careers. And, they were good roles to sink your teeth into. There were things that suited everybody, the guys got to be very athletic, swimming and biking, and running around in their cars, and fighting with each other. It was a little different then, wasn't it?

How did the character of Nancy fit for you?
Amy: Oh, pretty easily. I think I went to the audition with my hair in those braids stuck on the side of my head, and I think he really liked that. You never know, you walk in, and there's so many people being considered for the part. I didn't know, that was just the way I was wearing my hair at the time. It seemed like the character was just someone like myself. But the hairdo kind of sealed the deal, I think.

Did you make up an accent, a small town kind of accent?
Amy: I worked on it a little bit trying to sound like them, a little bit. I didn't go to a coach for it, but I remember trying to get some of the sound of it. I mean, I'm from Chicago, so Bloomington is a little different. Chicago's very twangy, nasally. I remember getting a little bit of the accent.

Speaking of Chicago, with all the cast members were from big cities, was that a culture shock to go to Bloomington?
Amy: For me, no, because I grew up at the University of Chicago. I grew up in academics, in a university town. It was different from Hyde Park in Chicago, but it still had a lot of the same things going on, but more sports-oriented, very different architecture. I remember driving from the airport to where we were staying, just the smell of the cornfields. I'm like, man, this is home. I felt right at home, because I'm from the Midwest. The first time, it did hit me by surprise. Oh boy, does that smell familiar, seems familiar.

I described the character of Nancy as an angel, would you agree?
Amy: Oh, why is she an angel?

Because she's so sweet, and she does everything for Moocher, and she pays the $4 out of five for the marriage license.
Amy: Oh, yes, she does. "Oh, Fudge, you have a dollar." You don't really know what bag of tricks you stick your hand in to come up with a character. But, it was very well-written.

It was a fairly short shoot, about eight weeks. Did you get a sense that this was a low-budget movie?
Amy: I got the feeling it was. I think they told me it was a medium-budget movie. For that time, it was a lot of money to me. I know that pretty soon after that, bigger movies were like 50 million dollars.

You've worked with so many incredible directors. How would you rate Peter Yates?
Amy: Oh, great. I mean, I have been very lucky. They all have their own way, I guess. He was very nice. One time he said to me, "Amy, the camera's over here. Would you please play to the camera? No one can see your face

if you're looking the other way." I was still at that time maybe a little shy of the camera. I had mostly done stage work, so I got nervous. I felt like, oh, somebody's watching me so closely here. I guess he was happy with what was happening, because he didn't say much to me.

Speaking of movies that I call real, I really loved "Crossing Delancey", by Joan Micklin Silver. Can you compare "Breaking Away" to it, a simple story with real people?
Amy: Yes, it's that kind of film. Regular old people, doing what they are involved in, living their lives.

You had two movies come out in the following year. Was "Breaking Away" instrumental in your career?
Amy: "The Deer Hunter" came out the year before. Until the early 80s, I was being seriously considered for parts. And that was just based on, I think, my work in New York on stage and some of these films. I was getting the jobs, and that would push you to get more auditions for another one, so I was in the running, let's put it that way.

Any stories about the movie to share?
Amy: If I think of something, some funny story, I'll call you. I haven't looked at the film for a while. I should watch it again with my grandchild, she's seven, I think she's too young.

Give her a warning about the language.
Amy: Oh, I'm sure she's heard some bad language. Is there a lot of bad language?

Just, here and there, a couple times.
Amy: That's a good idea, I'll watch it again, that would be fun.

CHAPTER 7

EDDY VAN GUYSE, THE ITALIAN VILLAIN

THANKS TO Dr. Ben Pearl, Eddy joined me for an interview in August of 2024. A photo of Eddy and his three Italian teammates in the Cinzano 100 race appears in John Schwarb's book. His exploits in the Little 500 race are prominent in the book, including competing while very sick in a disappointing second place finish in 1972.

How did you first get involved in the movie?
Eddy: That was pretty neat, that was a surprise. Okay, so I'm announcing the 1978 National Cycling Championships in Milwaukee, Wisconsin. And I'm doing the usual combination stuff I did in cycling. I'm doing radio interviews, some TV interviews, hooking people up with key racers who know nothing about cycling. And then I'm on stage being the voice, the MC of the event in front of the live audience. And after this race, and it goes on for several days, the juniors and category one, too, my mom calls me up with her Belgium accent from Chicago:

> Mom: *Eddy, Eddy, Eddy. 20th Century Fox call up. They want you to try out for a movie.*
> Eddy: *Mom, what did you tell them?*
> Mom: *Oh, I told them. He want to try out.*
> Eddy: *Mom, did you get a number?*
> Mom: *Eddy, I have a number. Okay, you have to give them a call.*
> Eddy: *Okay, Mom. I'm going to be done working in another day.*

And give me the number I can call.
Mom: *You want to call them, eh? I want you to call them. You were a good actor in theater, Eddy.*
Eddy: *Okay, Mom. I know. Okay, so I'll call them.*

And I called up, and these people say that Gary Rybar gave us a picture of you, because we put an ad in the Bloomington paper for the last four principal parts to be cast in "Bambino"—the working title of the movie throughout the entire month on the Bloomington campus film, not "Breaking Away"—the Cinzano cycling team. We'd like you to be a good cyclist, an avid cyclist, and you must be Italian or look Italian. And if you have any acting background, let us know about it. I called up, and I said, "Yeah, I said, yeah, I just co-starred and starred in some plays. I'm not talking grade school, high school, I'm talking Roosevelt University and professional theater in Chicago." "All right, Eddy, would you come for an audition?" So, the audition was in two weeks. Being a sportscaster, broadcaster, announcer, whatever you want to call it, we know that you can get wined and dined very well by sponsors. And I hadn't been on a bike in a while, and I needed to lose weight to look good. I was born in Belgium, and beer is part of my culture. So, I needed to lose weight. So, in two weeks leading up, I said, okay Eddy, no brewskis for a while. I went and laid out at Foster Beach in Chicago to get a tan to look like a real dark Italian. And I had my long curly hair, my mom's curls. And then I go to the audition. Gary picks me up, and I go to the audition, there's over 100 Italian-looking guys there at the Best Western in Bloomington. And you signed in, and I'm waiting. And when my time came to be called in, I go in there, and I wore a white shirt. I'm tan like crazy. I got my shirt open, and it's a big collared white shirt. I look like a disco duck Italian. So, I go in there, and …

Peter Yates, with his English accent: *My, haven't we got quite the Italian here.*

Eddy: *Excuse me sir, are you Mr. Yates, the director?*
Peter: *I am, Eddy. Just call me Peter, and this is my first assistant, Mike Grillo.*
Eddy: *Hi Peter, hi Mike, I can't lie to you, I was born in Belgium, I get mistaken all the time for Italian.*
Peter: *Do you speak any Italian?*
Eddy: *No, but I'm fluent in Flemish, Dutch, and I do pretty well in German. But with the right coaching, I know that I can do a good job Italian for you.*

And then they asked me a couple other questions, because I was a high school math teacher in the inner city at the time. And then they talked about acting, what I had done in the plays "Critic's Choice" and "The Happy Time", co-star and starring roles. And then I asked the question which was very key …

Eddy: *Is this bike race, this Cinzano 100, a serious bike race or sort of a tour?*
Peter: *Eddy, why are you asking me that?*
Eddy: *Well, you've got guys out there on 10-speed bicycles. Some of them have reflectors in their wheels. Some of them have a 10-speed with straight handlebars, not drop handlebars. If it was a real bike race, you wouldn't want this to be seen in your movie.*
Peter: *Eddy, it's a real bike race. Then we wouldn't want that to be seen in the movie.*

Anyway, long story short, he says, "Eddy, it's been nice talking to you. Can you wait back in the lobby there? We'd like to talk to you later". So, another hour goes by, and everybody gets seen, and he calls me in …

Peter: *Eddy, I'd like to congratulate you as the first team member of Team Cinzano.*
Eddy: *I'm thrilled. I'm really happy.*
Peter: *Eddy, I'm not that thrilled with all the Italians I saw here. I either have to go to New York or a place where there's lots of Italians in New York. But I know that there are Italians in Chicago. Is there any chance you can recommend any real cyclists, Italian-looking who could fit the role to be your teammates?*
Eddy: *I can't believe you're asking me that, because I have to go and MC an event called the Tour of Elk Grove Village in a suburb of Chicago. There are three guys who stand out. One is Pete Lazzara, a real Italian. The other one is John Vande Velde, who's dark-featured like me, whose grandparents were immigrants from Belgium. And then there's Carlos Sintes, he's of Cuban descent.*
Peter: *Eddy, I'm going to have Mary Gaffney, our casting director, give you this Polaroid camera. Eddy, will you take pictures of those three guys, three together, in a straight shot? Will you then get individual straight-on shots? Will you also get a profile of the three guys? And will you mail them, FedEx, 24 hours?*
Eddy: *Yeah, I'll do it.*
Peter: *But, I really need you to do it. Please, will you do it immediately, Eddy, sorry to put the pressure on you.*
Eddy: *No, no, no, I'm a responsible person. I'll take care of it.*

So, I go to this race, and I go to these guys, and I go, "Hey, I just got a role in a movie," and they start razzing me. And I go, "No, no, no, this is for real. Let me take pictures of you guys." And they're laughing at that, and I take my pictures, and I send them in, and all of a sudden, I get a call in my apartment in Chicago about a week later. And it's, "Eddy, Peter loved the pictures. Can we send you the contracts for the boys? And can you get it to them? And then can you send it back as a package? Here are our film dates."

And that's it, that's the story.

Talk about Gary Rybar, the stunt rider for Dennis Christopher?
Eddy: Gary is a Delta Chi fraternity brother who, like me, was a Hall of Famer for the Little 500 bike race, and he's the guy who gave a picture of me that led to my audition, and my mom got the call. So, Gary picks me up at the Bloomington Airport before the audition. I wouldn't have been in "Breaking Away" if it wasn't for Gary, and Gary wouldn't have been in "Breaking Away" if it wasn't for Eddy, because after I get the role, Gary drives me to the audition, he's tells me he's a film major, and he says, "I've been knocking on the casting, where they have their office set up, and I said, 'Hey, I'm a Hall of Famer from a Little 500, and I graduated in film. If I can be involved with this movie at all …', but they ignored me, but I hope you get a part." So anyway, after they brought me in at the end of the night and said I was the first member of Team Cinzano, and Peter asked me for the favor with the Polaroid camera for the upcoming race in Elk Grove, I said, "Peter, can I ask you a small favor? I've got a fraternity brother here named Gary Rybar, he is a most accomplished cyclist, he's an Indiana State champion, he's a Hall of Famer for Little 500, and he's graduated with a major in film, and he's approached your offices at least three times, saying can I get involved in any way. I wouldn't be here today if it wasn't for Gary, and he picked me up at the Bloomington Airport, he drove me here, he's been waiting in that lobby for the last two and a half hours, and I just wonder, can you meet Gary at all?" Peter tells me to bring Gary in, and the words out of Mike Grillo's mouth exactly are, "Oh, my God, Peter, we just found our double for Dennis Christopher." Gary worked the entire movie many more days and was also used like me as a technical consultant.

How did you become the villain?
Eddy: So, we get there a couple days before shooting, and all four of us are handed a script. And we're reading this, and there's one guy who is the jerk, the featured guy. And Peter didn't say who the bad guy is, and I got to tell you, I want to be the bad guy. I did the audition, I got the boys in. I'm watching them shoot, because having acted, I just want to see them shoot the scenes at the quarries. When the day of shooting is done, and Peter's watching me watch, I'm just watching intently a Hollywood movie up close, I can watch this. And then I ask him, "Peter, I have one question. Who's going to play the bad guy from the four?" He said, "Eddy, I'll let you know that after you guys ride by me tomorrow. You'll ride by me." So I leave, and I'm like, I wish he would have told me that I'm the bad guy, but he didn't. And I'm just hoping, because the other guys are riding along. And then we come to shooting day, and Peter says, "Team Cinzano, get on your bikes, and I'd like you to ride by me, not just once, but twice, have your hands in the drops, and look up at me." So, we do that twice, and then he announces, "Eddy, you're my villain." And my heart was, "Yay, I scored that role." I know how important bad guys are in movies. You and I are movie buffs, we love our heroes, but, man, when somebody plays a great bad guy and you hate him, that's awesome.

And after that, I went to Peter, and I said, "Peter, can you tell me why you chose me as your villain now?" And he said, "Your eyes, Eddy, strictly your eyes." And I made a quip, and I said, "Well, Peter, that explains it. I am a bachelor, and no gal that I've dated has ever said to me, you've got bedroom eyes." And he said, "No, you don't."

Walk us through the Cinzano 100 mile race.
Eddy: So, now we're going to start shooting, the first scene is the start of the Cinzano 100, and he didn't direct us in any way, do what you want to do, and so I took my water bottle and sprinkled it on my head. I also think that I blew a kiss to the crowd. It was typical Hollywood, do a few takes of

us arriving and the fans at the start line cheering, and then, all of a sudden, it's: we're going to shoot the gun, we're going to shoot all the way. Team Cinzano, you and the rest of the pack heading very fast at turn number one, making a right turn. They just shot different things and segments of the race, I'd say, probably shooting 30 seconds, 45 seconds minimum and maximum us arriving, them getting their closeups. That would have been day one, nothing was going on between Team Cinzano and Dave. Then on day two or day three, we had some rain that delayed something, but I think that we were there for about seven, eight, nine days of shooting.

Who were some of the racers in the Cinzano 100 race?
Eddy: Oh, my God. It was like a Delta Chi fraternity, that was my fraternity, and all of us that rode in a Little 500 … Steve Dayton, my wonderful teammate for my senior year, and he was a national road racing champion, his brother, Mark Dayton, Randy Strong, Joel Stetina, Greg Silence, Dave Blase, Gary Rybar—the double for the Dennis Christopher cycling scenes—Bill Brissman, the double for Hart Bochner, Chris Gutowsky were in there. Isn't that something, little Delta Chi? There's no other fraternity that I think contributed more to the success of "Breaking Away" in these two cycling scenes, the Cinzano 100 and the Little 500. So, I take great pride in the involvement of my fraternity brothers who were involved in that.

There were other cyclists from Indianapolis, because they had published it and said, we need extras. We need a bunch of bike racers for this movie. It was phenomenal to see so many of my friends and acquaintances, the cycling community, again, that was making up the Peloton for the Cinzano 100. There were so many people. I mean, it just made my heart jump for joy. My head was like, is this really happening? Is this a Hollywood movie, and all my buddies and we're all involved in this? Yeah, it was a pretty happy time.

Describe the scene of the insulting gesture to Dave?
Eddy: Peter Yates, when we're leading up to that scene, comes to talk to me. This is after the scene of Dave catching up, and me shifting his gears, and he drops behind. And then he catches up again, he's all happy, and he wants to talk in Italian to his heroes, who he's looked forward to racing forever in his life. Peter Yates is such a distinguished man, the Englishman. I just had so much respect for him. And so …

> Peter: *Eddy, in this scene, here's what you're going to do. Dennis is going to come up to you. And he's going to talk in Italian to you. Eddy, I want you to do the bent elbow. You know, the Italian bent elbow, with your left hand. You're going to be riding with your left hand in the drops. And take your right arm, and go bend it.*
> Eddy: *The real way to do that is I got to take my left hand, put it by the elbow. The way the Italians really do it.*
> Peter: *But Eddy, then you'd have to take your hands off the handlebars.*
> Eddy: *Peter, that's no problem, riding without my hands in the bars.*
> Peter: *So you can do that?*
> Eddy: *Yes, Peter.*
> Peter: *Fantastic.*

So, that's what happened there. He originally thought for safety, I had to have my left hand in the drop handlebars and then look up at Dennis. So, we did a couple of takes of that, and Peter was happy.

Talk about the scenes of messing with the gear shift and the pump through the wheel?
Eddy: When we shot the scene where I reach over to shift Dave's gears and put it in high as we're climbing, I see Dennis Christopher doesn't have a

front wheel in his bike, his fork is on a dolly with wheels, it's being pulled by a car. So, of course, me being inquisitive, I have to ask, "Peter, how come we didn't do it with Dennis having a front wheel in there?" And he says, "Eddy, if something went wrong with you shifting his gears, and he crashed, our filming is done, we lost our star." So, we do however many takes of that, five, six, seven, whatever. They shoot Dave dropping back, and Team Cinzano is in the lead, he's got to catch back up to us. Dave comes up and wants to talk Italian to me, and I give him the big "Get the heck out of here."

In the script, it says that I am putting the pump in his rear wheel. And I'm like, oh my God, I said to Peter, "It's got to be in the front wheel, to have him flip over." And that's how we did it. Conrad Palmisano, a very accomplished Hollywood stuntman, is going to be the guy who's on the bike as Dave. I couldn't believe how they had this rigged up, they had a cable attached to his left front fork blade, and that cable was not like we know, round cables, it was a Slinky, it was so cool not to get bound up, it was a flat steel cable, and it was jacked in the ground when we started to shoot this, it was maybe a hundred yards or over a hundred yards away, and they measured it out, and they threw the big mattress for Conrad to flop on after the stunt to make sure that he fell there, buried under leaves and stuff. So, we do the first take, and Peter told me, "Eddy, I'll cue you an audio cue, when I go 'now', you thrust that pump towards that wheel, but you don't put that in the wheel." We did that take, and it looked bad with the bike sliding sideways, so Peter comes up to me, and he says, "Eddy, would it be possible for you to put the pump in the wheel?" I say, "I'd love to do that", and he says, "But we have to make sure that Conrad falls on his mattress, or we are in big trouble." I said, "Okay, can I make a suggestion? Instead of your audio cue, can we measure out again exactly where Conrad's mattress is to fall, and can I take a branch, something clearly visible, instead of your audio cue? Can I see something lying alongside the road that I know that is visible for me as we're coming up to it, and I know that's where I want to put the pump in the front wheel?" And he says, "Lovely, great idea." So, they did that, it was big enough for me to see, and they hand me a pump that was a silca pump that was filled with lead wrapped with tape, I mean a regular silca pump in the wheels would have done the job. By the way, the rules of the stunt were that we're going slightly downhill, we could go no more than 15 miles an hour, that was Conrad's stipulation, a guy who had just finished doing a roller coaster movie where he's tucked in a roller coaster and gets thrown off the rails, and he's tucked in, and he's a pretty neat stuntman, he and Diamond Farnsworth, two stuntman from Hollywood, involved in "Breaking Away". So, we do the second take, and everybody roars, the crew, Matt Leonetti, the cinematographer, and Conrad gets up and has a fist pump, and so that's a keeper. Earlier in the shooting, when we did several takes on shifting his gears, I had to ask Peter, "When you say that's a keeper, I know what you mean, that's good, you like it, but then you say let's do it again. Can you explain that to me?" He says, "Well, of course, Eddy, if I don't have more than one, I can't make any choices."

You should have been a director yourself!
Eddy: You know what, somebody else said that during the filming, and that's a compliment, thank you.

Talk about the pothole scene, which is in the script but did not make it into the movie?
Eddy: There was a pothole scene, after I shift Dave's gears, and I'm drafting off of him, and then he pulls away, and I get jarred in the pothole. Well, the reason that got left off was the guys from 20th Century Fox make a pothole, they dig a hole, and I tell them, "This is too big, this is dangerous, it's got to be a smaller pothole." And then Peter Yates is there, and I go, "Guys, I could fall, this is a little bit too big." And Peter says, "Well, Eddy, will you give it a shot?" Well, I hit that pothole, my front wheel collapses,

I go down, my elbow is bleeding, thank God I didn't break anything, and I get up, and I'm mad. Peter felt so terrible, "I'm sorry, Eddy, are you okay?" I go, "I'll be alright, but I told you that that hole was too big, you know?" They call the medical crew for my elbow that's bleeding, and thus that scene is not in a movie. Once I fall, I'm no longer in the race, I'm out of it.

Talk about the photos of you and your buddies, the four Italians, in the magazine that Dave gets and in the poster above his bed.
Eddy: They took pictures of us, they did that immediately. After the race, Dave's tearing down all his posters, after I knock him down, right, he's mad, he's in his room, tearing down all these posters, he had all these cycling posters, including Team Cinzano. At the world premiere at Indiana University, Peter Yates hands something to me and says, "Eddy, you were an awesome villain for me, I want to present this to you." The picture I have framed upstairs that Peter Yates gave me, it's Team Cinzano, just the four of us, and we're toasting champagne, and that was one of the pictures that was hanging up in Dave's room. He tears it up in the movie, but they made a copy of it, and Peter gave it to me.

What other stars did you meet?
Eddy: Everyone was wonderful during the filming. Dennis Quaid was great, Daniel Stern was awesome, Jackie Earle Haley … just mingling with them was so good. After Steve Tesich died, there was a special event in Beverly Hills, in a theater to honor Steve. People were going to do a reading out of his last book, "Kazoo". And so, I go walking in there. And there's Daniel Stern. I hadn't seen him in so many, many years. And he's standing next to the actor James Woods, who I like as an actor. So, I go walking in, and I look at tall Daniel Stern. And I have a smile. And …

> Eddy: *Daniel, I don't know if you remember me.*
> Daniel: *Of course, Eddy. I remember you.*

Eddy: *How are you?*
Daniel: *I'm doing good, Eddy, good to see you.* [To James Woods], *This is Eddy, who played the villain in Breaking Away.*

James Woods sticks out his hand and goes, "Hi, Eddy, Jimmy Woods." And I go, "James, I know who you are. I'm such a fan of you. You're an awesome actor." And he says, "Thanks a lot".

You must be very proud of the fact of creating the Cutters name for the new team in 1984 and by so doing, you're keeping the movie relevant, probably forever, so talk about the pride you must feel for that?
Eddy: I'm announcing bike races all over the country, because of the successful cyclist I was, but now being a villain in "Breaking Away", there's more people who say, "Hey, Eddy, will you do some TV stuff, will you do radio stuff?" You know how that goes, you being a sportscaster. So, anyway I'm announcing at the Encino Velodrome in Southern California, which I love. When I was an 18 year-old boy in 1968, I was here from National Championships and Olympic trials, and I was the Illinois State 10 mile champion, the longest event on a velodrome in our National Championships individually as a 10 mile event, and I ended up getting third as a skinny 18 year-old boy in August of 1968 before I'm going to start my freshman year at IU in September, and later, I come back to that track and announce, as well as announcing at the 7-11 Olympic Velodrome, the track built for the 1984 Olympic Games.

One day at the velodrome, Gary Rybar has been coming out, he is so happy, he says, "I've been working 'Breaking Away', the TV show", which was a disaster with Shaun Cassidy. He's been in Georgia, working, making money and loving it, and he comes on, stays with me and my roommate. We were bachelors at a great place that has pools and everything here in Long Beach. We get a call from Randy Reisinger–Billy Brissman was with us, too–and he says that two Delta Chis got kicked out of the house, and they're going to form an independent team, and they asked me if I had any ideas on what to call the new team, and there wasn't a hesitation, I said, "My God, you've got to be the Cutters. That was made famous in the movie, and if you boys win as the Cutters, you will get so much more publicity than you would get using any other name". And one of the boys says Hey, Eddy, you're putting a lot of pressure on us. I say you're good bike racers, what do you mean, pressure, you're the best, you guys can win this thing. I said I don't know if they can guarantee you white jerseys with "Cutters" on them, I doubt that, you got to have what the Student Foundation gives you, but the key is I hope that they let you call yourselves the Cutters, and, lo and behold, they're the Cutters, and they win.

And this is unbelievable: the paper here in Long Beach is the *Long Beach Press-Telegram*, and that paper that I've been getting for years, and the only reason I still get it is because I had an award-winning sport show called Sports Break that I produced and wrote and hosted at the pleasure of covering so many sports clubs here. They win on Saturday, on Monday, I look at the paper, and above the headline at the very top of the paper, just like in the Academy Award winning movie "Breaking Away", is "The Cutters Win Indiana University's Little 500". It blew me away, I call up the boys, I said, "Guys, I want to take a picture of this, (there weren't cellphones), and send it to you, this is unbelievable."

Talk about Steve Tesich?
Eddy: I love Steve Tesich, and I'm so sad that he died early, because I want to tell you that I was communicating with him often. One day, I'm announcing in Encino, and I see him walking in the Encino Velodrome. The stands are always packed, it's the most exciting little track in the West Coast, it's a fifth of a mile, about 250 meters and banked properly, and I'm in the announcing booth doing the live play-by-play announcing, and I see Tesich walking in, in blue jeans and a T-shirt. And I go, as he walks,

"Ladies and gentlemen, give a big hand to the Academy award-winning writer for best original screenplay, Steve Tesich, for the movie 'Breaking Away'. Steve, this is Eddy Van Guyse up here, come and join us." And he works his way up the steps, I do a little interview with him, and he stayed up in the booth until the races are done, and when I'm finally done, he says, "I tried to get a hold of you. I'm wrapping up my next movie, where the heck were you living? I had your number in Chicago." And I say, "Wow, that's on me, I can't believe it. I should have stayed in touch with you. I should have stayed in Chicago. I would have been in another Tesich movie." I was out here, bit parts and stuff after "Breaking Away", I moved out here for that reason. And I said, "What's your movie about?" He says it's called "American Flyers", and he says we're wrapping in a week, and you would have been key in it, I would have used you. He says, "Well, go see the movie, you're going to like it. I'm going to name someone in the movie after you." I say, "Give me a clue, will you, Steve, tell me, give me a clue will you?" He says, "You go see it, you'll know, and don't tell anybody that I named someone in the movie after you." So, we exchanged numbers, and I say, "Hey, Steve, let me audition if there's a third Tesich movie, OK?"

I moved out here in 1979, so we got married five years later in 1985, Christina, my wonderful wife, and we go watch "American Flyers" for who's this Eddy? Finally, a scene comes up where one guy says to the other, "Hey we're going to go training with Eddy today." And they're riding in the country, and, all of a sudden, one of the cyclists whistles and says, "Hey Eddy!" And here comes this friggin' pit bull chasing them! So, Steve Tesich had a big laugh on that.

After that, he and I stayed in touch. He was living in New York with his wife Becky and their one child, not far from his Hollywood agent. I said to him, "Hey, Steve, if you ever do a sequel for 'Breaking Away', I just have the right ending." And he says "Eddy, I know it's going to have to wait, because I made the mistake of doing that short-lived TV series called 'Breaking Away' with Shaun Cassidy. If I had not done that project, we would be seriously talking about a sequel to 'Breaking Away', but go ahead, Eddy, tell me what you're thinking." I say, "Well, it has to be that after Dave got knocked down in his hometown race, he came home crying to his dad, we know the key scene, with him and his dad, the shyster used car salesman, to bring them close like they never were, and everybody cheats." And I said, "Here it is, the world championships are in Italy, and off this big climb, it's Dave Stohler with the jerk from Team Cinzano. One of them is going to wear the rainbow jersey, one of them is going to be world champion, and it's in Italy, and as the Italian tries to drop Dave, he can't, and there's a flashback that shows him getting put down with a pump in the front wheel, and here is Dave Stohler in the world championships, a professional cyclist after 150 miles, a mountaintop finish, he takes out his pump, and he thinks about putting it in the wheel of the Italian, and instead he throws his pump away in the ditch. He accelerates, he breaks away alone and comes across the finish line with his arms up as world champion." Tesich says, "Eddy, I love it, it's awesome, it's great." We didn't talk after that, then he died in Nova Scotia, he was out on a family vacation with Becky when he had his massive heart attack, but that's the last time I talked to him.

How accurately is the Little 500 race depicted in the movie?
Eddy: Oh, I think that the depiction was great. Totally accurate? I loved it, because you had to look at the contrast. Not accurate: the difference in seat position between little Moocher and geeky, tall Cyril. No, you're not going to hang with them, with that discrepancy in seat position, but mind you now, in the movie, that they didn't do a bike exchange that is now allowed. In my day, you had to ride the same bike, so you better have teammates whose legs are close in length, not a great discrepancy. Now, for many years, they've had a bike exchange where they touch hands, and you can go to a guy who is 5' 8", 5' 9", you can go to a guy who is 6' 4",

6' 3", whatever with a bike exchange. In my day, you couldn't. You had to line up your team, you had to be close. It's hilarious in the movie to see the closeups they shot of seeing Moocher's face and his little body stretched out and to see geeky Cyril and then, of course, Dennis Quaid was the jock of the four Cutter boys. Dennis Christopher was the bike stud who looked best, but then the old football jock Dennis Quaid, who talks in the movie about football when they are sitting on the hill and not getting his chance, but very athletically-built Quaid, so, yeah, that wasn't realistic. And, also, giving up the inside of the track at the end, when Hart Bochner, the big shot fraternity guy, the good-looking boy, for them to lose that race to the Cutters as they go wide, and all of a sudden here's the Cutters winning the race. Nobody should go wide.

Is it realistic to expect anyone to ride all 200 laps?
Eddy: No, because the speeds during this relay race, on a single geared coaster brake bike, are incredible. Asking one individual to cover all the opposing teams' attacks and sprints to the pits with fresh bodies constantly getting on the bike would make it impossible.

Dave is doing 60 miles per hour on the highway chasing the truck. How realistic is that?
Eddy: In the gear he was in, not realistic. With the proper gearing, very realistic, with the big chain ring up front and a very little sprocket in the back, no problem, but the blooper was the close-up they showed before drafting, the inside front chain ring that you used to climb a hill. I got to go to the world premiere in 1979 at the auditorium by Showalter Fountain, what a thrill it was to see it for the first time before anybody else, and to see that close-up of Dave's road bike, he's got it on the inside chain ring that you would use to climb hills. They show that, and then he's drafting at 60 miles an hour behind the truck. So, wherever I went, announcing races around the country, it was, "Eddy what a blooper, the

big 'Breaking Away' blooper, did you see it?" I said, "Of course, I saw it, it is a big blooper."

Talk about the Delta Chi fraternity?
Eddy: I just want to share that I'm so proud of Delta Chi's involvement in the movie. When I arrived on campus as a pledge in 1968, at little Delta Chi, we were insulted, because the common question was, if someone asked how many fraternities are there here at IU, the way they would insult us was that they would say 32 fraternities, plus Delta Chi. That was the insult, we were the smallest, we did not excel in grade point average, we were a little Animal House, party boys, and that was it, basically.

Why is the movie so popular to this day?
Eddy: That's a great question. It's so real, everybody loves the underdog winning … "Hoosiers", "Rudy", and "Rocky", I love them … and the humanity.

I'm a guy who likes some of the old-fashioned movies, and we live in an era of special effects. And I enjoy them, too, and they're necessary. There are so many movies, I'm not going to name them, but I've gone to a lot of movies that are "bang, boom", and I walk away, and I'm empty, and then I go, God, what is Tesich doing? And I'm just like, you know what, I think the heart and soul of a movie is when you have a storyline, character development, great dialogue between the characters, and in then "Breaking Away", when you add to this, outstanding acting by the cast, and then great direction by Peter Yates. I think that people forget that with the heart and soul of movies, you don't need special effects. And this is a great example of that.

CHAPTER 8
IN THEIR WORDS

SEVERAL PEOPLE ASSOCIATED with the movie granted me interviews. I am honored that Amy Wright agreed to one. With all due respect to the others, I gave Amy Wright and Eddy Van Guyse their own chapters.

Carlos Sintes was one of the Team Cinzano racers, recruited by Eddy Van Guyse.

Randy Strong was an extra who appeared in the Cinzano 100 race, appearing right behind Dennis Christopher in one scene. He was 16 years old at the time; he had a driver's license, so he drove between Indianapolis and Bloomington for three days of filming. He was on the winning Cutters team in the 1984 Little 500 race and on the Delta Chi team that finished second "by a spoke", as a newspaper headline described it, in the 1982 race. In the CBS telecast of that 1982 race, Ken Squier identified him several times, and it included a brief taped interview with him. In the interview, where "RANDY STRONG, DELTA CHI-SOPHOMORE" appears on the screen, he talked about the success of Delta Chi: "It's put us in a position where everybody's going to be expecting us to do good, and if we don't, there's going to be a lot of disappointed people."

Bill Brissman was the stunt double for Hart Bochner and was on three Little 500 championship teams with Delta Chi between 1978 and 1981, including crossing the finish line to win in 1979, between the filming of the race and the release of the movie. He is a member of the Little 500 Hall of Fame.

Bob and Debbie Broeking, husband and wife, were extras, with Little 500 experience. Bob competed for the Willkie South X team in 1978 and was a Little 500 racer in the movie, and Debbie competed in the Mini 500 tricycle race and cheered in the stands in the movie.

Doug Bruce appeared in several scenes, the fight scene in the student union, as a racer in the Cinzano 100 race, and in the crowd at the Little 500 race.

Jim Kirkham was a four year rider for The Cutters teams; the team finished second in 1991 and first in 1992. He started coaching the team in 1997 and has been a part of 12 winning teams. His photo and quotes from the 2024 race appear in an online *Washington Post* story.

Dr. Ben Pearl connected me to several participants in a Little 500 race. He was a Little 500 racer in 1987 with the Zeta Beta Tau fraternity.

Dr. James Pivarnik, retired Professor at Michigan State University, competed for the Pi Kappa Phi fraternity from 1971-1973 and has the perspective of a hometown Bloomington South High School graduate. He rode qualifications in 1971, and the race and qualifications in 1972 and 1973.

Judah Thompson is an Indiana University junior as of this writing in the Fall of 2024. He was a freshman on the Cutters team that won the Little 500 race in 2023, decided by just 0.133 seconds, and a sophomore on the team that finished second in 2024. His photo and quotes from the 2024 race also appear in an online *Washington Post* story. He has the perspective of competing in the race and analyzing a movie that is over 40 years before his time.

Dennis Robinson writes: "I was a student at the time of filming. I was also working for the *Indiana Daily Student* newspaper as an advertising salesperson and sales manager. I was intrigued with the movie filming process, and watched them set up and film several scenes. My one weird observation was that there was a strong sense from some on campus that resented the Hollywood business taking this story away. I remember maybe a negative story in the *Indiana Daily Student*. I went to the premiere showing in the local theater (von Lee or Indiana Theater?) Got a standing ovation. I loved it!"

Dan Levinson writes [Note: My hometown is Columbus, Ohio, and I recall the filming of "Teachers" quite well.]:

> My father, Art Levinson, was the associate producer on "Breaking Away". In 1984 I went to visit my father in Columbus when he was working on "Teachers". I appeared in one scene in that film as well - and had a line ('oh - excuse me'). It's the scene where JoBeth Williams follows Nick Nolte into the men's room. I come out of one of the stalls and say that line. Alas, my three-second segment - which would no doubt have made me a star - ended up on the editing room floor. But, I still ended up in the credits.
>
> I was on set during the filming of "Mr. Mom", and remember meeting Michael Keaton and Teri Garr. "My Favorite Year" was Dad's favorite of all the films he worked on, and I was around for quite a bit of that. They re-created the 1954 New York NBC studios on a soundstage at MGM in Culver City, and I watched them shoot the Boss Hijack sketch and the scene with the lawyers on the terrace ("He's beneath us"). I also visited New York City for the first time while Dad was working on "My Favorite Year". That was the first of five films he did with Dick Benjamin. Ten years after "Breaking Away", I was in Memphis while Dad was working on "Great Balls of Fire" with a now-established Dennis Quaid.

How did you get involved in the movie?
Randy Strong: I was in high school at the time, which was, you know, a pretty hot thing for anybody who would have been in the 70s being a bike racer in high school. I think that I was the only kid in the school of

3,500 kids who raced bicycles. And my teammates, the Stetina brothers, called me up and said, they're filming a movie down in Bloomington, and Gary Rybar, who's the double for Dennis Christopher, was my teammate as well. But, he made sure I got into all the shots, the team jersey, and through all the Italian bike race shots that they could. So, I got like three extra days of pay to go down there and shoot some of the scenes that weren't with everybody else. It was a little bit of an extra two days' pay for the shoot. But, I was able to get my face in the effort, a few frames, and it was a lot of fun. I had a lot of notoriety in my high school for being in the movie. They did a big story about it in the yearbook, and a lot of people who didn't know who I was were getting to know who I was after that. I ended up going to IU and riding the Little 500, and started the first team that had ever won the race as an independent team, and we ended up calling ourselves the Cutters, and we won that year, in 1984. So, we brought the movie to life. And then in the true sense, ever since then, we'd be the winningest team of the Little 500's. So, we've won 15 times since 1984, in the 40 years of the team's history. Nobody's even come close in the number of victories. Eight victories by Delta Chi was the second most victories. The Cutters have stamped their name on the race in more ways than the movie.

Bill Brissman: I had a long-time friend and a fraternity brother in Gary Rybar. Gary graduated out of Delta Chi, the year I pledged. So, we knew each other from bike racing, and Gary had gotten the role of the stunt double for Dennis Christopher, and he recommended me, and he called me down and looked at me, and I was close enough to looking like Hart Bochner that they said, okay, fine, he'll do. And I was probably one of the only people in Bloomington that had ridden a Little 500 that could give Gary a reasonable sprint, because Gary was a very formidable rider, and I was kind of an up-and-coming sprinter myself. So, it was a good match, and it was due to Gary's recommendation.

IN THEIR WORDS

Carlos Sintes: When Eddy Van Guyse asked me to be in the movie, I was like, okay, sure. I had no idea really what it meant, or what it was going to be throughout my life, but Eddy just said, would you like to be in a movie? Are you free? I said sure, and off we went from there. Eddy picked me up at our house and drove me to Bloomington, and when we got there, half the town was in line for a part as an extra. And Eddy says, well, where are we supposed to go, but why don't you go in line and save our spot for us? And he went off, I'm in line, high-fiving other people. This is pretty cool, blah, blah, blah. And then about a half hour later, a lady shows up and says to me, "Mr. Sintes", and at the time I was like 19, I wasn't used to being called Mr. Sintes. "You don't need to wait in this line". So, they took me to a suite, gave me a drink and a copy of the script, and then asked me, where's your agent? I looked at Eddy, "Agent?" I didn't know it was going to be quite as big as it was. I just thought it would be like an extra's part, riding in the movie, etc.

Bob Broeking: I was a rider in the Little 500 in the spring of 1978. I was on the Willkie Deca team; on our jersey, it was "Willkie Deca", but on the paperwork it was "Willkie South X". The name of our team was Willkie Deca, because we were on the tenth floor of a Willkie residence hall. We started making fun of the fraternities by saying Deca, but we were Willkie Deca. It was our team name. In the summer of 1978, when they started the filming, they asked for riders who had ridden in the last race to be extras in the movie if we wanted to be. I was a rider in the Little 500 race scenes, but my face did not get in the movie. We think we get to see my helmet in one of the scenes. I was paid for it by 20th Century Fox. I remember getting a pay stub that we wish we would have kept. I received $250 as an extra for two days of filming, that was a lot of money back then, it came in handy in 1978.

Dan Levinson: I was 13, and I went to visit my dad in Bloomington. I spent about a week there. That was the first film he received associate producer credit for.

Doug Bruce: I heard they were going to film this bike movie, and as a 15-year-old in the 1978 summer of my freshman year in high school, and back then, the only way I got to bicycle races was with the college kids from Little Five, and I would practice on the Little Five stadium, and I just ran circles around these guys, and so I got to know guys, and they would throw my bike in the back of a van and drive me to the Tour of Kettering, different races in this three state area, and it truly was almost like the movie. I'm a true townie, although no one really uses that term, and my brother is actually a limestone carver, so we were fascinated with this movie and what they were making up, "Cutters" and stuff. I just knew very little about the Little Five. I just knew where the stadium was, and so I was interested in it, and they were really hurting for extras. So, that's really kind of how I got interested, I was just being a bike racer, and my claim to fame is that Greg LeMond and his team Avocet came from Minnesota where he lived at that time, and they came down and raced this race in Cincinnati—Racing superstars Wayne and Dale Stetina were there racing and selling prizes they won in Europe out of their van or bus, too—and against us, and they lapped us 10 times easily, and that's when I realized that I might have been good, but I wasn't incredibly good. I was a bike racer at the age of 15, so I was interested in the film for that reason. I got paid two days as an extra, and then I spent two days at the stadium on the weekend when they were filming the movie, so that gave me four days of being in the film, and then we just tried to be in the background where we could.

James Pivarnik: When I was a grad student working on my PhD, I was kind of the faculty advisor for my fraternity, and one of the guys who was sort of a local guy helping to get riders together for all of those scenes, I knew him pretty well, and he said, "Jim, you want to be in the movie?", so all of those kind of things sort of put it together.

How did the movie influence you?
Jim Kirkham: I saw the movie when I was in middle school, I knew about the Little 500 through the movie, and there was this fictitious story, this bike team, and this really cool event. So, it was in my head, and I was not involved in cycling or anything at that time. It was kind of like, it was a cool story. And then I made my way to Indiana University and had some friends that rode on the bike team called the Cutters, and of course I knew the name Cutters through the movie, and I just instantly knew that I wanted to do that. And there was this dream, and it was coming true. So I started riding on the bike team and rode four years on the bike team. And then I started backfilling the history, like where the Cutters team came from. I met more people that were involved in the movie. And so I got to, just really study the movie more and kind of got to know all the characters and then became a fan of the movie on a deeper level, because I was now involved with this bike team that kind of came from the movie indirectly, they borrowed their name from the movie team. So, it was kind of arts and real life coming together.

Ben Pearl: Coming out of high school, it put IU on the radar for me. I would have known nothing about Indiana University. I had applied to the University of Virginia, an early decision, in fact, but I had the intrigue and the mystique with the movie and just the connection with these outsiders and underdogs, and that's basically what it was. It was a great underdog movie. I loved the movie "Rocky", and this was like "Rocky" on bicycles. I was a runner, so I didn't initially conceive that I would be doing bike racing at IU. I had actually ended up getting rejected at the University of Virginia, which was the best thing that could have ever happened to me, because then my second choice was IU, and I ended up being a walk-on on track, getting injured, and then looking more seriously at bike racing, particularly as I saw the ways that you needed to get connected to ride on a bike team, which was primarily through either a legacy or an independent team or a fraternity, and, initially, I had not pledged to a fraternity, because I wasn't interested in joining a fraternity, but I found out that you needed a more organized team to have a better chance to make the race. Most of the fraternities had the most established programs, so that's why I ended up joining the Zeta Beta Tau and pursuing the Little 500 bike race.

> **What about your cohorts? Were you aware of others who saw the movie and decided to come to IU for the bike racing?**
> Ben Pearl: It's a good question. I think that it creates, certainly, a lot of intrigue and interest and especially at that time in the Indiana area, in the adjacent Chicago area, because they're so close to Indiana University, and, in some cases, when you have really accomplished riders who are already riding at category level before they attend college, they might specifically seek out Indiana University at that time because of the movie. For students like me, I think it was a little less common, because I was so far from Indiana. I was on East Coast, but the movie had such a strong impact on me about not only being able to see the bike race but to see how Bloomington was, how the Midwest was, to see the kind of a mystique of the quarries and the beautiful campus and just getting a sense of what Indiana University and the bike race were all about.

Judah Thompson: I watched the movie when I was younger, when I was just growing up, because my dad is also from Bloomington. He grew up in the quarries, swam there before the movie was even made. He was actually an extra. He was in the scene at the very end where Dave is walking with his girlfriend, and he's sitting on a rock, a quick little cameo, and there's one other scene where it's on Route 446 at the Cinzano 100 race, just cheering on, and funny enough, he actually did not enjoy that experience. When my grandpa picked him up, he was like "I'm never going to be in a movie again", but anyways, he was very proud of being in that film, as it was so successful, and it meant a lot with it being in town. I believe my dad didn't enjoy it because it was a long day of filming, and he was an impatient teen. He showed me the film early on in my childhood, so it was super cool seeing my dad in the film, and it's also just a film that's based in Bloomington, the place I grew up in, seeing these landmarks, pointing stuff out they're like, "Oh, I know where that's at." It influenced my cycling career quite a bit, just seeing the main character Dave, living a pretty relaxed, low-ley, lifestyle, just biking around, something I really admired.

As a current Indiana University student watching the movie, are you saying to yourself: this is an old movie, or it's just a movie?
Judah Thompson: When I think of "Breaking Away", I definitely think of it as an older movie, just the way it was filmed, just like the times, because Bloomington has really changed, there's a lot more apartment complexes, it's definitely a little more busy, housing is a little more pricey. It's just different. I wasn't born back then, but you can really see that Bloomington has changed a lot, so I'd say it's an older movie.

As a coach, do you invoke the movie as an inspiration?
Jim Kirkham: As a coach, I've been involved in a Little 500 since 1990. So, a long time, and I see the movies about the coming of age of adolescence. And when I was going through it, you don't realize this much. Now that I'm older, I see that every athlete on the team, everyone, especially in that age group is doing the same thing while coming of age. They come to IU, green, leaving their parents, and some joined a bike team. And so,

invoking the movie in the sense that everyone is struggling with identity, the uncertainty of life in how to kind of lean into that and use the movie as a kind of a source of comedy, but let the kids know like this: you're not the first one to go through this. We've all had to do this, and here's this really cool movie related to bikes. It shows that none of us are exempt from this transformation.

What was your Little 500 experience?
James Pivarnik: I competed in 1972 and 1973 when I was an undergrad, and then I coached my fraternity team when I was a grad student. I had moved to Virginia for a few years, and when I came back in 1978, I was a much better coach, because I had really good riders, and we finished like third, ninth, and second the years that I coached, which was pretty good. When I rode the first year, we were kind of crummy. It was a two-day race, it rained, then the next year we finished 12th, I think.

Do you know of any other colleges that come close to the passion of Little 500, perhaps in a different sport?
Jim Kirkham: There have been many schools that try to replicate Little 500, but it's never stuck. Others, maybe non-traditional sports, not that I am aware of, really. The Little 500 is a really unique event. Bill Armstrong had this idea, he understood that investing in kids, the experiences would pay dividends in the future. So, the experience and creating this event and giving something for kids to train towards, but also getting the campus involved and coming out to cheer for your friends. So, creating experiences. And then, when COVID hit, universities were kind of figuring out, what was their role in kids' lives? They were cutting back on experiences like that, and things were kind of going away. You could just as easily get an education online and save a lot of money. But then when COVID hit, this is my opinion only, the smart universities, especially Indiana University, realized they had this tradition, this experience that

is unmatched. And since COVID, they've really doubled down on it and really enhanced it and built it back up. And it gives kids a reason to come to IU and to be part of it, and something to look forward to in April as the school year is coming to a close. So, just the experience of it, I think, is magical. And I think the university now kind of has a better understanding of what they have on their hands.

Actors came from all around the country, metropolises, like yourself. What was your impression of small-town Bloomington, Indiana?
Dan Levinson: I grew up in the Brentwood section of Los Angeles, so it was quite different. And I visited my father at several locations by that time. I knew that the university was there and it was a university town.

Talk about how the Cutters became an independent team that broke away from Delta Chi in real life?
Randy Strong: The whole culture of Little 500 was pretty much developed around the Delta Chi team of the early 1970s. The team that is kind of pictured in the movie, that would have been Delta Chi in real life. I was part of Delta Chi, the fraternity. Randy and Steve Reisinger were the two brothers that started that team and had coached it for these seven years. They won seven out of 10 years during the 70s. By the time the movie came out, it won six times. I think a lot of the patterning of the race and the fraternity came out to a Delta Chi program. And that was the same program that we brought over to the Cutters. My teammates, Adam Giles, Scott Senese, and Adam Beck, who are all Cutters, were not allowed to return in the fall, so they got kicked out of the fraternity. And I had to make the decision whether I came back to the fraternity or not. It kind of made for an interesting story. And then the entire Delta Chi program got behind us as we break away from the fraternity. And so, we've brought that program forward all the way up to 2024. And, that's kind of an interesting side note to the whole evolution of the Little 500. Before 1981, they were

wearing wool shorts; I brought Lycra shorts to the race to bring it into the modern day. I actually went to the world premiere event at the IU auditorium by Showalter Fountain the night they had the world premiere, and I have the original program in my scrapbook.

How did your scenes in the Cinzano 100 race shape up?
Carlos Sintes: We were there, I think, about eight days but only filmed for four or so, because of rain. So, whenever there was rain, they filmed indoor scenes, and we'd be on call. At the start of the Cinzano 100–I was an elite cyclist back in the day, as were the rest of the Italians—and no 100 mile race ever started that fast. We were supposed to get to the front and make the turn. And we had to film that scene seven times, and finally Peter Yates walked out in front and told everybody, "Hey, I'm sure you're all fine racers, but this is a movie, and the Italians have to get to that corner first." And we finally got that scene done, but it was everybody sprinting out like mad men just to get their face in the movie. But that's how the movie really kicked off, was filming that scene of the start of the race. And then all the other scenes, it seemed like we would film in segments and then wait around for two hours. They would start us from being cold to 30 miles an hour, so it was pretty hard riding for the most part. Dennis Christopher was, in a lot of the scenes, being pulled by a truck, basically. They had this gizmo where his fork would go into a hitch, and he'd get pulled along, and we're riding pretty fast. It was realistic riding and hard riding, and multiple scenes. It was tiring, but realistically fast.

Randy Strong: I showed up, and they were at the start line, down and over by the east side of Bloomington, and there was a hotel out there. And I thought I missed the filming. So, I ran up, and the lady at the counter said, now we've got three more days of shooting, so, just come back tomorrow, and I came back the next day, and my teammates had secured me at the front with all the other teammates so that we could get our jerseys in the shot. And then Gary Rybar wanted me to kind of guide him up through the middle of the pack, because there's a lot of squirrely riders, and so kind of pushing guys out of the way, so he'd get through as the stunt double. And then they'd cut the Dennis Christopher role into the shots. Gary wasn't able to get a chase in. And there was a lot of fun there. We met a lot of the guys from the Little 500 who were hanging out there, and, for being a high schooler, it was kind of eyes wide-open, the whole movie scene. They kept telling us to slow down, because they could always make it look faster in the edits. And everybody wanted to go much faster. We kind of came around, and we were kind of acting that we were chasing him. But he was going pretty darn slow.

Doug Bruce: They got a hold of the Bloomington bicycle club and asked us to help put on their race. I tried out to be one of those guys, but I didn't have dark enough hair, and I obviously looked way too young. If you look at the guys they got, they got Eddy Van Guyse and some guys in there who were good and who looked really Italian, but parts of that scene, those of us who are riding in the pack, they had to yell at us to slow down, because we were all antsy. We were all in a bike race, and we wanted to catch those guys, but they were trying to film a movie, it was easy to forget that and try to ride fast. So, they kept yelling at us from their support vehicles that we had to slow down and slow down, as we were getting too close, and Team Cinzano had to look like they were as good as they were supposed to be. The start/finish line is actually out on East Third Street right near route 446 and Bruster's Ice Cream, and there's a pack scene of us, and we're all racing down the hill on route 446 towards the causeway, then they took us into Clear Creek, and, if you pay attention, there in Clear Creek, we're riding as a pack over the railroad tracks, and then again, because it was low budget, they didn't want to move the cameras. They made us ride back, didn't move the cameras, and they had us going in the other direction. That's the scene where the dog walks out in front of everybody as we come through there. Again, cycling wasn't a big thing, it was hard to get anybody to show up to act like a bike rider.

Bill Brissman: They wanted to be very sure that they limited my face time, because they were concerned that somebody might see an inconsistency or see my face and put it together. I was in that mass start scene, which they had to shoot four times, that big race start, and the filmmakers were so frustrated on it, because, of course, here are all these Indiana bike riders grouped like crazy on this line, and everybody knows that the only way that you're going to get in this movie is if you're up front, so everybody clamored to get right on the front line, and when they said go, everybody was going full gas from the very beginning, and they wanted to show these Cinzano riders as being clearly better than everyone else and going out on time, and they just couldn't keep up with the group, and finally they had to give them a head start after three times had failed, and I'm in that mass, and I think I'm seven guys through that corner, but only I could pick myself out of that scene, because it's such a mass.

What cast members did you interact with?
Carlos Sintes: I did a little bit with Dennis Christopher. I interacted with a lot of them. I actually got to spend some time just hanging out with Dennis Quaid. He was at the front of a hotel, he had bought a used car, and he had bought himself a dog while he was there, I think it was a little basset hound that he called Bluebonnet, I think that was the name that he called it. It was neat to talk to him, he was very reserved and quiet. And I never met a real actor before. And I had no idea he'd become the actor he became, at the time. Daniel Stern, his personality is very similar to the Cyril character. Jackie Earle Haley, his character, he seemed like the kind of guy who had a chip out of his shoulder. It was really neat to meet these people and to watch them work. We watched them do scenes that we weren't in, and it was interesting to see them change personality and

become their character. They would sort of stand around reading their lines, kind of meditating or getting into character. And then they would change. It would become who their character was. I had no idea about acting. I was in a room next to one of the actresses, the Nancy character. And we both had little balconies, and we were just making small talk. She asked, "So, where did you go to school?" And I said, "Well, I go to business school at Loyola University." She goes, "No, school for acting". And I said, "You go to school for acting?" And she got mad, turned around, walked in, never talked to me again.

Randy Strong: I met Dennis Christopher. He was a little aloof to all the extras. Didn't really talk or interact with us too much. He didn't say hi to us. But he was pretty squirrelly on the bike. He was really nervous that he was going to crash. So, everybody was kind of like, just stay off his wheel, don't get close to him, let him just ride and let the cameras do the work. I knew Eddy Van Guyse from years of racing. Dennis Quaid, Daniel Stern, and Jackie Earle Haley were in the Little 500 event, but they weren't in the Cinzano race, so I didn't get to see those guys, they weren't there. Gary Rybar, who was the stunt double, and I knew each other real well, we had raced together.

Bill Brissman: I was the stunt double for Hart Bochner, and I met him, but the funny thing is we didn't have many interactions, because they just kind of wanted me for the riding, but they didn't really care so much about the interaction between the stunt double and the actual actor. He actually came to the race in 1979, of course, he was there for the premiere, which was the night after the race and congratulated me after the race, and we chatted a little bit, but he was very nice, an approachable guy. I did not meet the four boys, but some of my other friends had a chance to get together with them and party a little bit with them, but I never did.

Dan Levinson: I remember briefly talking to the stunt man who was doubling for Dennis Christopher and telling people how he had to fall off his bike. For a 13-year-old, I was just taking it all in. I didn't have the perspective of someone who understands how all that's done. And I think at the time I was speaking to him, I may not have realized that was a stunt double, because I think I said something to Dennis Christopher like, "So you're going to fall off your bike today?", and he looked at me, "What?" And Hart Bochner, I saw him years later when I was playing soccer. He was coaching the soccer team that we were playing against. And I thought, oh, that's sort of strange. To me, he was a Hollywood movie star. There was no delineation between having a role in the film and being a Hollywood star. Jackie Earle Haley was especially friendly with me, as though we were just buddies. And at the end of my weekday, when I said, "Can I have your autograph?", he just said, "Oh, come on, really, after this?", and that was when he let me take his picture. I should have asked him to give me an autograph. It would mean something to me today. But we were just hanging out. I don't know how old he was at the time, maybe what, 16 or 17? Sure wasn't that much older than me. But he was a star in the film. And Paul Dooley, wasn't he wonderful? … "REFUND! REFUND! REFUND!"

Doug Bruce: One of the ways that we would find out where they were filming the next day was because we were all standing around outside the Union watching them film, and my brother showed up on his unicycle one day, just kind of seeing what was going on, and we lived only maybe three or four blocks south of the campus. Jackie Earle Haley came walking over and wanted to borrow the unicycle from my brother and ride it around, and so we got to know him a little bit, and he would tell us where they were filming. He seemed to be kind off on his own, like he was the kid I remembered him from "Bad News Bears", and we were all that age where you're playing backyard baseball, and that was the movie that was for us a coming of age kind of thing, and he wandered away from everybody else.

I met Dennis Christopher and Robyn Douglass during the filming. I'm a Little Five safety director now, I rode in the Little Five later on in life, then went off to architecture school at Ball State and wrote collegiately for Ball State and then rode on the Velodrome in Indy, a race there. I've coached Little Five teams, and for the last 20 some years, I've been a safety director, doing just what they had me doing in the race back in the film. We had the 20th or 25th anniversary of the film, and Robyn Douglass and Dennis Christopher came back. We were pretty good scavengers; after they filmed the race scenes at the stadium, I kept a couple of the wooden bike placards that were just laying around. I brought my part from the wooden number piece from the bicycle, and I had them autograph that at that event, and I got a picture taken with them.

James Pivarnik: All of them except Robyn Douglas, she wasn't in the Little 500 race scenes, but Dennis Quaid, Dennis Christopher, Jackie Earle Haley, and Daniel Stern, those guys, they were all fairly friendly. We didn't hang out with them or anything, they came in and they say their lines, and really there weren't that many lines in the racing scene, there were just a couple when Dennis Christopher got in that wreck and said "Give me the bike and tape my feet to the pedals" and all of that, but beyond that, there weren't a lot of vocalization or lines.

Did you interact with Peter Yates?
Carlos Sintes: He was pretty cool, he was very business-like. I'd never met a director in my life. So, he just seemed like a nice guy who knew what he was talking about. I still remember, we Italians didn't even know the terminology. One of the first scenes that we started filming, he said, "Roll it", and we started thinking that meant that we rolled it. And, we didn't understand that when they say "Roll it", that means get the cameras rolling. And then they say "Action". So, we quickly learned that he explained it to us. He probably rolled his eyes.

Randy Strong: Just briefly, he came over and talked to us as a group. And he kind of just gave us some guidance on how to approach the scene from a rough racing perspective. And there were, I think, 12 of us who got paid extra for the shot, where we were coming down the hill and kind of swooping around. And then that was the scene where Dennis Christopher breaks away from our group to go up to the Italians. And I was right on his wheel when he was breaking away, that was where I was.

Bill Brissman: Yes, I met Peter, and one of the funny stories about him and one of my few stories about the filming, really, but it was a very hot time of the year, it was the fall, so there was a tent in the middle of the field at the track, and the filming days went on and on and on, and not much seemed to be happening, because they had to do all this setup, and some cog was turning in the wheel at all points, but as a participant in the scene, you don't really see very much going on. We're just horsing around and doing other things, and somebody had a squirt bottle, and I had a squirt bottle, and we're kind of messing around near the tent, and then I hear this British accent, "Someone is squirting me", and Peter Yates looks over his shoulder right at me, and I say "So sorry". You know, this is the guy who had just gotten done directing "Bullitt" with Steve McQueen, so I'm just a kid. And then we talked about the final scene, and Gary and I were all dressed up, and they had to make sure that everything that I had on was just perfect with what parts the character had on, and Peter said, "You two work this out", but he looked right at me, and he pointed at me and said, "Don't win", because they have helicopters in the air, and they had the people positioned, and it took a couple hours to get the scene set up, so those were his only words to me, and then Gary and I talked about it, and I said, "Okay, I'll let you kind of lead it out, and I'll let you in, and I'll let you underneath", and that's how we rode it.

Doug Bruce: No, and that's one I wanted to meet, because he was the director for "Bullitt". I race vintage cars now, and I run all kinds of GoPro cameras and cameras in my helmet, and I remember all those scenes from "Bullitt", and you could see how he took the camera and put the camera on different places on the bicycle to really put you in the action, and I really wanted to meet him. I got a t-shirt and tried to meet everybody we could, but as a 15-year-old, maybe I was more of a rules follower than I probably should have been, but if something said stay back, we didn't try to sneak in, we didn't get too pushy, we were just little kids.

James Pivarnik: I met Peter Yates, as a matter of fact, it's pretty funny, he was great, the one time that I was on that stationary bike, I told him, "Peter, I going to be acting now, when the other guy says his line to catch up with the leader, I'm going to be nodding intelligently." He said, "That's good, Jim, just keep doing that." So, yeah, he was good.

Did your father say how he ranked Peter Yates among all the directors he had worked with?
Dan Levinson: I know he enjoyed working with Peter Yates. I know that they got along very well. And for the first time in my father's career, the director gave him one point. I'm not sure about this, you'd have to verify it, but the director gets a certain number of points. And each point represents a residual amount. And my father got one point, which represented a significant amount of income for him after the film became a success. So, that was very nice for Peter Yates to do, he didn't have to do that. So, I know my father appreciated it. And he got a credit in the beginning of the film. I think that was the first time he got a credit in the beginning. It meant a lot to have him to be part of that project. It wasn't the first film he worked on that was a hit, because he'd already worked on "All the President's Men", "Shampoo", and "Harry and Tonto". But

this was the first film my father did as an associate producer. And the fact that it became a hit meant a lot to him. And he was such a major part of it.

Your father has had a major role in so many movies. Did he say how "Breaking Away" ranked among all the movies he had done?
Dan Levinson: At that point, it was the most successful one. Nobody expected it to do well. It was, I guess, what is called a B movie. And it surprised everybody, because it became a huge success and developed a following. Somewhere in storage, I have a script that says "Bambino".

Why do you think that the movie is so popular, to this day?
Randy Strong: I think it's the identification of coming of age, that awkward stage between high school, college, what are you going to do with your life? Small town versus college, kind of the antagonist of the fraternity against a kid who's just trying to make it in his own town, and he's being bullied in his own town by these college kids. I think there was a lot of identification with the characters in general. And I think, the underdog coming from 34 to win is always the big identifier to a successful movie, and they gave a really good job. Even though they have a full stadium of people, they're moving the people around in the stadium. So, get the shots. They did a really good job of especially the music choices they have at the end, which was really good, and the finish was super exciting. Bill Brissman and Gary Rybar were actually playing that whole lap, and Peter Yates made it clear to Bill Brissman that he was not to win, no matter what. He had to let Gary Rybar win. And Bill just did a spectacular job of pulling off a very believable, very close at-the-line win by Gary Rybar, aka Dennis Christopher.

Bill Brissman: That's a really good question. I think it's known as one of the Holy Trinity of Indiana sports movies along with "Hoosiers" and

"Rudy", but I think it's that a lot of people can relate to the exhilaration and also the hard side of sports, and it also really is a movie that isn't so much about bike racing as it is about the relationships of these high school kids, and there are funny, funny points and poignant points, and there's a little bit of something for everyone. It's corny, but it's corny in a way that everyone can embrace.

Debbie Broeking: I think it definitely is the story of the underdogs being triumphant. It was heartwarming. And Dave's family, it's just typical Midwest values. I really liked that part.

Bob Broeking: And then I think at the end when the fraternity boys smiled and acknowledged the Cutters had won, that's what sort of tied the whole movie together at the end, because they were the enemies up to that point.

Dan Levinson: If I knew what the public wanted, I'd probably be much more successful as a musician. It's a great movie. It's great actors, like Dennis Quaid, and that was his first hit. And it just resonated with people, and it's funny, and it was a great script. An underdog movie, like my father told it, a sleeper.

Doug Bruce: I think it's the nostalgia, as those of us who grew up here in Bloomington look at our town as before "Breaking Away" and after "Breaking Away", that "Breaking Away" was kind of the coming of age of our town; it really started to develop after that movie. I think that the nostalgia of the film helped the sleepy town that we were, but I also think it hits every sensibility that you've got. There's a little bit of a love story, but it's not too overblown; there's action, there's the kind of the villains in a way, which are the fraternity guys. I mean, it's just so well written, how can you not like it?

Ben Pearl: Everyone loves a good underdog story, whether it's a sports story or just a coming of age story. And this movie has both. The actors were a great ensemble, they worked together well. And there's a certain authenticity that you see with the characters. You see that there is almost a real paternal relationship between the actors, Dennis Christopher and Paul Dooley. And I know that they had done other films in the past. So, it's just a really authentic presentation of the family and the kids being the outsiders trying to fit in. And I think there's another aspect. It's not just about being an underdog, but just trying to fit in. And I think that even today, with movies that are out, post-millennium, it's a lot about being able to fit into the rest of the crowd for those who are kind of on the fringe. So, I think those are the strongest elements. And then, as far as the action, you have Peter Yates, who was arguably one of the best action directors at the time, with the "Bullitt" movie, and he really was able to convey a sense of realism, particularly in the race scenes of the Little 500 race itself. He did a nice job, too, on the road scenes. Those are less intimate than the race scenes, where you really get in the pack with the Little 500 bike race as a culmination to the movie. So, I think those are the elements that still make this an iconic movie. It's only a few years away from being a 50-year classic. And, although some of the younger riders and younger people who aren't associated with Indiana University and the culture of the Little 500 may not know the movie, once they are introduced to the movie, they realize why it is the classic that it is.

James Pivarnik: It's just, I guess, a love story, maybe, and exciting, you want to know if the local kid is going to win? Just the whole idea that the local cutter kids could do that.

Jim Kirkham: It goes back to a coming of age, and everyone has to go through that. And they found a great way to make it funny to tie into a unique sporting event. And there's a victory at the end, which we all don't get in life. But when you do get a victory in life, it's important to celebrate and savor it. But sometimes those victories are hard to come by.

Carlos Sintes: The theme is timeless, the growing up theme, moving on with life, that type of theme. The line that Dennis Quaid has by the football stadium that the college students, they always stay young, they always keep getting replaced. And that's so true. It's just a good movie. There's no violence, other than Dennis Christopher getting knocked off of his bike. It's just a good family movie that has a great ending. And it just leaves you feeling good. It has so many great quotes, my favorite is Cyril's line when the brother asked him how they were doing, and he says, "Well, we're a little disturbed by the developments in the Middle East." And gosh, that applies to any time period, I think so.

Judah Thompson: I think the movie is so popular nowadays because they do a really good job with the storytelling, and they do a really good job with the character selections, the actors who play them do a phenomenal job of really embodying that role, the college student, the dad, the mom. Everything just fits in pretty well, and that story of four friends growing up in a college town, not really knowing what they want to do with their lives as they get older. I feel like that's something that pretty much everyone experiences. I can say that I'm experiencing that right now, because I'm a junior. I know in the future, I have to start planning my life, I don't know exactly what I want to do. That does a really good job of encapsulating that growth and that coming of age, and also the camera work, the humor, and all that stuff really goes into telling that narrative.

What was the reaction to the movie?
James Pivarnik: It was kind of a surprise to us. I talked to people who say, "That's dumb, that didn't work, that would never happen, that's over there, didn't you see they went down the same street twice?" You don't look for

that stuff when you're seeing a movie, but we were the insiders, so it turned out pretty good. From an Oscar standpoint, I was moderately surprised. It went up against "Kramer vs. Kramer" for the best picture, and that's the one that got it. When I talk to people about it, they say "Oh, you were in Breaking Away, that's my favorite movie", it's kind of humorous.

After the movie came out, is there a measuring stick if the movie accelerated the interest in the Little 500?
Jim Kirkham: I think it did, at least the stories that I heard. When I started riding in the Little 500, there were like 54 teams or so trying to compete for 33 spots, and that's a lot. It's a lot of kids, training, trying to qualify, putting a lot into it. It builds the whole culture of cycling in this little town. And then in 1982, CBS broadcast the race, that was a really big deal, national coverage of this real life event. And then 1984 was the first year for the Cutter team, a couple years following the movie. And we were fortunate with some grace that we won the very first year that we were a team. So, that was kind of cool, and that kept the team going in many ways. It's definitely created a bike culture in our town, which has ripple effects of health and fitness and wellness. I think it teaches kids who come through here, how to take care of their bodies, how to train, how to stay in shape, and it can take that for the rest of your life. You can ride bikes until you're really old. So, the movie "Breaking Away" really took the Little 500 from this little midwestern, small IU event, and it really propelled it to a national level. I think it really expanded the interest of the bike race and all the good ripple effects from that.

At Indiana University, obviously, men's basketball is king, but where do the Little 500 athletes rank?
Jim Kirkham: Basketball used to be king, for sure, and we would love to see it return to maybe be at least be a prince [laughs]. But the athletes involved in the Little 500, they put a lot of time into it. The top teams,

IN THEIR WORDS

they're riding their bike upwards of 20 hours a week, including weightlifting and focusing on their diet. They really treat themselves like Division One athletes. They put a lot into this one day, this little intramural event. And I would certainly compare that to a basketball player who practices a lot. The basketball team has a lot more resources at your hands, they get all the doctors and equipment and the food and study halls and everything. But no NIL money in the Little 500, it's still pretty pure in that way.

Having done the Little 500 race yourself, how realistic was it to expect Dave to do all 200 laps?
Bill Brissman: Well, there's a rule that you can't do that, so you've got to have 10 exchanges, so there's that, but with the right kind of rider back then, it might have been possible, but you would have to be an Olympic-caliber rider doing it, because it really is a series of shorter sprints. It's like, the best marathon runners run nearly four-minute miles for the 26 miles, but not quite, and so it's very much like that. I think it would be implausible for one rider to be able to ride against teams of riders for the entire race, it's 50 miles on a low-gear bike.

Bob Broeking: That's definitely Hollywood. They do have amateur racers who go to Indiana University, students who end up in the Little 500 race, and they can ride 20 or 30 laps at a time, no problem. But, for the majority of us who were either recreational cyclists or just quasi-intramural athletes, it's a struggle. It was a cinder track at the time, it was not asphalt. And you had to do exchanges. I see now in the Little 500, they actually exchange a bike that one rider will come in, and another rider will just tag and take off on a second bike. We had to do exchanges, and those are obviously fraught with some danger when you're coming in at high speeds and skidding to a stop, getting off the side you're not used to getting off the bike, and another guy grabbing the handlebars and taking off with it and hopping on.

Jim Kirkham: I think that certainly it was very realistic. There was a timeframe early in the Little 500 where one rider could do that, because the Little 500 started as an intramural event, and they try to still claim that it still is, but it's kind of exceeded that. But you could have a bunch of really good athletes in the Little 500. But if one guy came along who had some cycling experience, and maybe did some races, regional races in the summer, he could certainly propel himself to a higher level than just the athletes, just the football players and so forth. That could certainly happen. And it has happened through the years. One year, when I rode in the race in 1991, there was a man named Mike Lantz who rode 180 laps of the race. He got third, he was right there at the end.

Ben Pearl: He rode a bulk of the race, so as the movie goes, you saw how Moocher was having some trouble, they had issues with the different heights of the bike, they weren't changing the bikes out, which you can do today. At that time, I'm not sure if the rules specified whether you could have switched out bikes during the race with different pre-ordained saddle heights. Obviously, the movie does show that Dave ends up doing the majority of the race, it looks like he does at least about 185 laps, and that the other guys, including Mike, only did a handful of laps, compared to Dave. To think that a rider would be able to ride that much and win the race is unlikely with today's competition. There have been riders who have ridden well over a hundred laps, but to get closer to doing sets that would accumulate to 175 laps or 160 laps, is probably not that realistic.

James Pivarnik: My senior year, there was a guy on a very good team who rode 150 laps, and he was actually an Olympic cyclist, they just recruited him, the Delta Chis, kind of a crappy fraternity, but they rode bikes pretty well. They recruited him to their fraternity basically just for the race, and he was really good. There were another couple guys who were okay on the team, but he rode 150 laps, not straight, but he wrote 90 before he ever got off, which is a lot, and if you rode 20 laps, 25 maybe before exchanging, that was a lot, because it was pretty brutal, the speed was pretty good. We were college students, so it's not like we were a trained-cyclists kind of a thing, we were just training then.

Randy Strong: Very unrealistic, especially on those bikes. It's incredibly difficult for one person to ride the entire race. I think the most laps that were ever ridden by one rider in the actual Little 500 was by Wayne Stetina, who had just come back from the Olympics. And he rode 156 laps of the 200 in the race, but even that was probably too much for Wayne. You need two or three riders to really pull off the victory, who can pull their weight in that race, because you're spinning so fast, the gears are so low, and your bike is heavy. Everybody's got the same disadvantage. And so, when you go out there, you're spinning 130, 140 revolutions a minute with your legs. And, you're drafting off the pack, and to be out there by yourself for 200 laps, I don't think it can be pulled off. I don't think anybody outside of maybe somebody like Mathieu van der Poel could probably pull it off in today's world.

Judah Thompson: That part is pretty unrealistic, you actually have to make 10 exchanges in order to complete the race, because that's one of the rules. You can't have someone just sitting on the bike doing 200 laps, although you can have a rider do a majority of the laps; that was kind of my role this year. In one of my sets, I ended up doing 46 laps, so that was a long time to be on the bike, and I ended up being on there for 76 laps in total, but I know some guys on other teams who have done like 146 laps, which is almost there to 200.

Overall, how accurate was the depiction of the Little 500 race in the movie, compared to a real race?
Bill Brissman: Oh, it was absolutely not like a real race. There's no time to

tape the feet on pedals, even if it were legal, and there were many, many, many things that were changed to make it a more dramatic movie, but it's not so much like the race. The race even then was much more like a real bike race, and today it's perhaps even more so, because there are so many teams that are training all year round for it. There are probably 15 or 20 teams, and it's an all-year effort to prepare for this one race.

Bob Broeking: Oh, it's pretty accurate. The interesting thing during the filming was that it was all slow speed. It makes it look like it's fast in the movie at real time, real speed. It sort of surprised us. When we formed up in a pack, and they wanted us to do the riding scenes, we were going so slow, it seemed totally unrealistic to me. So, I think it's funny how, in Hollywood, they can transform fiction into fact, and the scene comes out in the movie, and you're racing around at 30 miles an hour, we really weren't doing that.

Ben Pearl: I think there was a lot that was done spot-on, and that was primarily because of Tom Shwoegler and Eddy Van Guyse to make sure that the bikes looked the part, and the riders who were doing the race scenes actually had experience. There were some notable things about the movie that we, of course, know are not true, and the first being the premise of the movie that they would invite a local group of kids who are not students at Indiana University to ride in the Little 500. You need to be a student at Indiana University, and that, of course, was not the case with the fictitious Cutters team. The real Cutters team, of course, was an independent team that came in 1984, not long after the movie, and, of course, with the intrigue of the movie, this influenced the name that they chose, and the fact that one of the principal riders who was in the movie played the Italian, Eddy Van Guyse, was a legacy member of the team Delta Chi, which was a fragment of the team that became the Cutter team when they split off from the Delta Chi fraternity. Other things that were not accurate in the movie included the taping of the feet to the pedals, that would not be allowed in the Little 500 rules. Those were some things that were not accurate about the race, but they got a lot right about that race, and, of course, their intention was not to completely duplicate what the actual race was a hundred percent; they wanted to have the romance of an outsider, underdog team being able to get involved in this race and win the race.

James Pivarnik: Not accurately; well, the race, if you looked at the jumping on and off of the bikes, that was right on, that's how you did it, it got crazy, and there were some accidents, and stuff like that would happen in the race. As a matter of fact, I still have some cinders in my knee from way back, because of the cinder track, but the fact that the guy was like a lap and a half up or something halfway through, nobody ever broke away like that, rarely, rarely, rarely, rarely. It's called breaking away, and that's the play on words there with breaking away, getting out of Bloomington versus breaking away in the race, that's why they did it that way. But Dave got so far away, and when I rode, there were a couple of guys who were actually part of the Italian team, the cheaters, that rode back when I did, and they were good, but even with them, they won it at least one of those years. Really, I just can't remember too many times when anybody would get a whole lap and whatever ahead, one or one and a half laps, two laps, that just didn't happen, because the pack went with you, nobody was that much better than everybody else, because when you lead on your own, you had nobody breaking the wind for you, eventually the pack would catch up with you, just kind of like the Tour de France, it just doesn't happen on that kind of a track, you can't get away.

Jim Kirkham: Just like any sports movie, you can pick it apart and say, oh, that's not realistic, you can't really do that. And there are some scenes in the movie where, like the Cutters are in the pits, taping up the feet to the pedals, and the amount of time that passes doing that, you've lost the race, essentially. The little things like that, of course, you could pick them apart. But all in all, I think they did a great job, certainly, of capturing the spirit of the Little 500 and the intensity of it.

Judah Thompson: The Little 500 has changed so, so much from that one. The track is different, it's at the Bill Armstrong Stadium now, it's no longer by the Wells Library. The track is a little wider, it's a little safer. I think the movie does a really good job of depicting the pressure of having family there and the fans. They also do a good job of just getting that atmosphere, the electric crowd, a lot of people, all sorts of people in the stands. It gets pretty crowded, it's pretty chaotic. They do a good job of the music and the soundtrack, like lining up the fast-pace camera work with all the cyclists whizzing by. So, I think they do a pretty good job with depicting the Little 500.

In the Little 500 scenes, there were racers making hard tumbles onto the track on exchanges. Were those stand-in actors or true racers?
Bill Brissman: Those were just guys messing up with no direction.

In the scene where Mike refuses to get on the bike to take a set, how are you reacting?
Jim Kirkham: In any high-level team in any event, you want athletes to want to step into the spotlight, right? Not hide behind the curtains. But that's part of that transformation story. Like, he didn't believe in himself or his team or who he was until that moment. And then he stepped in and changed his future, in a sense.

Judah Thompson: Some parts, yeah, come on, but as a team, we all know that you have to be completely honest with each other and completely open, so if there's a guy who can't go on the bike, you just have to communicate that and let the team know that you're not ready to go in. We've had that happen a couple times. I was almost one of those guys who said I couldn't go back in my freshman year, because I was so terrified after my first set that I was going to mess something up, but just being open about it is the biggest thing.

I remember that when I saw the movie, I said to myself "That last turn looks kind of wide." Did it look out of the ordinary to you?
Bill Brissman: Oh maybe, yeah, and I also noticed that Gary Rybar coasted a little bit in that corner, too. We did it in just one take; if we did it again, we probably could have improved all of that, but we did one take, and they liked it. They were trying to get this movie done, and this was not designed to be an Academy Award winning film, it was a low-budget, kind of a feel-good summer movie that was going to spend a little money and make a little money, and no big deal, so they just wanted to move on to the next scenes and wrap the thing up, so it's good.

Describe your role as an extra in the Little 500 race?
Doug Bruce: There were seven different places, you'd really have to look for me. I've got pretty long hair. I'm in the infield, I jumped over a fence, and I'm walking up to like a race flagger, a safety person, and I'm supposed to walk up and talk to them like in the background, like I'm bothering them, and they're kind of like, "Get away", and you could just see that in the background, and probably the easiest way to see me is I'm in the Cutters pit just down from them with a shirt that says "Indiana Indiana Indiana", and I've got really long hair, and I'm clapping really strangely like only a 15-year-old awkward teenager would. We changed shirts, and then when the race ended, my friend Chip and I both jumped over the wall, and we're congratulating them when they won, and I'm in the background there. My friend Chip, I don't think he has a shirt on, and he's wearing a black batter's cap that says "White Sox", I think, and

he's just bumping into everybody just trying to get on camera. You never see a full view of the stadium, because there weren't enough people to fill the entire stadium, so they moved us around and made us wear different shirts, so they would show different scenes with everybody in the background.

James Pivarnik: I actually have a picture, it's kind of funny, I think it was on the cover or maybe like a foldout in Bicycling magazine maybe the next year, of me right behind Dennis Quaid, and I always tell people there's me and Dennis Quaid, we're both in the movies, he just went a little farther than I did. I decided to teach college instead, so that's kind of a funny joke. I was in probably a half a dozen scenes if you know what you're looking for. One was, actually if you dig around enough with Little 500 pictures, you can find me, but the funny thing is, when you're doing a movie, it's like this is going to be terrible, this is phony, and we know that's not right, no that's not right, well nobody out there in the world knows other than the people riding in the race, so don't worry about it. We switched jerseys occasionally, depending on when the scene was, and whether you got a big scene with a lot of people, or were you just kind of on the sidelines. I was on a stationary bicycle on the side, and actually the guy that I knew really well was whispering to one of my co-riders something stupid in reality, but to the viewer, it made sense, he said something about "We'll take the exchange, and go ahead and catch the guy that's leading", well duh, but I was on the stationary bike, and I'm just kind of sitting there pedaling, so that's the only scene I was in without a helmet on, so you could really tell it was me. Some of the other ones, you kind of had to look and kind of know I was coming, but different color jerseys, a blue jersey one day and this one I think was a gold jersey with brown sleeves or brown jersey, gold sleeves or something. I didn't have any lines. We were extras, $2.65 an hour, ten hours a day for four days, big bucks.

IN THEIR WORDS

Describe the weekend of filming the Little 500 race scenes?
Bob Broeking: On that Saturday and Sunday, they invited girlfriends and boyfriends and everyone to come to the stadium to try to fill it up as much as possible, but it was probably only like a quarter filled at any given time, and they kept moving the crowd scenes down to make sure that the camera could make it look like it was completely crowded. During the actual Little 500, it's a madhouse. There's 20,000 kids there.

Debbie Broeking: It was hot, and they were long days, but it was exciting.

James Pivarnik: It was in the fall, so we're lucky it didn't rain on us, it was right when school started, and the way they got people into the stands, they didn't pan anything, the start of the race and the end of the race is where they did a lot of the crowd shots, the big crowd. They advertised to the students in the newspaper or something before the internet back then, so I don't know how we figured it out, but that they're going to have bands, and they're going to have drawings for prizes, and it was early in the semester, and a bunch of students said, "A party, we'll go watch the movie, and we'll act as stupid as we normally do", it's perfect, so that's when they shot those scenes, that was like a Saturday and a Sunday to get all the students there, and then the up close and personal ones where you just saw the faces of riders, like the Dennis Quaid one, that was taken from a camera from a truck that was on the track, and those were Monday and Tuesday ones when there really wasn't any crowd, if there was any crowd at all in the stands. I mean, that's when they did that one when I was on the stationary bike, and it looked like a bunch of people, because of the way they spliced it, you thought was in the race, but really they had like 25 extras who were right behind us, so the stands look crowded, but the camera was only focusing on those 25 people, so it was kind of fascinating how they did that kind of stuff.

What other filming did you see?
Debbie Broeking: We got to watch the filming around campus, like the frisbee scene in front of the fountain. I thought it was so realistic, everything around campus. It was very, very well done with the quarry and all of that. I mean, that's Bloomington.

Bob Broeking: I saw the filming where Dave and his dad are walking in front of the library. That was at night, they're having a talk, and I think I was just coming through campus in the evening or coming from work, maybe. And I saw them filming, and so I watched that.

Describe your role as an extra in the student union fight scene?
Doug Bruce: I'm harder to spot there, stuff happens so dang quick, but those were the scenes where they're inside, they've got the bowling ball, there's just a crowd of us in there packed in, and I'm a short little kid trying to look over everybody to see what's going on, but just to hang out there brings back a great flood of memories and a great time in Bloomington. We were all just crowded in there, and, honestly, for those of us who were in there as extras in the back, I remember seeing around me people who just wanted to get their face on camera, so that's one of the things that got them mad is that people are looking at the camera and not watching the action, and then it doesn't look real, and so it was hard to get up close, because there were so many people packed in there, and you could hear them calling out the directions of what they were doing. I just remember that it was just chaos of people trying to push their way up front, like we were all getting into a mosh pit at a concert. I didn't get close enough up front, because I just was too little of a guy, and there were pushy college students all around me. It seemed like they spent forever just kind of going through the motions trying to figure out which way do you swing, who stands where, where the camera angle is, and then the hardest part was it's so much brighter than the movie shows, because they have lights in there

basically glaring into your eyes. I never got a chance to pick up the bowling ball, so I can't tell you if that was a real heavy bowling ball.

Talk about the quarry scenes?
Doug Bruce: When we found out when they were filming at the quarries, and they were jumping off, that was my elementary school. I'd been going to those quarries, I'd ride my bicycle out there. First of all, the students never come there, and it's never us versus them. The quarry that they filmed, we used to call it Slant Rock, because of the big rock that they were laying against which would face south, and it would get really warm, and those quarries are really cold. It was truly amazing to see what they did there, because some of us would jump off of it, and it just killed you to land in the water anyway. We used to climb up on top of it and just sit and hang our legs, and then anybody who ever climbed up to where they dove down from, when you climbed up through kind of a passageway to get up there, you couldn't climb down. I mean, you were going to get harassed, you had to jump from there. I remember after they filmed it going back just to see the refrigerator, because they placed that in there as part of the movie, but then they didn't take it out when they left, which I thought was interesting. Like they said in the movie, it had no back to it, but that was kind of weird, going back there and seeing it, and thinking, wait a minute, why did they leave this here?

How realistic was it that Dave could do up to 60 miles per hour, chasing the truck?
Carlos Sintes: It was really realistic. Gary Rybar was the rider double for Dennis Christopher, and I think Gary actually went like 50 miles an hour, 55, maybe. But it was realistic. He really did ride behind the Cinzano truck. And Gary was a very good bike racer at the time. So, that was realistic. The only glitch, of course, was the editing glitch where they show him switching into a small chain ring, but the riding was realistic.

And you can tell when Gary is riding, because he's got real muscles in his legs.

Ben Pearl: Drafting does enable you to achieve great speeds, and that's a great point that you bring up. I'm not sure what the record for slipstream or drafting behind a truck is and what speeds that they are able to achieve, but I think that is likely a tall order to achieve that speed, and, remember, this kid was not a pro racer at the time either, so he could certainly hang with the pack, but, yes, it certainly tests the limits of credibility to reach that speed, drafting.

Randy Strong: That's realistic. I've done that before. One time, Bill Brissman and I were down on Route 446, which is a popular ride, and we were coming back. And there was a semi that was kind of creeping up the hill. We caught on to it, and we latched onto it the whole way back to town. And even with the hills and everything, we were probably going at least 55 at some point. Well, it's very realistic to do that.

[Note: the Cinzano 100 race begins on Route 446.]

Bill Brissman: Oh, that's completely doable. A lot of us have done that.

Bob Broeking: That is actually doable, but not going on a level road. That's not really doable. They can descend at 60 miles an hour. You can descend at 50 miles an hour, but not pedaling. You would pedal out of your gear, you wouldn't be able to keep up with the truck. So, that's not realistic.

James Pivarnik: Just thinking physics-wise, I don't think you can keep up with it, I don't think the suction would be enough to block the wind for you to go 60 miles an hour.

Jim Kirkham: We do something similar to that in training, it's called motor pacing, where the cyclist gets behind a vehicle, either a small car or a motorcycle, and you ramp up the pace, and you do it on a Little 500 bike. It gets pretty tough, because those bikes have one gear. There's like a speed limit as a governor on those bikes. We do that as a training way to get the cyclists to go faster than they normally would, so they pedal that bike, that cadence is quicker. We do that out in the country roads in Indiana. We don't get up to 60. We get those Little 500 bikes up to 40, and if I can get a kid to do that, then I know we have a good chance of winning the race.

Judah Thompson: Oh, I've had plenty of times like that. A couple of funny stories, usually when I'm riding, I try to eye up those semi-trucks or box trucks that I can hop on for a little bit, especially on the busier, flatter roads, like Route 45 or Route 46. There was this one fun moment in Colorado where we're going down a mountain highway. We do a team training trip there in Colorado Springs, and we're racing on that highway, and all of us just grabbed onto a car or a box truck, and we had this intersection that we were supposed to pull off on, but my teammate, Torin Kray-Mawhorr, hopped on to a box truck on the left lane, and he was going like 70 miles per hour probably, and he just whizzes by the off ramp. And a funny thing about that was that he was actually taped in, because his cleat broke during that ride, so he was taped in like Dave in the final scene, going 70 miles per hour behind a box truck on a Colorado highway down a mountain. I actually have a plan to try to jump behind a box truck or a semi-truck on the road where it was filmed, because there's a pretty good off ramp that you can sneak behind the semi-truck going on I-69, it's relatively flat there, so I think it could work, but it would be pretty dangerous to try.

Talk about growing up in Bloomington?
James Pivarnik: The funny part was they call themselves the Cutters, and that's from stone cutters, but there is a town south of Bloomington called Bedford, they changed schools and they changed their name, but their nickname used to be the Cutters, because that's where most of the stone cutting was done, down in Bedford. The quarries that they were swimming in, nobody swam with suits on, that part was fake, "Why are they wearing bathing suits?", that was the nude swimming place. That's just what it was, nobody cared if you just went out there and took your clothes off and sunbathed and swam and dove off those crazy cliffs and all of that.

Were you aware of any friction between students and the townies when you were there as a student?
Bill Brissman: Not so much, but there was certainly a pejorative for the Bloomington natives, they were just called "Stonies", and they just couldn't use that in the movie, because there was just too much of a drug connotation, so they changed it to "Cutters".

Bob Broeking: No, we were not. We were from Fort Wayne, Indiana. We were friends with the owner of a drug store, and he invited us into their house. We always felt welcome in Bloomington.

Doug Bruce: No, no one ever called us Cutters, and, like I said, we laugh, because my brother's a true carver. He's down in Bedford and lives in Mitchell, and his whole life, that's all he's done. Back in the day, later when I was in high school and I started driving, we would cruise up and down Kirkwood Avenue in our cars. The college students were there, too, we were in front of all the bars, and we were 16, 17 years old, and there weren't fights, we didn't do the whole frisbee scene. Honestly, the college students just kind of kept to themselves, and occasionally you see a few of them out at the quarries. As kids growing up just south of campus, we always joke that we own the campus. I know where every steam tunnel is and how to access them, and it's as 13-year-old, 14-year-old, 15-year-old kids, we were running around, skateboarding inside the Musical Arts Center, we were probably doing things that we sometimes shouldn't have done, but there were never college students telling us to get off campus.

Ben Pearl: No, I really didn't. The only thing that occasionally happened would be, you would get a nasty car incident of yelling or getting a little too close, but that didn't happen often, and, in fact, that happens with cyclists everywhere, where you can potentially have somebody who just doesn't like the idea of cyclists and sharing the road, but it wasn't a common thing, and the most common thing that would happen to people who were training out on the roads was the dogs that might be roaming around a house or some of the farmland and would come out and chase you down on the bike, and I, like many cyclists who were training for the race, did have an incident or two with a dog, and you did end up high-tailing it when those dogs came out, because you didn't know how rough they were, and it was a certainly an added incentive to pick up your speed.

James Pivarnik: No, my father was in the service, that was an interesting time in the country, it was 1969 when I graduated from high school, and there was a lot going on over in Vietnam, and he was in charge of Air Force ROTC, so there's enough friction on campus at that time, but no, I mean, we used to talk about that once in a while, but it wasn't just really a big deal. I went to Bloomington South High School my senior year of high school, because that's when my dad got stationed in Bloomington, and a lot of people didn't go to college, but a lot of my friends went to IU, but no, I don't really remember a lot of that at all. Actually, they would be the Bedford kids coming up, because they were the cutters, and they'd come up for the weekend, they didn't bother IU kids, they would bother us Bloomington kids.

Are you aware of any stats or any stories to see if the movie was motivating a boom in biking after that?
Randy Strong: Well, it was. It was a huge boom to the attendance at Little 5. If you're looking for some kind of a statistic, you can look at the attendance before "Breaking Away" and the attendance after "Breaking Away", and the popularity just kept growing, to the point where they had to cut off. It got too popular, and there were too many incidents of drunk and disorderly conduct around the campus. They kind of shut down a lot of the big parties and everything associated with the weekend in the mid 80s time frame. And then they actually tore down the big stadium that they had. They had a huge grandstand on the front five, and they tore it down, because it wasn't safe. They found structural damage to it, and they were afraid it was going to collapse with the kind of crowd that they were getting. Now it's kind of scaled back. It used to be, like in 1982, the year that I was a sophomore, there were 30,000 people there at the event. And now, with the stands and the way it's set up, there might be 18,000 to 20,000 at most, but that was by design. You can't put 30,000 every year.

What about nationwide, any inkling that more people wanted to be bike racers or started riding bikes?
Randy Strong: I think, overall, that was kind of a high period. I don't know if it could be attributed to "Breaking Away" or to Greg LeMond as being a catalyst for that. But Greg LeMond came along at that same time and won the Tour de France in 1986. And, that was a real big boom to the cycling business. And then in the 90s, it became Lance Armstrong who drove the culture in bike races. But, I think, empirically, you could see the races around the Midwest were getting bigger. The peak was right around 1981, 1982. It could have had a lot of impact on a lot of kids' motivation, getting a bike and going out and racing. A lot of Little 500 riders came in from other states who had never heard of the event, because of the movie. I definitely feel like there were a lot of people who came to IU, with the

idea of having seen the movie, they wanted to be a part of that. IU is super popular now, I can't believe the housing prices in Bloomington. It's outrageous, because it's become one of the most popular schools in the Big Ten for kids to attend.

What was the Mini 500 race like?
Debbie Broeking: I rode in the women's trike, the Mini 500. They had that before they gave women bicycles in 1988. It was brutal. We trained for it behind the dorms in the parking lot. We had a little oval set up, our team of four. They gave us specialized trikes that are big adult-sized trikes. And we had to do exchanges as well. So, you talk about getting bruised, jumping off and on that hard trike. But then the actual race was in the Assembly Hall, so it was indoors, and we didn't do very well, but we sure had fun. I think I rode for two or three years. And they even gave us sponsors.

Any stories that you can share?
Dan Levinson: I know that my father and Katie Larson, the WTIU host, were dating at the time. And my understanding was that she was going to come back to Los Angeles and live with him, but that didn't happen. She backed out at the last minute. She didn't want to leave Bloomington. That never happened, and he remarried a few years later. I remember that I thought the girl who played Hart Bochner's girlfriend, Robyn Douglass, was really hot. I took a picture of the two of them in the car. Blowing up balloons at the Little 500, that felt like to me I was helping the film, doing something significant, but really, they had people to blow up balloons, I was just there, and I should do it. I didn't get paid for anything. I got a blister on my finger, because I think that I blew up balloons for two days.

I thought that the extras were supposed to get $2.65 per hour?
Dan Levinson: Yeah, well, I don't know. I don't think I got paid. I was a

minor, and I'm sure the others did, the professionals, the ones who were officially hired. I just happened to be there.

Doug Bruce: If you remember the part of the movie in the beginning where Katherine is getting on the scooter and riding away, and she drops her book, so Dave picks it up, and he chases her through campus over to the sorority house. If you pay attention, you'll see that they've got her riding the scooter going eastbound on the south side of the union towards Ballentine Hall, and then they don't move the camera, and if you watch it, you'll see they've got her going westbound in front of the same spot, just to try to couple it together to make it look like she's on one long scooter ride. If you weren't from Bloomington, you wouldn't really notice that that's from the same spot, just two different directions. They kept having to film it, when she rides off on her scooter, the book sometimes didn't fall off, or sometimes it fell off too early, or they just couldn't get it right. We were all standing there in kind of the wooded area back from the filming, and I remember that there was a road then, now it's the Sample Gates, the entry to IU. Somebody who was part of the crew took a whole bunch of rubber bands and laced them together, and then they hooked them to the books, and they hooked them to the ground and put something in the ground to hold them, and she puts the books on her scooter, and when she rides away, these rubber bands then stretch just enough, and then the book falls off onto the sidewalk, and if you look in the movie, you can see the string of rubber bands connected to the books when that scene comes up, and it was hilarious, because they filmed that thing like 10 times until they finally got it right.

Randy Strong: I don't know if you remember in the movie, there was that dog that ran across the railroad track. I was right at the front, towards the front of that. I came within an inch of hitting that dog. I thought it was going to take down the whole pack. I mean, it was like, where did that dog come from? It wasn't even part of the movie, it was just a stray, it just came out of nowhere, it could have destroyed the whole movie. People could have really gotten seriously hurt, because they're coming across the railroad track, and there's a dog. I'm sitting right there in the middle of the track. I'm coming across right in front of the track.

So it wasn't staged?
Randy Strong: It wasn't. It definitely added to the tense situation right there.

Did you come close to hitting the dog in that scene?
Bill Brissman: I wasn't in that dog scene, that was later. After that first scene, they cut it down to maybe 20 riders or so, and because I had another role in the movie, they kept me out of that.

Talk about Eddy Van Guyse?
Bill Brissman: It's kind of a post script, but Eddy Van Guyse, who was the mean Italian guy who puts the pump in the spokes, and Gary Rybar and I all lived in Southern California a couple of years after the race, and we got together from time to time over at Eddy's apartment in Long Beach, and we were keeping in touch with the Delta Chi bike team, and they called us up when we all happened to be together. They said, hey guys, we're going to split with the house, and there were all these problems with it and everything else, or they had split with the house, and this was a big deal, because the Delta Chi bike team had been this juggernaut, this dynasty. We'd won seven out of nine years, and then we came in second in 1982, and then they missed the race in 1983, and about that time, there was kind of a schism with the house, and the bike team didn't really gel with the rest of the house, and it became kind of a fraternity within the fraternity, and two of them were kicked out, and the other two left in sympathy, and they had to create a new team, and they said, "Hey, you

know, we're thinking about a team name", and here are these three Hall of Fame riders out in California, and they said "We're thinking about maybe calling us ourselves the Barons, which, you know kind of connects with something with Delta Chi, but Eddy didn't miss a beat, he said "No, call yourself the Cutters", which is a brilliant stroke, because there is no team name that has any kind of marketing value anywhere near calling yourself the Cutters when you're an IU Little 500 team, but I was there on the call, and it was kind of a funny, funny moment that even brings back to the history that we see today.

Ben Pearl: The principal actor that I came into contact through the movie was Eddy Van Guyse, and our meeting was more happenstance. I was going to the Ben Clarendon Cup bike race (now the Armed Forces Cycling Classic's Clarendon Cup race), because I was a fan of cycling, and this was years after graduation, and I didn't know that the race announcer was in fact the Eddy Van Guyse who was in the movie. In fact, I didn't even know the actor's name at the time, and then when I saw him, I thought that he looked familiar from somewhere, and after talking to some of the race directors, it was revealed to me that that was the Eddy Van Guyse who played the Italian villain in the movie. I was at that time doing some sponsorship of that race, because I was doing some things to help improve cyclists' performance as a podiatrist, and biomechanical things that I was doing in the cycling cleats, and just to also generally be a resource for cyclists who had any kind of foot or lower extremity issues. So, that was my introduction to meeting the first principal who had a very large role in the movie, and he shared plenty of stories with me. One of things that I will share with you is that he told me that when he met Peter Yates, he sort of got into a costume of what he felt that would resonate with the character in the movie. So, Eddy's a very swarthy-looking character, he's Belgian, but he looks like he could be Italian, and so he's wearing this button-down shirt, and he's got a couple of these buttons at the neckline unbuttoned, to show a little bit of chest hair, looking like one of these Italian guys that's, how should I describe it, like a smooth operator and having a bit of bravado. So, I joked with Eddy, I said, you had everything, you had the curly locks, you had the loose buttons on the top of the shirt with your chest hair popping out a little bit. I said all you needed was the Italian horn, and so we got a chuckle out of that, that he could wear either a cross or an Italian horn as part of his character. Then from Eddy, I met many of the Delta Chi riders that he either rode with or was a legacy rider consigliere to, including Randy Strong, who I was fortunate to be able to watch his race in 1984, which was my first year as a student at Indiana University.

Jim Kirkham: I love Eddy. Every time he comes back, he supports our bike team. I give him a big hug and kiss. Eddy was the reason why the Cutter team chose that name. He rode for a really famous team called Delta Chi, which won a lot of races. And then some of the riders from Delta Chi decided: we got kicked out of the fraternity, like there's a whole story there, but they formed a new team, but it needed a name for the team. And then Eddy Van Guyse suggested they call themselves the Cutters, mainly because everyone knows that the Cutters are going to win the race coming out of turn four. So, it was a way to kind of plant a seed in every team's head that the Cutters are going to win. And they won the first year, so in many ways it works. But Eddy is a big part of our team history and still supports the guys.

You've had a few acting credits. Did Breaking Away inspire you for that, or would have it happened anyway?
Dan Levinson: Let's be real about that. I was a drama major at NYU, but I didn't do any acting after I graduated. And, really, by the time I was halfway through college, I realized I didn't want to be an actor. I wanted to be a musician. I had gone to NYU to study musical theater. But when

I was at Tisch School of the Arts, I wasn't interested in traditional musical theater. So, I wasn't getting much music. And I finally decided that I was going to learn how to play an instrument. So, when I was 20 years old, I started playing clarinet, not an easy instrument, but I loved old jazz. And I got to know a lot of musicians. So, the reason I mentioned that is my father wanted to get me into the union. So, I got one line in "Teachers", as you know, which ended up on the editing room floor. I didn't get into the union, because, I guess, my line didn't end up in the film. But I did get into the union the same year. I got a line in a movie about summer camp starring a pre-"Back to the Future" Michael J. Fox, before he was a star, a film called "Poison Ivy", it's not the one with Drew Barrymore. So, I didn't really do any acting, I did a line, I can't consider what I did in "Breaking Away" acting, although, as an extra in the scene in "Breaking Away", I talked about our motivation for walking down the street, I said, "All right, you're my mother, I'm your son, I'm talking about what I did at school that day." And I took it very seriously. Although in 1978, I had, at that time, no aspirations of being an actor yet. So, I was just 13, I loved music, I loved performance. But I hadn't really figured out what I was going to do with my life.

With music being your life, could you describe how integral the music in Breaking Away was to the movie?
Dan Levinson: That all happened in post-production. So, I wasn't there for any of that, in fact, I don't think I really paid attention to it. And when I saw it, I was interested in seeing how the scenes I had watched fit into the film, because when you are watching films being shot, they are shot out of order, and I hadn't read the script. So, I didn't know what was going on plot-wise. My memory is as a 13-year-old watching the scenes being shot and seeing the actors. And then, at that time, I hadn't been on sets with my father, and I had no idea this film would be such a hit.

IN THEIR WORDS

The possible "Bambino" title
Doug Bruce: When the movie first came out, the pizza joint in town was founded locally, it was Noble Roman's Pizza back in the day, by the Mobley family, and the Mobley kid and I were in high school together, and so Noble Roman's was kind of a sponsor, and they gave out T-shirts, that I wish I still had, that said "Bambino", and it was going to be a new pizza, but that was originally what was supposed to be the name of the movie, as far as I had heard, and I've said this to everybody I've ever talked to, thank God they changed the name to "Breaking Away", which was certainly more cycling related.

How would you sum up the experience?
James Pivarnik: It was just quite an experience, it was an entertaining four days, and it was fun, it went really, really well.

How did the movie affect your life?
Carlos Sintes: It was a life-changing thing for me, being in a movie and being an actor, of course. I never realized how much it would follow me through my cycling career. And, when I was racing, at every race, people always wanted to see you, and, of course, the announcers would announce it. I didn't have to win a race, I was going to be on the podium no matter what, they would call me up and interview me and introduce me to the crowd, that sort of thing. What was weird is that, after a while, my fellow competitors, it started to irk them, because here is someone who will win a race, and who gets more attention than some guy who was in the movie? And, they'd grumble a little bit, or at the start of races when they call people up, they'd call me up. "Yeah, yeah, yeah, it's Carlos." At the time, I was racing, and Pete Lazzara was still racing. John Vande Velde and Eddy Van Guyse had both retired by that time. But that was kind of a weird thing. And even to this day, when I get introduced, people will bring up "Breaking Away". They love to hear that story. As a bike racer, I

remember one time I lapped the field, and all they kept talking about was me being in "Breaking Away". Someone would say, by the way, did you know that he's winning the race, things of that nature. And then, to this day, I'm on Team USA for USA Triathlon. I came back from the World Championship just a couple of weeks ago. And people still say, "You're here to race?" And then my wife would tell them, "Do you know that he was Breaking Away?" That's all they wanted to talk about. And all I wanted to talk about was, "Man, here I am at the World Championship representing the USA." My oldest son, still to this day, will say, "Dad, that's an old movie." But I never realized how much it would have an impact on my life. In fact, I think that my gravestone probably would say that he was in a movie. We're almost 50 years out, but it's a timeless classic. And I still get royalties, which is amazing, good enough for pizza and beer.

What is in the future?
Randy Strong: I'm actually putting together a documentary film on the [real-life] Cutters. I have been gathering all the footage of all the years that we won, moving forward from the 15 victories. The film will be called "The 15", and it will follow the evolution of the Cutters from the beginning to the current day. It's a labor of love.

POSTSCRIPT

"BREAKING AWAY" had its network television premiere on NBC on Monday, May 5, 1980. In the book, "Dennis Quaid", Gail Birnbaum writes:

> … it set a record for the quickest sale of a movie to network television; 20th Century Fox sold *Breaking Away* to NBC for $5 million just three weeks after it won the Academy Award for Best Original Screenplay and only two weeks after it had been sold to theaters for a second run. That meant that instead of the usual three-year lag, *Breaking Away* ran on network television just nine months after its original theatrical premiere, bypassing pay cable altogether.

According to my hometown newspaper, the *Columbus Dispatch*, our local affiliate showed the Cincinnati Reds vs. New York Mets game instead. An ad for it appears on a Twitter post by RetroNewsNow with "Just Two Weeks Ago It Won An Academy Award … Tonight NBC Brings It To You On Television!" It also has "Four underdogs with no jobs, no money, no future. Only four beatup bikes … faith in the American Dream and the will to win!" Except for the "four beatup bikes" and Paul Dooley missing from the list of stars, that's fairly appropriate.

"Breaking Away" is the perfect American movie … directed by a man who was born and died in England; written by a man who was born in

Yugoslavia, earned a bachelor's degree in Russian and a master's in Russian literature, and passed away in Canada; about a boy who wants to be Italian while battling university students who are in the Greek fraternity system; starring an actor who is half-Italian; with supposed Italian racers played by extras with diverse backgrounds; based on the real-life racer (David K. Blase, who met his wife while riding a bike in Germany); with music from two German composers (Felix Mendelssohn and Friedrich von Flotow) and an Italian composer (Gioachino Rossini). In a *New York Times* article, Peter Yates saluted Gareth Wigan, another 20th Century-Fox executive who was born in England, for his support:[1]

> "Gareth Wigan at 20th was our champion on this picture. He steadfastly stuck to our decision not to use stars in the lead roles. So often studios try to compromise. They get cold feet and say, 'Let's safeguard ourselves, let's have one or two box-office names for insurance.'"

Why is "Breaking Away" the quintessential underdog movie? Like Dave battling the rich kids, its Oscars nominations had slim odds; it had the lowest budget of the Best Picture contenders, and Barbara Barrie was matched up against Meryl Streep, Jane Alexander, Candice Bergen, and Mariel Hemingway for the Actress in a Supporting Role award. Actually, against directors Robert Benton, Bob Fosse, and Francis Ford Coppola, Peter Yates can hold his own. Four years later, Coppola would make "The Outsiders" with a largely unknown cast that would elevate to stardom, including Rob Lowe (in his first theatrical movie), C. Thomas Howell (second), Patrick Swayze (second), Ralph Macchio (second), Emilio Estevez (third), Tom Cruise (fourth), Sofia Coppola (fourth), Matt Dillon (sixth), and Diane Lane (eighth). "Breaking Away" and "Apocalypse Now"

---

[1] https://www.nytimes.com/1979/07/15/archives/a-hot-director-breaks-away-from-the-mainstream.html

POSTSCRIPT

were the only two movies nominated for Best Picture where the producer was also the director, although "Apocalypse Now" had three co-producers.

As monumental as the movie is, it is hard to believe that it may not have even happened. In the *Houston Post*, film writer Eric Gerber wrote that for eight years, Yates and Tesich "... fiddled and faddled with the script and Yates waited for an opportunity to get the project bankrolled."[2] The *New York Times* reported:[3]

> [Bloomington mayor] Mr. McCloskey says that Mr. Yates and screenwriter Steve Tesich were about to give up and return to Southern California to shoot the film when they walked into his office last year. "They were having a little trouble making contact with the university," he recalls. "We talked for about an hour. I wanted to make sure there wouldn't be anything, you know, pornographic, in the movie, and when I was satisfied there wasn't, I called someone at the university. And that's how it started."

Eric Gerber of the *Houston Post* added, "Actually the university officials were only concerned about this being another rowdy, Animal House movie. So we submitted a script and they said, 'But there are no panty raids, no pot smoking! … you'll never get a picture like this made.' 'Let us worry about that,' we said."[4]

The noted film critic Pauline Kael wrote:[5]

> "Peter Yates, the director of *Breaking Away*—a graceful, unpredictable comedy that pleases and satisfies audiences—took the

---

[2] Source: Indiana University Lilly Library Archives
[3] https://www.nytimes.com/1979/10/14/archives/what-breaking-away-has-done-to-bloomington-ind-breaking-away-and.html
[4] Source: Indiana University Lilly Library Archives
[5] https://scrapsfromtheloft.com/movies/why-are-movies-so-bad-pauline-kael/

project to one studio after another for almost six years before he could get the backing for it.

"Just about the only picture the studios made last year that the executives took a financial risk on was *Breaking Away*. And despite the fact that it cost what is now a pittance ($2,400,000) and received an Academy Award Best Picture nomination, Twentieth Century-Fox didn't give it a big theatrical re-release (the standard procedure for a nominated film) but sold it to NBC for immediate showing, for $5,000,000. So a couple of weeks after the Awards ceremony, just when many people had finally heard of *Breaking Away* and might have gone to a theatre to see it, it appeared, trashed in the usual manner, on television. The studio couldn't be sure how much more money might come in from box offices, and grabbed a sure thing. In order to accept the NBC offer, the studio even bypassed pay TV, where the picture could have been seen uncut. It was almost as if *Breaking Away* were being punished for not having stars and not having got a big advance TV sale."

It is also hard to believe that it wouldn't be called "Breaking Away". The original title was "Bambino", the Italian word for "child" and a nod to Dave's Italian persona. A photo of a clapboard from the set on August 31, 1978 shows "Bambino" as the title, and the original script shows "Bambino". Dave uses a variation of the word a few times, including to Katherine. Daniel Stern had told his parents that he got the part in a movie called "Bambino", and his mother wanted to know if it was a porno movie. Shortly before filming ended, 20th Century Fox wanted to change the title, and Tesich chose "Breaking Away", a double meaning relating to pulling away in a race and to moving on to the next stage of life. In John Schwarb's book, he writes that Tesich had written two screenplays—"The

POSTSCRIPT

Eagle of Naptown", about a boy obsessed with cycling and Italian culture, living at home—and "The Cutters", about class conflict. Yates told Tesich to combine the two. Tesich said, "I thought it was the most absurd idea that I had ever heard until I tried it."

The Weekly View community newspaper in Indianapolis has:[6]

> In the early 1970s, David [Blase] heard through mutual friends that his old frat brother and cycling teammate Steve Tesich had written a screenplay about him. The script was called "The Eagle of Naptown" and was about a bicycle racer in Indianapolis. In trying to sell it for production, Tesich was told by David Picker, head of United Artists, that it needed something and turned the project down. Tesich discarded that script and created another about four Bloomington boys who work the quarries, a script he called "The Cutters." Director Peter Yates advised Tesich to combine the two scripts and the Breaking Away story was born, although it was first titled "Bambino."

Likewise, the movie could have been constructed quite differently. The *New York Times* article by Lawrence Van Gelder had:[7]

> Peter Yates, the director of "Breaking Away," and Steve Tesich, who wrote the screenplay, had seen Mr. Christopher in "A Wedding," and expressed interest in having him in their new movie.
>
> "Originally," Mr. Christopher said, "I think they were thinking of me to play one of the other characters. I think someone

---

[6] http://weeklyview.net/2015/07/16/of-bicycles-biology-and-breaking-away-part-2/
[7] https://www.nytimes.com/1979/08/03/archives/new-face-dennis-christopher-getting-his-break-in-breaking-away.html

didn't show up, or someone was late, and they kind of asked me to read the part of Dave—to fill in.

"So I read the Dave part, and when I got to the Italian, I just kind of had some fun with it. With my experience of being an Italian and coming from an Italian household and being in Italy for a little while, I kind of knew the way Italians express themselves. I think Peter Yates liked that."

Without Dennis Christopher fighting for a major change, the movie may have been unrecognizable. In a story on the Pop Entertainment website, he shares:[8]

> ... I flew in on a red-eye special, not sleeping at all, and went right to the set. I was costumed, made up, my hair done and stuck into a scene immediately, because the studio wanted to replace me. They wanted to get the next actor that [Yates] was interested in because my absence had held up the movie so much. Nothing I could do about it, but it had. Peter was determined not to lose me.
>
> They stuck me in so that they could get some footage and send it off to Fox and placate everybody. They painted me brown. They darkened my skin with makeup. They colored my hair a dark, dark brown and slicked it back. They had skintight clothes on. A Banlon shirt unbuttoned almost down to my navel, with lots of gold chains around my neck. Pointy high-heeled black boots. Skintight pants. I looked like a reject from Saturday Night Fever. That's what they thought the character was like, so when he comes clean later in the movie and

---

[8] https://www.popentertainmentarchives.com/post/dennis-christopher-an-actor-s-life-from-fellini-to-breaking-away-to-django-unchained

confesses to the girl that he's not an Italian, he'd have someplace to go. He would take off those clothes, have his regular clothes and speak to her regularly. I shot a whole day like that, absolutely horrified at my appearance.

The next morning, I got out of the car on the set. I saw Peter Yates get out of his car. I ran over to him, and he ran over to me. The reserved Englishman gives me a great big hug and I burst into tears. I looked at him and I said, "Peter, I don't know what I'm doing. I don't like this boy that you've created. I don't think that I can play him, before we get in any deeper." I'm bawling, crying. He sends me back. He says, "You know what you need? You need to go to sleep. Go back to the hotel and get some sleep. You haven't slept in a few days. [Screenwriter] Steve Tesich and I will be over at the hotel room later on to talk with you."

They came over and talked to me and I told them where I thought we went wrong, or where it was not right for me. I didn't know who this character was. We had shot a whole day's footage like this, with me looking really bad. Like in a Halloween costume.

We did it differently. I washed the crap out of my hair, so I had my blond hair back again. They said, "How are you going to change when you finally tell the girl the truth?" With my whole being I will change. We don't need props to do that. You don't need costumes to be masquerading yourself. It turned out really well, I think, those notes. We went back the next day and started fresh with this brand-new character. They really listened to me, really took my input. I was surprised they would, but they were very, very open to it. I guess they understood where I was coming from and liked that a little bit more than where they thought the character was coming from. I think it very much changed the movie.

In his interview with Bob Babbitt on the Babbittville website, Dennis Christopher said that one of the takes with him in his outlandish outfit was the scene where he has dinner with Katherine in the student union.[9]

Jackie Earle Haley was considered for the role of Dave. A story on The Beautiful Bicycle website states that Dennis Christopher was originally cast as Cyril. And, it has:[10]

"... the way the script was originally penned, it was more a movie about an American kid wanting to be Italian to pick up girls in clubs (sort of like "Saturday Night Fever"), than a movie about family and cycling. Christopher says that he talked the director into changing the script—arguing that part of Dave Stoller's (*sic*) motivation for wanting to be Italian because he was an only child and wanted a bigger family."

The pbs.org website has this from Dennis Christopher's interview at the Virginia Film Festival to show how close he came to not getting the role:[11]

"I left another film I was working on to play this part.

"Then they sent me out to shoot, and I'd never tried out the accent before in front of anybody because I missed the rehearsal, and I felt really uncomfortable. I couldn't even look at myself in the mirror. I couldn't understand why they hired me and what they wanted out of me when they changed me so radically.

"I got up the next morning and went to the set. I had spent a sleepless night and called my agent asking to be out of the

---

[9] https://babbittville.com/classics-dennis-christopher/
[10] https://www.thebeautifulbicycle.com/2016/04/breaking-away-with-dennis-christopher/
[11] https://www.pbs.org/newshour/arts/breaking-away-was-this-actors-breakout-role-fans-say-it-changed-their-lives-too

POSTSCRIPT

movie. And she said, 'Are you kidding? This is a giant movie. You have to do this.' I got out of the car and ran to the director, Peter Yates, who is British, and he embraced me and I burst into tears. I said: 'I can't do this part, I don't know who this guy is, he seems like a cartoon to me, why would those other guys be my friend? The only thing missing is a trick-or-treat bag missing from my arm.' "

Pat McGuire, on the website velo.outsideonline.com, quoted Dennis Christopher with:[12]

"I don't want to do it. Cyril's the best character; this guy's a buffoon, he sings opera!"

McGuire quoted Paul Dooley on the same website with:

"They considered two other people who, to me, seemed very wrong for it. One was Henry Gibson [who had also worked in Robert Altman movies] .... Art Carney was the other guy; Art would have been very good, but a guy like Art carries with him a bit of an albatross: his fame. Every time you see him you have to work to forget that.

"I went out there two days early to listen to the Indiana accent. I hung around the feed store and the pool hall, just listening, and I found that it wasn't so different from the West Virginian accent I grew up with."

Similarly, Dennis Quaid came close to not being in the movie:[13]

---

[12] https://velo.outsideonline.com/road/road-culture/lookback-breaking-away/
[13] https://gardenandgun.com/articles/dennis-quaids-gospel-truth/

Monte Burke: I read that just as you were offered your first big role, in Breaking Away, you were also offered the role of Bo Duke in The Dukes of Hazzard and almost took that instead. Is that true?

Dennis Quaid: It is. I had a choice. And I was broke. But Peter Yates ... told me, "Listen, young man, this is the role you have to do." He became one of my great mentors.

He had to warm up to the football aspect of Mike. "The Ultimate Book Of Sports Movies", by Ray Didinger and Glen Macnow, has, "... and though he hails from Texas, he never made much of an effort to play football, saying, 'I hate getting hit.'"

THE MOVIE AS A COMEDY

The IMDb listing for "Breaking Away" has the tags of Coming-of-Age, Comedy, Teen Drama, Drama, and Sport. Is it a comedy, a drama, or a sport movie? On the Sneak Previews show, Roger Ebert called it a comedy, but Gene Siskel said that it was hard to categorize. The RogerEbert.com website described it as "... wonderfully sunny, funny, goofy, intelligent movie that makes you feel about as good as any movie in a long time. It is, in fact, a treasure ..."[14] Reporting on the Today website, "Remembering Director Peter Yates: His Five Greatest Films", Emmy-nominated filmmaker and journalist Josh Grossberg called it a "cycling drama", not a comedy.[15] No question, the Little 500 race ending is quite dramatic. Vincent Canby, the noted movie critic of the *New York Times* described it as "a gentle, hilarious, thoroughly winning comedy."[16] One poster for the movie has "A Human Comedy Directed by Peter Yates".

---

[14] https://www.rogerebert.com/reviews/breaking-away-1979

[15] https://www.today.com/popculture/remembering-director-peter-yates-his-five-greatest-films-wbna41007707

[16] https://www.nytimes.com/1979/09/02/archives/film-view-a-comedy-in-which-class-tells.html

POSTSCRIPT

In his "Home and Alone" book, Daniel Stern writes: "The Oscar-winning script was as solid as a rock, the perfect blend of comedy, action, heart, and romance." In an interview with the American Film Institute, he said, "It's interesting that it's considered a sports movie, because I think of the sports part of the movie as the secondary part of the story, and the heart of the movie and the character of the movie and the comedy of the movie. There were a lot of big laughs in that movie."[17]

Pat McGuire, on the website velo.outsideonline.com, quoted Paul Dooley with, "... there were no jokes, *per se*. It was all character humor."[18] There are hardly any comedic episodes after the REFUND! scene, with 41 minutes remaining in the movie. We smile when Ray describes becoming a father and at the look on his face when Dave calls out to him in French. Appropriately, he gets the last laugh.

The year 1979 had a bumper crop of comedy movies; most of these are laugh-out-loud hilarious, starring comedic geniuses: "The Jerk" (with Steve Martin), "Meatballs" (Bill Murray), "Life of Brian" (the Monty Python troupe), "The In-Laws" (Peter Falk and Alan Arkin), "10" (Dudley Moore), "The Frisco Kid" (Gene Wilder), "Going in Style" (George Burns and Art Carney), and "Being There" (Peter Sellers). Two others deserve special mention: the hilarious "Rock 'n' Roll High School", starring P.J. Soles, and the underrated "Rich Kids", which had Paul Dooley and served as an appropriate follow-up to "Breaking Away" for him. Other than "The Jerk", "Life of Brian", and "10", which had R ratings, the other seven were rated PG, which would be like needles in the haystack of the anything-goes comedy movies of these days. The previous year had the release of "National Lampoon's Animal House", and the following year had "Airplane!", "Caddyshack", and "The Blues Brothers".

---

[17] https://www.youtube.com/watch?v=S77dwl06ZLg

[18] https://velo.outsideonline.com/road/road-culture/lookback-breaking-away/?-scope=anon

How does "Breaking Away" compare to these as a comedy? It doesn't have the physical humor or the slapstick of Steve Martin and Dudley Moore. We smile throughout the movie, because it is a feel-good story. Though we rarely laugh out loud, it *is* a comedy, with the humor mainly supplied by Ray, with his comments, his facial expressions, and his caricature. Evelyn makes us laugh with her dry humor, and Cyril with his wisecracks.

It came out almost exactly a year after "National Lampoon's Animal House", which has the only tag of "Comedy" on IMDb, was released. Comparing the two movies that take place in a college setting, "Animal House" wins across the board as a comedy. John Belushi or any of the fraternity guys vs. the evil Rod in "Breaking Away"? Dean Wormer vs. President Ryan? Double-secret probation vs. letting the townies compete in a bicycle race? The fights in the dining hall? The guitar scenes? (At least, Cyril's guitar didn't get smashed to bits by Rod's henchmen, we assume.) "Louie, Louie" (the song) vs. Felix and Gioachino (Mendelssohn and Rossini)? No contest. In the *Houston Post*, film writer Eric Gerber quoted Yates, "People feel the need to classify your film. This, for instance, is being called 'Animal House meets Rocky' ... Well, that's silly, isn't it? It's not very much like either. I would rather die than look like something that's been made before!"[19]

Ray appears in 18 scenes, with the "REFUND!" scene the most hilarious. In only a few scenes is he not wearing a tie—his first and last scenes, the one where he is tended to by the doctor, the one where he is in his robe when Dave comes home from the Cinzano 100 race, and the heart-to-heart talk. That scene outside the Wells Library is absent of any humor, although he is still wearing his pocket protector. As Ray sits on a limestone bench …

Ray: *I cut the stone for this building.*
Dave: *You did?*

---

[19] Source: Indiana University Lilly Library Archives

POSTSCRIPT

Ray: *Yeah. I was one fine stonecutter ... Mike's dad ... Moocher's, Cyril's ... all of us. Well, Cyril's dad ... never mind. The thing of it was, I loved it. I was young and slim and strong, and I was damn proud of my work. And the buildings went up. When they were finished, the damndest thing happened. It was like the buildings was too good for us. Nobody told us that. Just, just felt uncomfortable, that's all. Even now, I'd like to be able to stroll through the campus and look at the limestone, but I just feel out of place. You guys still go swimming in the quarries?*
Dave: *Sure.*
Ray: *So, the only thing you got to show from my twenty years of work is the holes we left behind.*
Dave: *I don't mind.*
Ray: *I do. Cyril's dad says he took that college exam.*
Dave: *We both took it.*
Ray: *How did both of us do?*
Dave: *Well, I don't know. One of us did OK. But neither of us ... Hell, I don't want to go to college, Dad. To hell with them. I'm proud of being a Cutter.*
Ray: *You're not a Cutter, I'm a Cutter. What, are you afraid?*
Dave: *Yeah, a little bit. And then, there's the rest of the guys.*
Ray: *Well, you took the exam. Did all right, didn't you?*
Dave: *Yes.*
Ray: *Well, that's ... that's good.*

In his "Movie Dad" book, Paul Dooley writes, "he runs his hands along that stone bench ... *his hands remembering.*"

Dave may be thinking, "Hey, I'm young and slim and strong, too." He has no fear when it comes to risking his life following a semi-truck at 60 miles an hour or outracing a bus through an intersection, but he is a little afraid of college. He is also afraid of breaking away from his friends.

Ray's lament about not being appreciated as a limestone cutter and Mike's "Mean old man Mike" monologue at the football practice are the two most serious moments in the movie, and both are 80 seconds in length. That scene is the exception for Ray; all the others make us laugh or smile. Ray is holding the cat when Evelyn calls him to the dinner table, where a meal with Ray's health in mind awaits him:

Ray: *What is this?*
Evelyn: *It's, um, sauteed zucchini.*
Ray: *It's Ity food! I don't want no Ity food!*
Evelyn: *It's not. I got it at the A&P. It's like, uh, squash.*
Ray: *I know Ity food when I hear it. It's all them "eeni" foods. Zucchini and linguine and fettuccine. I want some American food, damn it. I want French fries* [The cat jumps up on the table.]
Evelyn: *Oh, get off the table, Fellini.*
Ray: *That's my cat! His name is Jake, not Fellini. I won't have any "eeni" in this house.* [To the cat] *Your name is Jake, you understand?* [The cat meows]

Note: according to the IMDb entry for "A Perfect Couple", Paul Dooley was seriously allergic to cats![20] The aversion to things Italian was an act, too. In his "Movie Dad" book, he writes that as a student at West Virginia University, he did so well in Italian that he switched his minor from Art to Italian. He had all A's and was fluent after two years. And, his first wife was Italian.

Ray tells Evelyn about the near-collision with Dave on his bike, when he is test-driving a car with a customer

Ray: *I should have hit him when I had the chance. He'd be dead now. No more worries.*

---

[20] https://www.imdb.com/title/tt0079710/

POSTSCRIPT

Ray is always confounded by Dave.

Evelyn: *What's the matter?*
Ray: *He's shaving.*
Evelyn: *Well... so what?*
Ray: *His legs. He's shaving his legs.*

Ray: *Speaking of flies, you brought in a hell of a lot of flies in with you.*
Dave: *Did you know that fly in Italian is 'mosca'?*
Ray: *Did you know that in English it's pest.*

Ray: *That's because he never went to college! Besides, he's probably too stupid to get in.*
Evelyn: *Shh, he'll hear you.*
Ray: *I don't care. It's my house. Besides, he doesn't speak English anyway.*

Ray: *I'm just tired of it, Evelyn. I'm tired of worrying about him. Who'd hire a guy like that? He'll wind up a bum, an Italian bum.*

To Ray, when it comes to jobs, being tired and miserable is a red badge of courage.

Ray: *Let him look at least. Let him come home tired from looking. He's never tired. He's never miserable.*
Evelyn: *He's young.*
Ray: *When I was young, I was tired and miserable. I had my own place at seventeen.*

Dave is working in Ray's car lot, washing the cars, but is not miserable like his dad. He has his Italian Phrases book in one back pocket and his yellow Campagnolo cap in the other, as he whistles the familiar Italian

"La Tarantella" tune, sharing a common bond with the wedding scene in "The Godfather", which Peter Yates was considered to direct.

Ray: *Hey, no whistling. You're supposed to be a shag boy, so shag. If I wanted whistling, I'd get a bird.*

Dave is working at the car lot; he wants to race against the Italians:

Dave: *Papa...can I have this Saturday off?*
Ray: *Hell no.*
Dave: *Just this once, Papa. The Italians are coming Saturday.*
Ray: *I don't care if the second coming's coming.*
Dave: *But I've waited so long.*
Ray: *No. N-double 'o' NO-0.*

Dave has come home from the race against the Italians and is more concerned about his dad, who is recovering from his meltdown, than he is about his injuries.

Ray: *No, I don't feel lucky to be alive. I feel lucky I'm not dead. There's a difference.*

Ray: *Well, I'll tell you how I'm feeling, son. I had nightmares all night that everybody I ever sold a car to came in to ask for a refund. And you were there handing out the checks. One for you...and one for you.*

Dave gets emotional when Ray asks him where the trophy is; he breaks into tears and finds comfort in hugging his dad.

POSTSCRIPT

Ray: *What's the matter? What are you crying for? You'd think you lost your wallet or something. I didn't want you to be this miserable. A little bit is all I asked for. Come on now. Talk to him, Evelyn.*

Evelyn can dish it out, too.

Ray: *I want an answer, Evelyn. What are we going to do about him?*
Evelyn: *I don't know, dear. We could always strangle him while he's asleep.*
Ray: *That's not funny, Evelyn.*

Dave: *Mama, Mama, Mama! The Italians are coming! The Italians are coming to race in Indianapolis. The Team CINZANO!* [He crosses himself]. *Grazia tante, Santa Maria.*
Evelyn: *Oh, Dave, try not to become Catholic on us.*

Ray: *I don't want him selling used cars.*
Evelyn: *Why not? It's good enough for you.*
Ray: *Who says it's good enough for me?*
Evelyn: *You do.*

Cyril is always ready with a wisecrack, usually directed at Mike, the two being on opposite ends of the spectrum.
At the quarry:

Cyril: *STOP! It was somewhere right along here that I lost all interest in life. Aha, it was right here. This is where I saw Dolores Reineke and fat Marvin!* [Stomps his feet.] *Why Dolores? Why?*
Moocher: *They're married now.*

Mike: *You see what I saved you from, Cyril? If I hadn't told you about the two of them, you never would have followed them out here.*
Cyril: *Yeah, well thanks, Mike. You made me lose all interest in life, and I'm grateful.*

When Mike shares where his happy spot is:

Mike: *Hey now, look at this. That's the place to be, right there, Wyoming. Nothing but prairies and mountains and nobody around. All you need is a bedroll and a good horse.*
Cyril: *Don't forget your toothbrush. You're still in your cavity-prone years.*

When Mike jabs Cyril:

Mike: *How did you get to be so stupid, Cyril?*
Cyril: *I don't know. I guess I have a dumb heredity or something. What's your excuse, Michael?*

Mike is outraged that the students have dared to come to the quarry.

Mike: *It's my goddamn quarry.*
Cyril: *This hole! This quarry hole is mine!*

Cyril brings back memories from when I read MAD magazine, which had a "Snappy Answers to Stupid Questions" ongoing feature. Mike's brother has warned Mike about hot-rodding on campus. Prophetically, the Iran revolution and hostage crisis would occur a few months after the release of the movie. As he leaves:

Mike's brother: *How're you doing, guys?*
Cyril: *Well, we're a little disturbed by the developments in the Middle East...but other than that...*

At the quarry:

Moocher: *Hey, come on in, Dave.*
Dave: *Naw, I read where this Italian coach said it's no good to go swimming right after a race.*
Cyril: *Who's swimming? I'm taking a leak.*

On the day after the serenade, the boys are together, and Mike is outraged at the look of Cyril's bruised face.

Mike: *I've seen that car. All right. They want a fight...we're going to give them a fight.*
Cyril: *We rednecks are few. College paleface students are many. I counsel peace.*

The boys are examining the bare-bones bike that they have to ride in the Little 500 race. Cyril examines a shredded tire, and a pedal breaks off:

Dave: *Am I supposed to ride this thing or what?*
Mike: *Well, that's the official issue, can't add or change anything.*
Dave: *Yeah, well, it's a piece of junk!*
Cyril: *Hey, it's got a lot of personality to it.*
Moocher: *It doesn't look that bad to me.*
Dave: *That's because you don't have to ride it.*
Moocher: *You don't have to ride it either, Dave. We're not going to beg you.*
Cyril: *We may plead, but we would never beg.*

Mike pulls a prank by pretending that he is trapped in a refrigerator in the quarry, but he doesn't have much of a sense of humor; when he does lighten up, it comes as a jab.

Cyril: *You know what I'd like to be?*
Mike: *Smart.*

Cyril: *Hey, are you really going to shave your legs?*
Dave: *Certo! All the Italians do it.*
Mike: *Ah. Some country. The women don't shave theirs.*

The only one of the four boys who does not crack a joke is … Dave!

THE MOVIE AS A SPORTS MOVIE

If you were to ask me what my favorite sports movies are, it would include the usual suspects: "The Natural", "Field of Dreams", "Bull Durham", "Bang the Drum Slowly", "Eight Men Out", "42", "Rudy", "Hoosiers", "A League of Their Own", and "Glory Road". "Fever Pitch" is a favorite, as it combines sports, comedy, and romance. Why not "Breaking Away"? The answer is that when you talk about sports movies, it does not automatically pop into my head as one. As I said, it's about class differences, honesty, pride, family, relationships, romance, changing attitudes, and life. The actual portion of the movie that portrays competition is quite small.

In John Schwarb's book, "The Little 500: The Story of the World's Greatest College Weekend", he writes a similar take:

> The writer and director agreed from the outset that the story would focus on the main characters—the Bloomington locals and their trials and tribulations—rather than on the bicycling. *Bambino*, as it was called, would be a movie with cycling but

POSTSCRIPT

not exactly a cycling movie. And, perhaps more than anything else, *Bambino* would be a *Bloomington movie*.

In the August 1979 Bicycling magazine review, Susan Weaver wrote that it is "... first about people and only secondarily about bicycle racing."[21]

OVERVIEW

In the television broadcast of the 1979 race, William Armstrong referred to the soon-to-be-released movie with pride, and Bill Brissman was identified as crossing the finish line to win for Delta Chi.[22]

The financial impact on Bloomington was significant. A headline in the *Bloomington Herald-Telephone* (now the *Herald-Times*) had, *Movie means $1.5 million for Bloomington economy*. The *New York Times* in October of 1979 reported:[23]

> "Last year, our gifts totaled $10.7 million," says Jerry Tardy, vice-president in charge of public relations for the Indiana University Foundation, the school's fund-raising agency and its link to generous alumni. "We're $2.7 million ahead of where we were last year already, and a lot of that has to be from the movie."

Jon Wertheim, a sports journalist and author, and a Bloomington native who was in the Little 500 race filming as a young child, wrote that "Thanks to the movie the country's best teenage cyclists began enrolling at IU."[24]

---

[21] https://www.bikeforums.net/classic-vintage/1298715-45-years-ago-august-1979-bicycling-magazine.html

[22] https://m.youtube.com/watch?v=kmrCoLoWmXI

[23] https://www.nytimes.com/1979/10/14/archives/what-breaking-away-has-done-to-bloomington-ind-breaking-away-and.html

[24] https://vault.si.com/vault/2004/02/16/wheels-of-fortune-a-classic-indiana-film-provided-the-author-with-an-acting-gig-and-a-new-love

Not all of the reviews were glowing. One story in the *Herald-Times* had the headline, *'Breaking Away' has its flaws, but overall it's a 'tough film'*, and another had, *Ecstasy and disappointment* with the subheading, *Audience members give 'Breaking Away' mixed reviews*. The review in the *Indiana Daily Student* newspaper had praise, but called it "superficial" and "trivial."[25] The News at IU website has:[26]

> While IU students were an integral part of the film production, many were not completely pleased with the finished product. In a review of the movie published in the Indiana Daily Student on April 23, 1979, Eve B. Rose argues that the film misses the mark on an accurate portrayal of Bloomington life.
>
> "The movie suggests that college kids and townspeople are constantly at each other's throats," she writes. "It is as if there are two huge youth gangs."

Amy Harris, who was a 19-year-old student at the time of the premiere, told the Herald-Times, "It was a good movie, but I'm not sure that people outside of Bloomington and IU will like it as much as people here."

Dan Levinson shared his video of the "30 Thirty Magazine" TV show produced by WTIU, the university station, during the filming period. Host Katie Larson had interviews with Peter Yates, David Blase, President Ryan, Chancellor Herman Wells, and William Armstrong. Peter told Katie, "We've tried to make this as un-Hollywood a picture as

---

[25] https://mediaschool.indiana.edu/news-events/news/item.html?n=alumni-produced-anthology-chronicles-ids-history

[26] https://news.iu.edu/live/news/25964-40-years-ago-iu-students-and-administrators-made

POSTSCRIPT

possible and really try to present Indiana University and Bloomington as it is."

Katie Larson: *How does this work relate to the other films that you've made, Bullitt, The Deep?*
Peter Yates: *It's a film I really want to do. It's much more fun making a movie like this. On The Deep, for instance, as an executive director, you have all sorts of groups, and you have all sorts of departments which you're running. You have the underwater department, and you have the special effects department, and you have the prop department, and you have a crew of about 125 people. And it's very difficult to keep control over absolutely everything. I mean, you'd do it, but it's not quite so easy. This is the kind of film that I was brought up with, which is a basically more controllable and slightly smaller in concept film, which therefore concentrates more, and one can keep more control over it, and have more of a sort of personal signature, if you like to use that awful word, over it.*

Katie Larson: *When you came to town, the movie was called Bambino. Now it's called Breaking Away. Why the name change?*
Peter Yates: *We actually decided to change the name sometime before we came here. It's untrue that we changed it because it's the name of a well-known pizza. We felt that Bambino was a good title, if you had read the script and seen the film. So often, if you go and see a film, you say, ah, that's a terrific title. But unfortunately, we're trying to appeal to people who haven't seen the film and will go and see the film. And I think Breaking Away sounds more intriguing, sounds more interesting, and also is more descriptive about what the story is about.*

Katie Larson: *What aspirations do you have for this movie?*
Peter Yates: *That people should enjoy it, that it should give them pleasure, that they should come and see it, because I believe that films about people who are enjoying themselves and are not necessarily behaving in a way that cannot be admired could be popular. That it's possible, in fact, to make a film about nice people having a good time and enjoying themselves without necessarily having to use bad language or any of the other things that all us human beings actually do.*

In the show, movie critic Barbara Cabot described that she and Dan were filmed in a scene where they are walking downtown on Walnut Street to buy him sneakers at Penney's, but the scene was cut out.

The story of fatherhood must have hit home for Steve Tesich and Paul Dooley. Tesich did not connect with his father, who was presumed dead in the war in his native country, until age 14, and his father, who worked in a steel mill, died five years later. In a story by Lawrence Van Gelder of the *New York Times*, Paul Dooley said of the part:[27]

"I had a very personal interest in the man I was playing, because 70 percent of him was my father completely—his personality. This man is a kind of gruff, blue-collar working man. He is not able to show his affection for his wife or his son directly, and his style is to sort of grumble in a kind of comic way, to sort of complain, to put his son down. It's a very subtle thing, because it doesn't seem to be mean-spirited. My father used to communicate that way, in an indirect way. You know that he cared for you, but he didn't show it directly. It's not an uncommon disease in our country. As soon as I read the script I said, 'I know this guy very well.' "

---

[27] https://www.nytimes.com/1979/07/23/archives/paul-dooley-a-household-theatrical-face-gets-used-to-being-a-name.html

POSTSCRIPT

A story in the *Los Angeles Daily News* about Dooley and his "Movie Dad" book has:[28]

> But the irony in all those paternal roles, and all the other onscreen fathers he played, was that off the screen, Dooley's own children vanished for most of a decade, a trauma he alludes to in the subtitle of the book: "Finding Myself and My Family On Screen and Off."
>
> For an actor so often typecast as a father, Dooley's own dad didn't provide much of a role model.
>
> "He was unable to share," Dooley says. "I really think my father was afraid of people. He didn't have friends. And his dad had left the family, so he had all that to deal with."
>
> "I became this kind of character to portray these guys on screen who were kind of withdrawn, stoic, kind of, you know, unfeeling people. Sometimes cranky guys."
>
> Then, one summer day in the early '70s, while Dooley's kids were on vacation with his ex-wife, a letter arrived. "I'm taking the kids," it read in part. "We're not coming back."
>
> Dooley hired detectives. He went to court and got an order granting him sole custody. Yet no traces of the children could be found.

---

[28] https://www.dailynews.com/2023/02/02/paul-dooley-became-movie-dad-even-as-his-own-children-disappeared-for-a-decade/

A decade or so passed. Then, a tip arrived with his daughter's location. Soon, though hesitantly at first, Dooley and his now-young adult children were reunited.

Dennis Christopher related to the father/son dynamic, too. An article on The Ultimate Rabbit website has:[29]

Christopher also told the audience about when he took his dad, whom he was estranged from at the time, to see "Breaking Away" when it was first released. After it was over, he said his dad came out of it "ruined" and looked quite frail. His dad could not believe how great the movie was, and when people outside the theater asked Christopher for his autograph, he got in line with the others. His dad even acted as his security chief in getting people in the line to move along.

The movie is about 99% fault-free. The movie has a PG rating—the PG-13 rating started 1984—but if it were made today, it would probably not include a few inappropriate comments. It has minimal violence; Cyril getting roughed up by Rod and his henchmen is not shown. It has no alcohol (though Dave has an empty Cinzano bottle in his bedroom), no smoking (though Mike often has an unlit cigarette, and, nice job, Dave, telling Katherine that she shouldn't smoke), and no sex … well, at least, not on screen and not involving who you would expect. The scenes flow easily and naturally.

There are a few bloopers. When the Italian villain knocks Dave out of the race, only two Italians are seen riding away. In that race, his socks alternated between long and short. When Dave is drafting behind the Cinzano semi-truck, his bike is on the small chain-ring, which would not let him get up to 60 miles per hour. An earlier shot shows the bike on the

---

[29] https://theultimaterabbit.com/2021/01/22/jason-reitman-talks-with-dennis-christopher-and-daniel-stern-about-breaking-away/

POSTSCRIPT

large, and correct, chain-ring. When the racers are lined up for the start of the Little 500 race, the first row has the correct jersey numbers of 1, 2, and 3, but the second row has a racer wearing jersey #27 next to racer #4.

The only scene that seems out of place is the one where Ray visits his former limestone cutter co-workers at the mill, but it serves to show that Ray really is a good guy when he is in his element. He needs a break, away from his wife, who is controlling his diet, and from his son, who thinks that he is Italian.

> Katie Larson: *What changes are you making in the film in response to what you're actually finding here?*
> Peter Yates: *We're always making changes slightly all the better. I find that the best films, when you start to shoot, they begin to take on a life better, and they begin to grow. And I've been very lucky, because in this film, Steve Tesich has been here with me the whole time during the filming for that reason. So that when we found things, he could write about them. When he saw things he didn't think that looked quite right, he could change them. For instance, originally, the mill, the limestone mill, wasn't in the script. But when we went down and saw Mr. Woolery's mill, we were so impressed, and we felt it had so much to do with the character of the father of the boy in the film that we wrote a short scene to be shot there.*

The Hollywood Chicago website has:[30]

> The scene where the character Ray goes back to … his old quarry mates wasn't well received by the studio, they didn't think it should be in the film – it didn't have anything to do with the family or the race. The director Peter Yates told them,

---

[30] https://www.hollywoodchicago.com/news/26685/interview-actor-paul-dooley-on-getting-to-portray-dad

'yeah, but it has everything to do with this guy.' He still wanted to be with those craftsmen.

The movie takes place in the spring, because the Little 500 is held in April, and Ray had talked about having given Dave a year off to sort things out, and the time lapse into the final scene makes sense. However, in the opening scene, Cyril says, "You know, this will be the first time nobody's going to ask us to write a theme about how we spent our summer.", as if it is taking place in Autumn. Football practice is taking place, though it could have been the spring practice.

THE CAST
Both Dennis Christopher and Paul Dooley had little downtime when they were selected for the movie. Dennis Christopher had just wrapped up "The Last Word", and Paul Dooley had just completed "A Perfect Couple". The casting of Paul Dooley as Ray was brilliant. Pat McGuire, on the website velo.outsideonline.com, quoted Dennis Christopher with:[31]

> They wanted to have a table reading, but they still hadn't cast the part of the father. So I said, "I know a guy who played my father in 'A Wedding' and he's a fantastic actor," and I got them in touch with Paul Dooley, just to read at the sitting. And two minutes after he started, I don't think they ever thought of getting anyone else. He was brilliant at the table; he's even more brilliant in the movie.

Dennis Christopher related that Charles Durning was considered for the part of Ray, but:[32]

---

[31] https://velo.outsideonline.com/road/road-culture/lookback-breaking-away/
[32] https://www.popentertainmentarchives.com/post/dennis-christopher-an-actor-s-life-from-fellini-to-breaking-away-to-django-unchained

POSTSCRIPT

I said, "You need somebody to read the father? I just did a movie for Bob Altman with this man who played my father, Paul Dooley. He's a really terrific New York actor." They said, "Would he do the reading for us as a favor, knowing that he's not going to play the part?" I asked, "Will you pay him?" I don't think anybody had ever said that before. (laughs) We're New York people. We don't give it away. They said, "Oh, for the reading? Well, umm... Well, yeah, yeah, I guess we will, but he'll understand that he's not playing the part, right?" I said, "You say that to him, and he will hear you. He'll get a day's work out of it." He came in and read it. There was nobody in the room that wasn't gob smacked by his performance. There was no question of the fact that he was going to play the father from that moment on. I don't think they ever even called Charles Durning back.

The movie was a springboard (which the Cutters did not have at the quarry) for several of the stars. Peter Yates's prophecy was right on the mark.

> Katie Larson: *You've also worked with a lot of glamorous stars, Barbra Streisand, Steve McQueen, Ali McGraw. But this group is relatively unknown. Is it difficult working with unknowns, or is it easier?*
> Peter Yates: *It's a difficult question, because you really treat actors as actors. If they happen to be big stars, yes. Obviously, there is a certain ego, and they have a certain knowledge of the kind of things that suit them. When you're dealing with young actors, they haven't always found what suits them, what doesn't suit them yet. Obviously, for a director, it is more interesting to work with young people. It's made me feel about 10 years younger, because you catch*

their vitality and their energy. And this is what we've tried to show in the film, the energy and the vitality of the young people. It's also nice to work with people with fresh ideas, and I think there are several actors in this film who, when this film comes out, will become names.

Several of them had movies released the following year. Daniel Stern may have set a record by quadrupling his previous credits count; he had "It's My Turn", "One-Trick Pony", "Stardust Memories", and "A Small Circle of Friends". Dennis Quaid had two, "The Long Riders" (alongside his brother, Randy) and "Gorp". Paul Dooley had two, "Popeye" and "HealtH", both directed by Robert Altman. Amy Wright had two, "Stardust Memories" and "Inside Moves"; she also appeared in the Broadway plays "Fifth of July", starting in 1980, and "Noises Off", starting in 1983. Dennis Christopher had "Fade to Black". Barbara Barrie had "Private Benjamin" and kept busy with the "Breaking Away" TV series. Jackie Earle Haley had no movies, but was also busy starring in the "Breaking Away" TV series.

Within three years, Daniel Stern was in another movie that featured up-and-coming actors, "Diner", which had Kevin Bacon, Mickey Rourke, Steve Guttenberg, Paul Reiser, and Ellen Barkin. "Breaking Away" was a good initiation for him to make another transformation in a movie. In "City Slickers", he committed adultery and lost his job and family. Clay Stone says, "You came out here as city slickers, you're going go home cowboys." And, he gets the girl in the end!

Dennis Christopher ("Chariots of Fire"), Dennis Quaid ("The Right Stuff"), Jackie Earle Haley ("Lincoln"), Amy Wright ("The Accidental Tourist"), and Peter Maloney ("JFK") all appeared in subsequent movies that were nominated for the Oscar for the Best Picture. For Amy Wright, "Breaking Away" was her second nominated movie, as she had been in "The Deer Hunter".

POSTSCRIPT

Dennis Christopher followed "Fade to Black" a year later with "Chariots of Fire", which takes place in the Paris 1924 Summer Olympics, another French reference for him. After playing a bike racer based on a real person, he portrayed a real-life person competing in another speed event, Charley Paddock, an American sprinter who was the world record holder for the 100-metre dash, the 200-metre dash, the 100-yard dash, and the 220-yard dash, and was a member of a world record-holding 4 × 100-metre team. His nickname was the "world's fastest human", and his autobiography, "The Fastest Human", was published in 1932.

In "The Ultimate Book Of Sports Movies", by Ray Didinger and Glen Macnow, Dennis Quaid said of the impact of "Breaking Away" on his career, "… it made it a lot easier to get jobs. Before that movie, I was a struggling actor, new to the scene, going from audition to audition. That movie gave me something for the resume. Beyond that, it remains one of my favorite movies I've done. Peter Yates, who directed it, became a mentor in my life."

It was the first theatrical screenplay for Steve Tesich. It was the first movie for Daniel Stern, the second for Hart Bochner, and the first theatrical movie for Robyn Douglass. Cyril is the least confident of the four, just as Daniel Stern was the least experienced actor, this being his first movie. It was a good fit for him; a *New York Times* article has that his parents:[33]

> … took a reasonably tolerant attitude toward their son's haphazard progress through adolescence — much of which, he reports, was spent lying on the sofa in the living room playing the guitar, sleeping and eating an inordinate amount.

---

[33] https://www.nytimes.com/1979/08/31/archives/new-face-daniel-stern-off-the-sofa-and-onto-the-movie-screen-in.html

Apparently, his metabolism ate five times a day.

In her *New York Times* review at the time, Janet Maslin wrote, "... the cast is unknown, the director has a spotty history."[34] "Spotty" is interesting, based on the popularity of "Bullitt", but she was referring to more questionable efforts, such as "For Pete's Sake", "The Deep", and "Mother, Jugs and Speed", which were not lacking for star power, including Barbra Streisand, Nick Nolte, Jacqueline Bisset, Robert Shaw, Bill Cosby, Raquel Welch, and Harvey Keitel.

In the July 1979 Vogue magazine, Rex Reed said, "... a smashing movie" and "It is one of the most rapturously funny, totally unique, and eccentric film experiences of this or any other year, and you'd be dead wrong to miss it."[35]

Jackie Earle Haley was only 17 years old when he played 19-year-old Moocher; he was the only teenager of the group. Daniel Stern turned 21 during the filming. Dennis Quaid was 24; four years later, he would portray astronaut Gordon Cooper, who was in his mid-thirties at the time of his Project Mercury spaceflight, in "The Right Stuff". Hart Bochner was fresh out of college at age 21. Jennifer K. Mickel, who appears in two scenes as Rod's new girlfriend after he loses Katherine, was a freshman at Indiana University. In John Schwarb's book, he writes that Mickel had signed up in the studio's production office on campus to be an extra. Robyn Douglass, P.J. Soles, and Amy Wright were closer to age 30.

In the book, "Dennis Quaid", Gail Birnbaum writes:

> It was one of Yates's conditions that there be no stars as the leads in *Breaking Away*. "I wanted the audience to be concerned only with the story, and not distracted by how well so-and-so looks and acts," he said. That quest took five months of casting,

---

[34] https://www.nytimes.com/1979/07/18/archives/film-breaking-away-a-classic-sleeperback-home-in-indiana.html
[35] Source: Indiana University news release, Indiana University Archives

during which "we looked at hundreds of photos, and interviewed scores of people on both coasts."

One of Robyn Douglass's efforts after the movie was in the Sta-Puf Fabric Softener commercial called "Cuddle Up", where, appropriately, she is caressing an infant *bambino*. Bart Harris, who produced and directed it, shared his experience:

> It was an interesting project in that it was a low-budget, 30-second spot shot for test market that scored so high in test market scores that it went national, even though it was shot 16mm for budgetary reasons. I was always a still photographer, but I loved live action and thinking continuity was a fun challenge for me.
>
> She was becoming popular because of the critical acclaim received from her wonderful performance in "Breaking Away". I shot it in one day because of her schedule. I used twin baby girls in order to ensure a one day shoot (babies were limited to short shooting days), and, as I remember, it was a union shoot.

Just as the cast was largely no-name, so are the characters. We know Dave's family name, although it is not spoken until he confesses to Katherine, and it is spoken later in the dinner scene with Moocher and a few times in the Little 500 race. We know that Katherine's last name is Bennett, spoken once, when she introduces herself to Dave. Otherwise, that is it. Ray's name is spoken only three times, barely audibly by a mill worker, when the doctor says before giving him an injection, "Easy, Ray", and when Evelyn calls him to dinner with "Raymond". His name of Raymond appears at the end, on the sign at the Cutter Cars lot. Rod's name is spoken only twice, in the frisbee scene and when Suzy calls him on the phone during the serenade. The Indiana University president's last name is not spoken. On the other hand, Ray says "Evelyn" nine times and calls her "Ev" at the Little 500 race. The closing credits list "Mom" and "Dad", instead of "Evelyn" and "Ray".

While the cast is relatively young and inexperienced, the quarry has a monumental history. The *Bloomington Herald-Times* reports that the Empire Quarry in Oolitic, Indiana supplied the limestone for Yankee Stadium.[36] In the book, "In Limestone Country", by Scott Russell Sanders, he writes that in the Bloomington area, "… there are gaping holes in the Earth from which the stone was dug for The Empire State Building, the Pentagon, Rockefeller Center, the National Cathedral, Grand Central Station, San Francisco's City Hall, Chicago's Tribune Tower, the Dallas Museum of Fine Arts, New York's Metropolitan Museum of Art, the Free Library of Philadelphia, Vanderbilt Mansions, fourteen state capitals, and countless other buildings grand or humble.", and "In Washington, Abraham Lincoln's statue is surrounded by walls of it, and his weighty words are carved into it. The Bureau of Internal Revenue toils through its endless piles of forms behind sturdy walls of Salem Stone and so do the Departments of State and Commerce and the United States Postal Service …". The *Indianapolis Star* reports that Indiana's limestone also can be found in "… the Biltmore Estate in North Carolina, parts of the Lincoln and Jefferson memorial in Washington D.C., the University of Texas clock tower …".[37]

PRAISE FOR PAUL DOOLEY

The "Movie Dad" book contains samples of the praise that Dooley received. Gene Siskel wrote that Dooley gave the performance of his lifetime, and that he was certain to receive an Oscar nomination as the best supporting actor (he did not). Roger Ebert wrote that Dooley could win

[36] https://www.heraldtimesonline.com/story/news/2017/06/22/oolitics-empire-quarry-a-source-of-pride/46754905/

[37] https://www.indystar.com/story/news/environment/2022/02/01/indiana-limestone-used-build-u-s-landmarks/9250023002/

POSTSCRIPT

an Oscar. Janet Maslin of the *New York Times* said that Dooley "… gives a fabulous supporting performance …".[38] Richard Schickel of Time magazine wrote of his "expert exasperation."[39]

MY TOP 10 PAUL DOOLEY FACIAL EXPRESSIONS

10. When Dave takes him by surprise with a hug, at home after being sabotaged in the Cinzano 100 race.
9. His "Get lost!" look when Dave calls out to him while he is with a customer.
8. When he says "What?" to Evelyn saying that Dave says that they should have another child.
7. His deadpan "What is this?" when he sees the zucchini for dinner.
6. His "Who are you?" to Dave when the students return the car.
5. His dumbfounded look when he tells Evelyn that Dave is shaving his legs.
4. His scowl when the car won't start in the intersection after almost hitting Dave on his bike.
3. Moaning with his head on the steering wheel while the stalled car is towed.
2. Getting squeamish when Dave kisses him on the cheek.
1. The final shot, when Dave calls out in French.

THE PRODUCTION

The location shooting for the first feature film shot in Bloomington started on August 14, 1978, following a press conference in Bloomington on August 7 to announce the filming. On July 24, a letter had gone out to

---

[38] https://www.nytimes.com/1979/07/18/archives/film-breaking-away-a-classic-sleeperback-home-in-indiana.html
[39] https://time.com/archive/6881613/cinema-cutups/

the 1978 Little 500 participants to invite them to participate as racers in the September 9 and 10 filming at Tenth Street Stadium.

The setting is in small-town Indiana, where folks sit on their front porch as Dave rides by. It was a change of scenery for Dennis Christopher from Philadelphia, Dennis Quaid from Houston, Texas, Jackie Earle Haley from Northridge, California, Daniel Stern from Bethesda, Maryland, Hart Bochner from Toronto, Ontario, and John Ashton from Springfield, Massachusetts. Robyn Douglass was born in Japan, and P.J. Soles was born in Germany. Except for Steve Tesich, the director and his staff were largely fish out of water. The roles suited the Cutter boys well in one respect, their minimal college experience; Dennis Quaid had dropped out of the University of Houston, Dennis Christopher had a short stint studying acting at Temple University, and Daniel Stern took acting courses at Catholic University in Washington, DC.

Bloomington was an excellent choice for the setting, not just because Steve Tesich and David Blase attended Indiana University. The City of Bloomington website in 2023 has:[40]

> On May 31st of this year, the League of American Bicyclists honored the efforts of Bloomington to build better places for people to bike with a gold-level Bicycle Friendly Community (BFC) award. BFC recognizes communities at five levels – diamond, platinum, gold, silver, and bronze (plus an honorable mention category), and Bloomington joins 506 communities across the country in the movement for safer streets and better bicycling for everyone. The award recognizes Bloomington for its commitment to creating transportation and recreational resources that benefit its residents of all ages and abilities while encouraging healthier and more sustainable transportation choices.

---

[40] https://bloomington.in.gov/news/2023/06/05/5641

POSTSCRIPT

The movie has a strong Chicago connection, both internally and externally. Katherine is moving to Chicago, where Moocher's dad is looking for a job. Barbara Barrie, Amy Wright, and Eddy Van Guyse and his three friends for the Cinzano team were from Chicago, and IMDb lists that Robyn Douglass was discovered by Peter Yates in Chicago, where she had moved from San Francisco. Peter Maloney, who played the doctor attending to Ray, was born in Chicago. Steve Tesich grew up in nearby East Chicago.

The scenery—the quarry, the woods, Dave's long bike rides, the college settings, the small-town atmosphere—is as significant as the characters and the story.

> Katie Larson: *Is there an atmosphere here in Bloomington or in Southern Indiana that you're trying to capture?*
> Peter Yates: *I think the background will surprise a lot of people. For so often, films about the Midwest have been made to look as if the Midwest was a sort of down place. I've seen these films like The Last Picture Show. And you will really look and you'll think, oh, I never want to go there. But really, we've tried to find locations which all exist around Bloomington, which are extremely colorful, like the quarries, and the Little 500 race, and so many of the buildings in the university, which I think are really beautiful. And I'm afraid we may be responsible for bringing an awful lot of tourists to Bloomington, looking for the beautiful surrounding countryside that they'll see in this picture.*

The Little 500 race scenes took four days to film. As James Pivarnik said, the *Indiana Daily Student* appealed to students to fill Tenth Street Stadium for the two days that required shots of fans in the stadium in a promotion in red letters:

20TH-C FOX IS SHOOTING AT IU!

"Bambino" is a full length motion picture being produced in Bloomington. And the Twentieth Century Fox cast and crew invite YOU to participate in the actual filming of a special scene.

You're invited to join two days of shooting at the Tenth Street Stadium, where the excitement will continue from 10am to 6pm on September 9th and 10th.

The scene centers around Indiana University Foundation's Little 500 Bicycle Race. And besides a 33 team race, activities include 20 lap sprint races, a performance by the "Wright Brothers Reunion," and other live entertainment. All you have to do is show up, relax, and have fun!

As an extra bonus, your participation will increase Student Scholarship funds. Each spectator represents a one dollar donation from 20th Century Fox to the I. U. Foundation. So, let's fill up the stadium!

Peter Yates, the director who's best known for "The Deep" and "Bullitt," wants to film Bloomington and Indiana University in a natural setting. That's why you're invited to play a part in the movie and promote student scholarship at the same time.

See you there at the Tenth Street Stadium, September 9th and 10th. Please, NO COOLERS!

For the dollar per person pledge by 20th Century Fox, the turnstile counts showed 11,654, to which the studio rounded the donation up to an even $15,000.

The News at IU website had:[41]

---

[41] https://news.iu.edu/live/news/25964-40-years-ago-iu-students-and-administrators-made

POSTSCRIPT

According to coverage in the *Indiana Daily Student* that summer, extras were paid an hourly rate of $2.65. This did not include extras used in the final race scene, who were instead compensated with prizes like NCAA basketball tournament tickets.

… Rex Reed for Vogue magazine wrote that the final race scene "is as exciting as any Olympic footage I've ever seen."

The filming of the Little 500 race was challenging and creative. A photo in the Indiana University Archives shows a camera operator filming closeup shots of Dave in the race from a pickup truck with "Doug's Auto Mart 807 Walnut St. South"–a stone's throw from the Stohler house and the same company that supplied Mike's Buick Skylark, as reported in the *Bloomington Herald-Times*[42]–on the driver's door. A video from WRTV in Indianapolis shows a camera mounted on the right side of Dave's rear wheel. The August 1979 Bicycling magazine had:[43]

> For close-ups of riders, the camera crew and technician Tom Schwoegler tried to mount a camera from the bike's front handlebars, but the heavy camera and battery pack made the bike unwieldy. So they put Jim Glennon, the cameraman, on the back of a motorcycle facing rear, and had him ride through the pack to shoot facial views.
>
> Close-in shooting of his feet pedaling and low perspective views of him going through the pack called for a camera to be

---

[42] https://www.heraldtimesonline.com/story/sports/2014/04/26/breaking-away-real-life-townies-gave-movie-valuable-authenticity/47503011/

[43] https://www.bikeforums.net/classic-vintage/1298715-45-years-ago-august-1979-bicycling-magazine.html#&gid=1&pid=12

mounted on [Gary] Rybar's rear wheel from the hub and from the point where the seatstays meet the seat tube ... the camera stuck out a foot and riders in the pack of 34 had to make sure they gave him plenty of room.

If the movie seems real, it should. Those really are Dennis Christopher's clothes, other than the racing outfits. That really is Dr. John Ryan portraying himself as the Indiana University president; in the WTIU interview, he says that he did not wear makeup. That really is Bob Woolery running his limestone mill that Ray visits. That really is William S. Armstrong and Howard S. Wilcox portraying themselves as the two Little 500 Race Officials. The *Bloomington Herald-Times* reported that the mailman whom Dave kisses after getting his magazine was the real-life mailman Jerry Mitchell, although he worked on the other side of town.[44]

Also reflecting the budget, saving on lighting, it is largely an "outdoors" movie. The only scenes indoors are in Dave's house, in the student union, in Dr. Ryan's office, in the limestone mill, and briefly in two scenes—the sorority house when Suzy calls Rod and in Ray's car lot office when Dave asks for the day off. The only outdoor scenes at night are the serenade, when Mike parks at the student union to look for Rod, when Ray and Evelyn chat about Dave getting a job as they walk in downtown, the heart-to-heart talk on campus, and when Dave goes on a training ride after a long day of work at the car lot.

On The Retro Set website:[45]

> ... Director of Photographer Matthew P. Leonetti remembered back to *Breaking Away*'s tight budget and production constraints that made shooting a lot more challenging than the typical

---

[44] https://www.heraldtimesonline.com/story/news/2004/04/18/revisiting-the-people-and-places-from-breaking-away/118134044/

[45] http://theretroset.com/?p=17036

POSTSCRIPT

"Hollywood" scenario. Even though 50% of the movie takes place "in action" with bicycle races and long stretches of bike riding, "…we didn't use a camera car because it was too expensive. We had a limited budget for that movie. They were efficient but frugal in their choices where we could spend money. It was pretty simple."

"We happened to have a motorcycle from Mike Weathers, the gaffer on the show… If we were on the back, we would shoot forward on the motorcycle or if we were in the lead, we'd put the camera operator on the back of the motorcycle. That's how we could weave through the bicycles. We were going to use a dune buggy, but it was too wide and you couldn't get into the middle of the pack. So I came up with the idea of using the motorcycle. It's simple. We tried to mount a camera to a bicycle first, but the cameras were too heavy. An Aeroflex, back in those days, didn't weigh much but it was still 10 or 15 pounds. It was impossible to try to keep balance with that weight pulling to the left or the right."

Regarding the pivotal tandem bike race all four characters participate in, Leonetti admitted, "We had about five cameras and Peter Yates storyboarded the whole race. He handed out an assignment to each camera operator. 'You get these shots, you get those shots, to the other guy, you get these shots, etc.' So that's how he cut the race in his head before we shot it. They would tell the camera operators what actors to focus on and they'd spread them out around the track. We never saw each other and one camera didn't photograph another camera. So it was very well planned out. We shot the race for three days. The whole movie took 39 days. It took a lot of pre-planning and people put their heads together to make it work. As I remember, our pre-production was about four weeks."

Despite its simple dialogue, the most compelling segments have no dialogue, often letting the music—which was nominated for the Oscar for "Original Song Score And Its Adaptation -Or- Adaptation Score"—take over. Dave's pursuit of Katherine on her scooter lasts 90 seconds, with the only words being his calling out "Signorina" to get her attention. The following scene is Dave pedaling in the woods with his head in the clouds, and it lasts 40 seconds. His race against the semi-truck lasts four minutes and 10 seconds, with the only words uttered when Dave says "faster", and the truck driver says "Damn" when he is caught for speeding. Between the scene where Dave tells Ray after his first day of work that he has to train and the next dialogue where Dave asks for the day off, a minute elapses. When Ray visits the limestone mill, he labors for 45 seconds, with the only sound the clamoring of the machinery. The scene of the swimming competition between Mike and Rod in the quarry is two minutes long with no music and only a few words of encouragement from their friends. The Cinzano 100 race is about five minutes long, with only a few words spoken when Dave banters with the Italians. When Dave crosses the finish line of the Little 500, a full minute of celebratory music follows. As some sportscasters say, let the pictures tell the story. There was no Al Michaels or Jack Buck to exclaim, "Do you believe in miracles? Yes!", no "I don't believe what I just saw!"

This is consistent for Peter Yates; in "Bullitt", the chase scene is ten minutes long, with no dialogue. He was also consistent with product placement; a Phillips 66 gas station appears in both the "Bullitt" chase scene and the Cinzano 100 race sequence.

The long shots are impressive—the diving scenes, Dave chasing the semi-truck, and the Cinzano 100 race on the country roads.

The closing credits conclude with, "The producer wishes to acknowledge the enormous help and cooperation of the Cinzano company whose contributions to this film were invaluable." The production was truly a team effort, similar to the effort of the racing teams.

THE SCRIPT

The story has an element of good guys vs. bad guys. A *New York Times* story on Steve Tesich spoke of his early days in Yugoslavia:[46]

> And he would go to the movies. "We all went to see John Wayne movies. The longest line I ever stood on was for 'Rio Grande.' Of course, as soon as you saw a movie, you played the game of that movie. Good guys and bad guys in the local ruin."

The generation gap is underscored by the fact that we rarely see boys and adults in the same scene; we see Dave with his parents; Moocher with Dave and Dave's parents together only once at the dinner table; the college students and President Ryan together in the peace meeting; Ray selling cars to students and convulsing when one student wants a REFUND!; the race competitors with the organizers; Moocher setting the record for the shortest employment period at the car wash; and the Cutter kids, students, and the police in the dining hall rumble. Dave really doesn't interact with the truck driver, who paces him. Evelyn is the only featured female adult. The only scenes with multiple adults are with the Stohler parents, with Ray's ill-fated test drive with a customer, with the limestone mill workers, with the Little 500 race organizers, and briefly when police officers break up the fight in the student union. Two adults, Mike's brother—who is probably not much older than Mike, but a responsible campus policeman—and President Ryan, have scenes where they hold the young men accountable.

---

[46] https://www.nytimes.com/1982/01/17/magazine/steve-tesich-turns-memories-into-movies.html

The two shorter Cutter boys are the most ambitious. Dave is supremely confident, pursuing the gorgeous coed and defying danger while chasing the semi-truck on the highway. He is driven and resourceful, training on rollers under cover while it is raining and Ray watches from his office, shaking his head. Moocher has the responsibility of maintaining the family house while his parents are in Chicago, and he is getting engaged. The two taller ones are a bitter underachiever—Mike, who would like to live in Wyoming as a Marlboro Man—and a laid-back, wise guy, non-achiever, Cyril. Cyril lags behind when the four are walking.

In an interesting choice of names, "Moocher" means "one who exploits the generosity of others", according to the Merriam-Webster dictionary. In the movie, Moocher is anything but that; he is quite independent. The origin of "Cyril" is "of the Lord", according to the Ancestry website.

In a story for Rolling Stone magazine, Tesich said "There were only two words added to the script that I didn't write … When the boy is sitting on the rock and is talking about his father selling the house, and he says we could use the money 'something fierce,' that was it. I was the writer, Peter was the director and the actors were actors."[47]

The original script has some scenes that do not appear in the movie. Suzy works at a florist shop and sells flowers for Katherine to Dave, which would explain Rod's comment that Suzy informed him of the flowers. The university bought Moocher's house, so he comes to the Stohler house to ask if he could stay, as Dave had promised; Cyril comes to sleep over, too. Katherine suggests that she goes to Italy with Dave, so he has to recover by saying that he will go to summer school. The job that Dave spoke about getting is at the car wash, but Ray vetoes that. Nancy had said that she may be promoted to head cashier; the cashier job is at Nick's Bar and Grill, and Ray goes there and indulges in forbidden food. Dave in fact

---

[47] https://www.rollingstone.com/tv-movies/tv-movie-news/breaking-away-77979/2/

POSTSCRIPT

does go to confession, despite not being Catholic. Katherine goes to the Little 500 race to observe, but not interact with, her two ex-boyfriends competing. Mike leaves Bloomington at the end of the movie, apparently for Wyoming.

The movie has several turning points. If Katherine's notebook doesn't fall off, Dave probably never meets her. If Dave's tire doesn't burst as he glides through the woods after first engaging with Katherine, she may not wave to him as she drives by, and Dave may not be encouraged to send her flowers and pursue her. If Cyril doesn't get roughed up by Rod's henchmen, Mike never goes looking for a fight, and President Ryan doesn't order the Little 500 organizers to include the Cutter team. If the college kid doesn't return his car for a REFUND, Dave probably doesn't race against the Italians. If the Italian racers don't mess with Dave, he doesn't shed his Italian persona, he maintains his relationship with Katherine, and Ray doesn't soften up. If the Italians don't come to Indiana … well, there is no movie.

THE THEMES

The movie is filled with opposites: American and Italian, students and young men in limbo, campus settings and idyllic settings, Dave and Ray, Ray and Evelyn, Mike and his brother. Even the four Cutter boys have four distinct personalities.

The theme of teams is prevalent. The boys watch the football team at practice. Rod is on the swimming team. In biking scenes, the Cinzano team appears and rides as a team, and the grand finale has the Little 500 race teams. The Cutters are a team in the race out of necessity but evolve into a team that wins the race.

Dave is the central figure of the foursome; there are scenes with Dave and Moocher, and scenes with Dave and Cyril (and the two of them took the college entrance exam), but no scenes of just Dave with Mike. When there is a scene with just three of them, in the student union fight, Dave is the one who is absent. The vast majority of scenes with just one of the boys entail Dave. Moocher has a few scenes with Nancy, and Cyril has one solo scene, where he gets chased after the serenade. There are no scenes of just Mike, and none with Mike and one other of the four. Two of the four don't back down from a fight; Cyril is a pacifist who reacts only in self defense, and Dave begs off when Mike wants to go on campus for a fight.

The story has a recurring theme of the number four. Four is the perfect number of main characters in a buddy movie. The Little 500 teams needed four for a relay. Four characters fit perfectly in a car. "Stand By Me" had four buddies, "Mean Girls" had a group of four, with an aggressive leader. In music, The Beatles had a Fab Four, the U2 band does, too. In college football, Notre Dame had the Four Horseman; when "Breaking Away" was filmed, the Wishbone offense with four players in the backfield was still popular with several successful teams.

Of the four featured young women in the movie, only the conniving Suzy does not have a positive character. Nancy is an angel to Moocher and may become the breadwinner of the marriage; she has a job and may get promoted to head cashier. Katherine ditches the evil Rod for a charming, supposed Italian exchange student. Rod's new girlfriend, played by Jennifer K. Mickel, is in only two scenes, with an air of innocence in Rod's car and cordial to Cyril in the dining hall when he asks her what her major is; she is the All-American girl, wearing red, white, and blue. The French girl seems to be a perfect match for Dave. Evelyn is the lone adult woman, the perfect mother and wife. She embraces Dave's Italian influence; she serves "eeni" food, she goes with Dave's choice of "Fellini" as the cat's name, and she is romanticized by the operas.

Continuing on the theme of four, the Stohlers will be a family of four at the end of the movie. The movie mainly has four types of vehicles, and all four are significant—bikes, both solo for Dave and *en masse* in the races; cars, both low-end (Mike's and those at Ray's lot) and high-end, Rod's Mercedes convertible and the highway patrol car; Katherine's

POSTSCRIPT

scooter, the target of Dave's first chase; and the Cinzano semi-truck, the target of Dave's training. In addition, Dave nearly hits a bus, and, in production, a camera operator on a motorcycle and in a pickup truck filmed the close-up shots of the Little 500 race. Dave has four chases on his bike, chasing Katherine on her scooter, the truck on the highway, the Italians in the Cinzano 100 race, and Rod at the end of the Little 500 race. Dave is downtown in four scenes, when Mike's brother warns Mike about hot-rodding on campus, when he sees Moocher and Nancy at the courthouse before nearly colliding with Ray, when he talks to Moocher about confessing to Katherine, and when Katherine reconciles with him. Mike and Rod have four confrontations, at the frisbee incident, in the dining hall fight, in the swimming competition, and in the Little 500 race. The Little 500 race track has four turns, and four wheels crossed the finish line in the last split second. Dave challenges four Italians in the Cinzano 100 mile race. Four students push the broken-down car into Ray's lot as Ray pushes back. Attaining a college degree typically takes four years. The music of *M' appari tutt' amor* plays four times, as Dave glides through the woods after first meeting Katherine, as Evelyn waxes the floor, as Dave and Cyril practice for the serenade, and concurrently when Dave serenades Katherine and Evelyn seduces Ray. The song is from Friedrich von Flotow's romantic comic opera, "Martha", which has four acts. Nancy, Mike's brother, and Fellini/Jake, the cat, each appear in four scenes. Robyn Douglass's character is called Katherine, Katherina, Kathy, and Kath at various times. The address on Moocher's house is 4.

On the theme of cars, in the two scenes involving law enforcement vehicles—the highway patrol stopping the truck driver for speeding and Mike's brother pulling up to the pizza place to warn Mike about hot-rodding—it does not turn out well for the characters.

On the theme of water, the quarry swimming scenes are instrumental to the movie, Dave splashes himself with water after chasing the truck, Moocher never did wash a car at the car wash, and Dave almost douses

Ray with water from the hose as he washes the cars on the lot, whistling like a bird.

On the theme of colors, the light blue theme is prevalent, usually in a negative way for the boys. Mike is tormented by the light blue of his brother's uniform and Rod's convertible. The owner of the car wash, where Moocher briefly has a job, wears a light blue shirt. When Dave wears a light blue shirt while riding downtown, he almost gets hit by Ray.

On the other hand, the light blue and the pink of Rod's Izod shirt, Suzy's sorority shirt, and the flowers in the Stohler house front yard, are colors associated with newborn children, perhaps a foreshadow of an addition to the Stohler family?

THE MUSIC

The opera "Martha" has some interesting, coincidental features, "masquerade" and "Nancy", as described on the Culturedarm website: "… it tells of two young noblewomen who to relieve their boredom attend a country fair and masquerade as maids. Lady Harriet Durham and her confidante Nancy are hired by two young farmers, half-brothers Lyonel and Plunkett. They give their names as Martha and Julia …".[48]

INTERNATIONALLY

The French poster calls the movie "La Bande Des Quatre", for "The Gang of Four", and the boys are wearing their CUTTERS T-shirts. The Belgian poster also has "La Bande Des Quatre", for "The Band of Four". The Spanish poster has "El Relevo", for "The Relay". On that poster, the boys have LOS PICAPEDREROS (The Stonecutters) on their T-shirts. The text has "Los llaman LOS PICAPEDREROS y son dinamita pura.", for "They are called LOS PICAPEDREROS and they are pure dynamite." The Denmark poster has "Udbrud", with a clever sketch of Dave and

---

[48] https://culturedarm.com/behind-the-song-mappari-friedrich-von-flotow-martha/

… Katherine—in red, white, and blue clothing—smooching on his bike atop Mike's car. In Sweden, it is "Loppet AR kort", for "The race is short". In Venezuela, it is "Los Muchachos Del verano" for "The Summer Boys". In Argentina, it was also "Los Muchachos del Verano", with the text "En algun lugar entre el crecimiento y la madurez", for "In some place between growth and maturation". In West Germany, it is "Vier irre typen", for "Four crazy guys". The Italian poster has "All-American Boys" in English, with the "Boys" lettering resembling the American flag.

THE LITTLE 500 RACE
In real life, a team called Cinzano was created in 1985 to compete in the race, a year following the creation of the independent Cutters team. As Randy Strong said, the Cutters team has won 15 titles—including three out of their first five years of 1984, 1986, and 1988—while never placing lower than 12th. Appropriately, 1984 was year #34 of the Little 500 race, matching the team number of the movie Cutters. The Cinzano team had steady improvement, winning in 1989, their fifth year.

In 2024, an adult ticket for the home football game against Indiana's rival, Purdue, cost $35, while the Advance Sales price for the public to the Little 500 race was $40.

THAT'S A WRAP!
The movie was filmed in the hot weather of late summer 1978, which was the 150th anniversary of "State Seminary" becoming "Indiana College", before later being renamed as Indiana University. The nationwide premiere was in August of 1979, but the world premiere was at 8:00 p.m. on April 21 at the Indiana University Auditorium, the night of the 29th Little 500 race. Peter Yates and Steve Tesich attended, along with a crowd of 4,000.

The settings in Indiana University and its surroundings have changed significantly since the movie was released. The Sanders Quarry has been filled in, due to the occurrences of trespassers getting seriously injured from jumping into the water. Tenth Street Stadium of the Little 500 race was demolished in 1982, and now the Jesse H. and Beulah Chanley Cox Arboretum occupies that space. Kirkwood Avenue, in front of Franklin Hall, where Dave fetched Katherine's notebook, is no longer; now it is a walkable area, with the Sample Gates dedicated in 1987 as a western entrance to the university. The revolving door entrance to the student union has been replaced with a swinging door. In the scene where Mike is angry with Cyril getting beat up, the old railroad tracks have since been removed. The railroad tracks on the Cinzano 100 race route where the dog scurried out of danger are also gone. The Opie Taylor's restaurant on North Walnut Street that was named Pagliai's Pizza for the movie, where the boys get a pizza slice, has closed. The Tovey's Shoes store on Kirkwood Avenue, seen in the background when the boys are eating their pizza, was one of several buildings replaced in the renovation project of the Fountain Square Mall, now known as just Fountain Square. Ray's car lot on South Walnut Street now has buildings in its place. The Campus Car Wash has been replaced with apartments. The viewpoint where the boys watched the football practice does not exist; permanent stadium seats now block that view. The A&P grocery chain, where Mike was fired and the other three quit out of solidarity, and where Evelyn bought zucchini, started its decline as the movie was filmed. The Britannica website shows, "The last remaining A&P supermarkets were closed or sold by November 2016."[49]

The *Herald-Times* reported of the mill:[50]

> The Woolery Stone Mill — the fantastic former workplace of "Raymond Stoller" (Paul Dooley) — is buzzing again. After closing in 1994, the building is now being renovated to include

---

[49] https://www.britannica.com/money/Great-Atlantic-and-Pacific-Tea-Company-Inc

[50] https://www.heraldtimesonline.com/story/news/2004/04/18/revisiting-the-people-and-places-from-breaking-away/118134044/

POSTSCRIPT

42 condominiums, a 55-room hotel and conference center, a climbing facility and a restaurant/pub.

But, the movie has lived on for decades, with cast reunions taking place, and not just in Indiana but across the country, and not just in the United States. The four stars often wore their "CUTTERS" T-shirts. Virtually all of the main cast is still going strong. John Ashton, who played Mike's brother, passed away in September of 2024. Tragically, Lisa Shure, who played the French coed, died from complications of diabetes a few years after the movie's release. She had been married to Klinton Spilsbury, whose only feature film was "The Legend of the Lone Ranger" in 1981. The director of that movie was William A. Fraker, who was the director of photography for "Bullitt".

In the 1989 Little 500 race, the tenth anniversary of the film's release, the Cinzano team won, with the Cutters team finishing second. That same weekend, a reunion took place in Bloomington, with Dennis Christopher, Robyn Douglass, and Jackie Earle Haley attending. As found in the archives at Indiana University, Peter Yates sent his regrets in a Western Union telegram and in a letter to the Indiana University Student Foundation. In that letter, he said that the reason for not attending was that he was starting a new film called "Hard Rain" with Tom Selleck, another case where the title would change, as it was released as "An Innocent Man".

On April 23, 1999, Dennis Christopher, Robyn Douglass, and David Blase came to Bloomington for a reception at the Fountain Square Ballroom and the re-premiere of the film in its 20th anniversary year, shown at the newly renovated Indiana Theater, later renamed the Buskirk-Chumley Theater, the same theater that Dave and Moocher passed by when Dave said that he should confess to Katherine. David Blase was the grand marshal of that Little 500 weekend.

In May of 2008, it was shown for free at The Showroom in Spartanburg, South Carolina.

As for the question, "How many low-budget movies can you name that were shown in a South American country, 31 years after its release?", it was shown 2,900 miles from Bloomington, at the National Gallery, Castellani House, in Georgetown, Guyana, in January of 2010.[51]

The producer/director Jason Reitman showed the movie in 2011 at the New Beverly Cinema in Los Angeles, with Dennis Christopher and Daniel Stern attending. It was the featured film at the Filmfare at the Main Library in Placerville, California in July of 2011. Robyn Douglass, who owned a bed and breakfast in Placerville, appeared and informed, in the *Placerville Mountain Democrat*:[52]

"I will be speaking before and after the film and during the intermission. And I will reveal hidden secrets about the film."

In 2012, the four stars, Paul Dooley, and Barbara Barrie reunited at the Encino Velodrome in California, where Eddy Van Guyse does the play-by-play for races. Joe Pugliese photographed the stars for *Entertainment Weekly* magazine. In that story, Dennis Christopher said that he kept the Masi racing bike from the movie, and he brought it with him to the *Entertainment Weekly* reunion shoot: "I had it restored, and it's been stuck up on the wall as an art piece for these many years."[53]

In February of 2013, it was shown as part of the Cinemapolis theater "Local Favorites" series in Ithaca, New York.

In September of 2014, it was shown at the Studio Movie Grill in Wheaton, Illinois, hosted by Film Critic Patrick McDonald of HollywoodChicago.com, an alumnus of Indiana University. In October of 2014, the San Luis Obispo International Film Festival had a screening

---

[51] https://www.stabroeknews.com/2010/01/09/the-scene/classic-tuesdays-selects-breaking-away-as-first-film-for-2010/

[52] https://www.mtdemocrat.com/news/breaking-away-actress-robyn-douglass-appeared-at-library-filmfare/article_917e9909-0950-514d-995d-92ad49f53ee5.

[53] https://ew.com/article/2012/10/05/breaking-away-1979/

POSTSCRIPT

at the Fremont Theater, with Dennis Christopher and Paul Dooley doing a Q&A afterwards; appropriately, they appeared at a meet-and-greet reception at Mama's Meatball, with classic Italian appetizers being served. In September of 2015, Dennis Christopher, Dennis Quaid, and Jackie Earle Haley reunited at the annual Interbike convention at the Mandalay Bay Convention Center in Las Vegas; there, Dennis Christopher told the *Las Vegas Review-Journal*, "I have a halo over my head because of this beautiful movie."[54]

In April of 2016, Dennis Christopher participated in the Eroica California vintage bike show in Paso Robles, California, with another showing of the movie at the Fremont Theater in San Luis Obispo. It was shown at the Normal Theater in Normal, Illinois in February of 2018. In May of 2018, The Varsity Center in Carbondale, Illinois helped celebrate the City of Carbondale's National Bike Month with a screening of "Breaking Away". If the attendees at the Carbondale event wanted to stay in the spirit, they could walk down South Illinois Avenue to Pagliai's Pizza, which had the same name as the pizza place on the courthouse square in the movie.

In August of 2019, it was shown at the Buskirk-Chumley theater in Bloomington, along with "Hoosiers" and "Rudy". In September of 2019, Dennis Christopher, Daniel Stern, Paul Dooley, and Hart Bochner appeared at the Egyptian Theater in Los Angeles for an interview and screening, with Dennis bringing his Masi bicycle. In the Front Row Flynn video with Jonah Ray as the moderator at the event, they shared which other actors were considered for the roles. For Dave, it was Richard Thomas, who had appeared in "September 30, 1955" with Dennis Christopher and Dennis Quaid two years previously, and Robby Benson, who had portrayed an underdog college basketball player in "One on One", also two years previously. Robert Preston and Charles Durning were considered

---

[54] https://www.reviewjournal.com/business/stars-of-breaking-away-reunite-at-interbike-in-las-vegas/

for the part of Ray, and Eva Marie Saint, who had no theatrical movies between 1972 and 1986, was considered for Evelyn.[55]

In October of 2019, with Dennis Christopher attending, it was screened in Indianapolis as the 40th anniversary honored movie at the 28th Annual Heartland International Film Festival, whose mission is to present "films that do more than entertain." Also in October, Dennis Christopher appeared for a discussion following a screening at the V. Earl Dickinson Theater on the Piedmont Virginia Community College campus in Charlottesville, Virginia.

In February of 2020, the Film Independent organization hosted a Live Read of the script at the Wallis Annenberg Center for the Performing Arts in Beverly Hills, with Dennis Christopher and Paul Dooley reading their parts and other actors reading other parts. A quartet of string players played music from the movie, and Film Independent's Cooper Hopkins appeared at numerous times to pedal on a stationary Masi bike.[56]

In 2023, it was shown at the Longwood Public Library in Middle Island, New York, in May and at the Revue Cinema in Toronto, Ontario, in August.

The 45th anniversary year of 2024 was eventful. On the Little 500 weekend in April, it was shown at the Buskirk-Chumley Theater in Bloomington. In May, the New Beverly Cinema in Los Angeles screened the movie, with Dennis Christopher and Paul Dooley, age 96 at the time, attending. Paul said that the movie was "the love of my life." He related a story of someone asking Peter Yates if it was his idea to have Paul do certain bits in the movie, and Yates said, "No, everything he did was his idea."[57] In July, it was featured at the Orchestra Hall at the Lakeside Chautauqua in Lakeside, Ohio. Also in July, in Portland,

[55] https://www.youtube.com/watch?v=foZ_YEF4N1s
[56] https://www.filmindependent.org/blog/live-read-recap-original-cast-and-surprise-cyclists-make-breaking-away-hard-to-forget/
[57] https://www.youtube.com/watch?v=4HEA-MiqxAo

POSTSCRIPT

Oregon, the anniversary was celebrated with a bike ride at 7:30, followed by the movie at 9:00.

THE LAST WORD

Symbolically, the movie makes a 180 degree change from the beginning to the end. It begins in a quarry and ends on the campus. The four boys are an aimless group in the beginning and a team in the end. Dave's first spoken words are in Italian as he praises Mike's singing, and his last spoken words are in French. It starts with a song, Mike's ode to the A&P, and ends with "Indiana, Our Indiana", Indiana University's official fight song, followed by a part of Rossini's The Barber of Seville that was played in the Cinzano 100 race. The first scene is of four boys who have not figured it out; the last shot is of an adult who thought that he had figured out his son, but now is not so sure.

Dave has made his own 180 degree turn. We know that he has a new life; he is a college student, he has a sibling on the way, and he has a new girlfriend. We know that Moocher is getting married and that his dad has a job in Chicago. We don't know what plans Mike and Cyril have.

At the end, have the four boys broken away from their teen days and from each other? Can we get a movie sequel to answer how they end up, *s'il vous plaît*?

PHOTOS

The quarry where the Cutter boys go to swim. *Courtesy: Indiana University Archives*

Dave preparing to chase Katherine on her scooter. *Courtesy: Indiana University Archives*

Dave confesses to Katherine and is about to be slapped. *Courtesy: Dan Levinson*

Ray's car stalls after almost hitting Dave. *Courtesy: Dan Levinson*

BREAKING AWAY

Hart Bochner and Jennifer K. Mickel. *Courtesy: Dan Levinson*

Nighttime filming in downtown Bloomington. *Courtesy: Indiana University Archives*

Producer/director Peter Yates, screenplay writer Steve Tesich, and Dennis Christopher. *Courtesy: Indiana University Archives*

Peter Yates, directing at Tenth Street Stadium for the Little 500 race scenes. *Courtesy: Indiana University Archives*

The motorcycle-mounted camera used for close-ups of the Little 500 race. *Courtesy: Indiana University Archives*

Creative camera work for close-ups of the Little 500 race. *Courtesy: Indiana University Archives*

ACKNOWLEDGMENTS

MY GRATITUDE goes to the following for contributing to this book.

Dr. Ben Pearl connected me to several participants in a Little 500 race, and without his assistance, this book would not have been possible. I first connected with him when I found his interview with Eddy Van Guyse and asked him if he could connect me with Eddy. Ben far exceeded my expectations by connecting me to several other participants. He started out as a walk-on for Indiana's track team his freshman year but after becoming injured, he switched over to bike racing. He has served as a consultant at the National Institutes of Health and is a fellow of the American Academy of Podiatric Sports Medicine. He has a sports medicine practice in Arlington, Virginia, and is active with running, biking, skiing, and soccer. He shared with me his video interviews with Eddy Van Guyse, Bill Brissman, and Randy Strong. The *Indiana Daily Student* newspaper had his photo showing the awkward exchange in the qualifiers in a year where they did not make the race. He says, "I was only able to do the race in my senior year because we had one guy that could not handle the exchanges. The cool thing about the race is no matter what team you are on, if you go back and you are passionate about it, it is like a big brotherhood. Everyone knows the experience of what the training was like, what the race was like, the pressure of qualifications, etc." He and I agree that the impact resembles that of the Army-Navy football game.

Thanks to Dan Levinson for sending photos, the video, and a copy of the script, which has "Bambino" on its red cover and the family name of "Blase" instead of "Stohler" throughout.

Thanks to Bill Brissman, Doug Bruce, Jim Kirkham, Randy Strong, Judah Thompson, and Eddy Van Guyse—all connected to me by Dr. Pearl—for their input on the movie.

Thanks also to Bob and Debbie Broeking, Dr. James Pivarnik, and Carlos Sintes for their input.

Thanks to Brad Cook of the Indiana University Archives and Helen Gunn of the Lilly Library at Indiana University for allowing me to access their materials on the movie.

BIBLIOGRAPHY

Birnbaum, G. (1988). *Dennis Quaid*. St. Martin's Press.

Didinger, R. and Glen Macnow, G. (2009). *The Ultimate Book Of Sports Movies*. Running Press Book Publishers.

Dooley, P. (2003). *Movie Dad: Finding Myself and My Family, On Screen and Off*. Globe Pequot Publishing Group.

Schwarb, J. (1999). *The Little 500: The Story of the World's Greatest College Weekend*. Indiana University Press.

Stern, D (2024). *Home and Alone*. Viva Editions.

Sanders, S. R. (1985). *In Limestone Country*. Beacon Press.

APPENDIX

TO LEARN MORE about the Little 500 race and bike racing, and to see interviews with David Blase, Bill Brissman, Jim Kirkham, Randy Strong, Judah Thompson, and Eddy Van Guyse, scan this QR code to access Dr. Ben Pearl's "Fit Foot U" podcasts:

To view the podcasts of Jim Kirkham, the coach of the real-life Cutters team, search the web for "Trophy Dash podcast".

ABOUT THE AUTHOR

STEVE BASFORD'S first three books are "Buckeye Memories: From the Couch, the Stands, and the Press Box ... and a Few Fun Facts", "2001 Games (And Counting): A Sports Odyssey", and "Ohio State Football 2002, The Improbable National Championship".

He is the play-by-play voice of Ohio Wesleyan University football, men's and women's basketball, baseball, and softball. He is the play-by-play voice of Dublin Jerome High School football and boys' and girls' basketball in central Ohio. He has been a statistician for Ohio State University football for Time Warner Cable in 1978 through 1980, for WOSU-TV from 1981 through 1990, and for the official stats crew for home games since 1993.

Despite his role in sports production and books, he says that he thinks that he knows more about movies than the X's and O's of sports.